"What an excellent set of writings! By turns insightful, inspirational, and critical, but always interesting, the book's method of looking back and looking ahead offers deep understanding of the present church in its messy, graced reality. So much is in bud. Read it and experience the maturing of the theological voice in North America."

Elizabeth A. Johnson
Distinguished Professor
Fordham University

"Nine first-rate theologians here offer their analysis and insights concerning key areas in Catholic ecclesiology, including authority, ministry, culture, gender, ethnicity, mission, liturgy, and ecumenism. The reader gains access to the most current state of theological discussion as the authors not only frankly acknowledge the seriousness of present challenges but also give solid advice concerning the future of the church."

Dennis M. Doyle
Professor of Religious Studies
University of Dayton

"If Pope John XXIII wanted to open a window into the church, Pope Francis wants to open its doors. This challenging book, the fruit of an extraordinary gathering of ecclesiologists brought together by Boston College, explores what the church of Pope Francis might mean for questions of evangelization, authority, ministry, gender, and ecumenism. Sensitive to cultural changes and demographic shifts, its starting point must always be mission with a special concern for those on the periphery."

Thomas P. Rausch, SJ
T. Marie Chilton Professor of Catholic Theology
Loyola Marymount University

"This book cracks open the doors of the church for a wide audience—students, parishioners, and seekers alike—with essays by the most respected US theologians, younger scholars and seasoned veterans, that explore the most challenging and most promising topics in the theology of the church today."

Bradford E. Hinze
Karl Rahner Chair in Theology
Fordham University

"An engaging collection that demonstrates the vibrancy, range, and continued promise of US ecclesiology today. As well as being a most valuable addition to any syllabus engaging the church of our times, it serves as a fitting tribute to Thomas O'Meara, OP, a true theological great whose own creative theological work and wider ecclesial service alike have embodied a vision of *A Church with Open Doors* across many fruitful years."

Gerard Mannion
Amaturo Chair in Catholic Studies
Georgetown University

A Church with Open Doors

Catholic Ecclesiology
for the Third Millennium

Edited by

Richard R. Gaillardetz

and

Edward P. Hahnenberg

A Michael Glazier Book

LITURGICAL PRESS

Collegeville, Minnesota

www.litpress.org

A Michael Glazier Book published by Liturgical Press

Cover design by Jodi Hendrickson. The Ludwigskirche in Munich, 1908, painting by Wassily Kandinsky, 1866–1944. © Carmen Thyssen-Bornemisza Collection, Thyssen-Bornemisza Museum/SCALA, Florence. © 2015.

Excerpts from the English translation of *The Roman Missal* © 2010, International Commission on English in the Liturgy Corporation. All rights reserved.

Excerpts from documents of the Second Vatican Council are from *Vatican Council II: Constitutions, Decrees, Declarations; The Basic Sixteen Documents*, edited by Austin Flannery, OP, © 1996. Used with permission of Liturgical Press, Collegeville, Minnesota.

Unless otherwise indicated, Scripture texts in this work are taken from the *New Revised Standard Version Bible*, © 1989, Division of Christian Education of the National Council of the Churches of Christ in the United States of America. Used by permission. All rights reserved.

1   2   3   4   5   6   7   8   9

Library of Congress Cataloging-in-Publication Data

A church with open doors : Catholic ecclesiology for the third millennium / edited by Richard R. Gaillardetz and Edward P. Hahnenberg.
   pages   cm
   "A Michael Glazier book."
   Includes bibliographical references.
   ISBN 978-0-8146-8304-0 — ISBN 978-0-8146-8329-3 (ebooks)
   1. Mission of the church.   2. Catholic Church—Doctrines.   I. Gaillardetz, Richard R., 1958– editor.

BX1746.C5155   2015
262'.02—dc23

2014048402

To Thomas F. O'Meara, OP,

who taught a whole generation of theologians
to engage the challenges of our age
in dialogue with the vital thought forms
of the great Christian tradition.

Contents

Part 3: Ecclesiological Openings

Abbreviations

AA	*Apostolicam Actuositatem*	Vatican II, Decree on the Apostolate of Lay People

AA   *Apostolicam Actuositatem*
Vatican II, Decree on the Apostolate of Lay People

AG   *Ad Gentes*
Vatican II, Decree on the Church's Missionary Activity

CD   *Christus Dominus*
Vatican II, Decree on the Pastoral Office of Bishops in the Church

DH   *Dignitatis Humanae*
Vatican II, Declaration on Religious Liberty

DV   *Dei Verbum*
Vatican II, Dogmatic Constitution on Divine Revelation

EG   *Evangelii Gaudium*
Pope Francis, On the Joy of the Gospel

EV   *Evangelium Vitae*
Pope John Paul II, The Gospel of Life

GS   *Gaudium et Spes*
Vatican II, Pastoral Constitution on the Church in the Modern World

LG   *Lumen Gentium*
Vatican II, Dogmatic Constitution on the Church

PO   *Presbyterorum Ordinis*
Vatican II, Decree on the Ministry and Life of Priests

SC   *Sacrosanctum Concilium*
Vatican II, Constitution on the Sacred Liturgy

UR   *Unitatis Redintegratio*
Vatican II, Decree on Ecumenism

Introduction

Richard R. Gaillardetz and Edward P. Hahnenberg

A Church which "goes forth" is a Church whose doors are open.

—Pope Francis, *Evangelii Gaudium*

In a speech to his fellow cardinals before the conclave that would elect him pope, Jorge Mario Bergoglio invoked the image of Jesus knocking at our door. He acknowledged that this metaphor, drawn from the book of Revelation, places Jesus on the outside waiting to come in. But then the future Pope Francis reversed the image and asked about all those times Jesus knocks from the inside trying to get out! He argued that the church must be a church with open doors, and not simply to welcome in those who might come. The church must open its doors so that the whole people of God can go out to a world sorely in need—out to those on all the peripheries of life, those on the edge of sin, pain, and injustice, those trapped in ignorance, indifference to religion, and all forms of suffering. This "going forth"—this mission of evangelization in its broadest sense—is the *raison d'etre* of the church, a church which, according to the Second Vatican Council, is missionary by its very nature.

Pope Francis's image of a church with open doors recalls a story now fifty years old. When Pope John XXIII was asked about his hopes for the Second Vatican Council, he went over to a window and threw it open, allowing light and fresh air into the room. Whether this dramatic gesture ever actually occurred, the image of throwing wide the windows of the church captured the spirit of openness, engagement, and mission that marked the time of the council. It also captures the spirit of Catholic theological reflection on the church over the intervening years. Catholic ecclesiology after Vatican II "opened up" in myriad ways—through ecumenical dialogue, through engagement with modern philosophy and historical-critical methodologies, through drawing on the insights of the social sciences, through greater attention to changing pastoral realities, through intercultural exchange and a growing awareness of the global dimensions of a world church, and through encounter with the profound context of injustice and human suffering that continue to define our time.

Today the Second Vatican Council, for all its many and real contributions to this ecclesiological renewal, remains a contested site, with significant disagreements lingering over the development of an adequate conciliar hermeneutics. At the same time, contemporary ecclesiology finds itself engaged in a series of debates regarding the place of the church in the present cultural moment often referred to as postmodernity. This postmodern engagement has taken ecclesiology in quite different directions. Some are eager to pursue a transdenominational ecclesiology that employs comparative methodologies that honor the integrity of diverse Christian traditions but that, its critics charge, may be abandoning the goal of full visible unity that has long been at the heart of the ecumenical movement. Others espouse a postliberal or postsecular turn that promises a rich *ressourcement* (return to the sources), but that is vulnerable to both sectarianism and neotriumphalist tendencies. Still others would call attention to the ecclesiological consequences of the tremendous growth of the church in the Global South and the important emancipatory impulses of various feminist and liberationist ecclesiologies. In the midst of these debates, Pope Francis has taken the new evangelization championed by his two immediate predecessors beyond a cramped pastoral program for shoring up Catholic numbers and a faltering Catholic identity. For Francis, a church that is focused in on itself fails to respond to the call of the Gospel. With doors and windows closed, such a self-referential church becomes pale and sick. Instead, Francis has refashioned the new evangelization as a call to a missionary discipleship animated by solidarity with the poor and marginalized and a commitment to building a "culture of encounter."

It was in light of the real challenges and opportunities of the present moment that the two editors of this volume imagined a project that would bring together theologians in North America for a symposium on the state of Catholic ecclesiology. The goals of the symposium were twofold. The first was to gather experts who could reflect on the development of Catholic ecclesiology over the fifty years since Vatican II, assess the present state of the field, and identify some of the more promising avenues for future theological work. The second goal was to honor the many contributions to Catholic ecclesiology made by Thomas F. O'Meara, OP, who, over the years, taught and mentored a number of students of ecclesiology, including the two editors of this volume and the other members of the symposium planning team, Stephen Bevans and Vincent Miller. In September 2014, over forty scholars gathered at Boston College's Connors Conference Center to engage in extended theological conversation.

The conversation at the symposium was oriented around nine essays that, after significant feedback and revision, appear as the chapters in this volume. In chapter 1, Stephen Bevans begins with a claim that will run throughout the volume: any ecclesiology adequate for the third millennium must take its starting point in *mission*. He approaches the mission of the church through the notion of the "new evangelization," tracing the development of this concept in the writings of Popes Paul VI, John Paul II, and Benedict XVI, arriving at the 2012 synod of bishops dedicated to this theme. There Bevans notices a shift in the center of gravity. It is the shift from the concerns of a secularized Europe to those of the growing Global South, and, with it, a shift on the part of the church from a posture of proclamation to one of listening and dialogue. Following the impulses of Pope Francis's witness, Bevans seeks to rethink all of ecclesiology in light of missiology, privileging the image of the church as "a community of missionary disciples." In chapter 2, Paul Lakeland affirms the fundamental orientation laid out by Bevans: the church exists not for its own sake, but for the sake of the world to which it is sent. Lakeland explores this "centrifugal" approach to ecclesiology in dialogue with the science of demography. But rather than summarize statistics, Lakeland is interested in what our response to the data reveals about our ecclesial self-understanding and, in particular, our understanding of the church's apostolic mission, or *apostolicity*. He organizes his analysis under three types—apostolicity seen as maintenance, as new evangelization, and as kenosis. Only in the third, with its christological pattern of death to new life and its humble confidence in divine grace permeating the whole world, does Lakeland find an ecclesiological posture adequate to our contemporary postmodern context.

In chapter 3, Natalia Imperatori-Lee carries forward Lakeland's attention to the concrete realities of the church in the United States but does so in a way that unsettles the stories we so often tell about American Catholicism. Drawing on the insights of Latino/a theologians, Imperatori-Lee challenges the historical narrative that begins in the

Northeast, ends in the West, and revolves around the assimilation of nineteenth-century European immigrants—while ignoring the presence of Spanish-speaking Catholics who lived in what is now the United States centuries before the Irish arrived in Boston. In their approach to inter-culturality, their engagement with pastoral theology, their attention to the sacredness of everyday life, popular religion, and forms of Christian praxis outside of the parish, Latino/a theologians like Imperatori-Lee disrupt the dominant narrative of Catholic ecclesiology, calling for a historical, methodological, and thematic reimagining of the field. Vincent Miller is also interested in the inculturation of Catholicism in the United States, but he invites us to push deeper, to get at the fundamental assumptions at work whenever we discuss "culture." Thus, chapter 4 situates contemporary ecclesiological concerns within the context of changing cultures and changing conceptions of culture. He argues that both the dialogical stance toward culture advanced by Vatican II's *Gaudium et Spes* (The Pastoral Constitution on the Church in the Modern World) and the more contrastive approach of Pope John Paul II's 1995 encyclical *Evangelium Vitae*—for all their obvious differences—nevertheless share a common horizon. They both assume that one of the challenges facing Christianity in the modern world is the threat of cultural homogenization. For Miller, this is no longer the case. As new forms of media, technology, and political niching split us into a million different subcultures, Miller argues that the real problem is not homogenization, but heterogenization. Thus the fundamental challenge of the present moment is to maintain the unity of the church amidst cultural fragmentation. In his call for a culture of encounter, Pope Francis seems keenly aware of this new challenge—offering not another subculture, but a way to draw human beings into communion.

If parts 1 and 2 treat the importance of mission and local context, respectively, then part 3 takes up several traditional ecclesiological themes, exploring potential openings for future theological development. Richard Gaillardetz's chapter 5 sketches the outlines of a constructive theology of power and authority in the church. Gaillardetz draws on Michel Foucault to critique a zero-sum conception of power that assumes power is inherently dominating and coercive. This critique opens up to a more positive account that, on the one hand, acknowledges the power that exists within all relational networks, and, on the other hand, emphasizes the way in which power can be disciplined toward certain ends. For the Christian, this disciplining of power need not constrain, but can in fact enable the free exercise of Christian discipleship. Such a reimagining of power along relational lines holds important implications for understanding the church's teaching office, and for a broader conception of authority as oriented toward the mission of the church. These issues of power and authority come front and center when considering the role of women in the church. In chapter 6, Mary Ann Hinsdale offers a feminist reading of ecclesiological developments since the Second Vatican Council. After surveying the involvement of women before, during, and after the council, Hinsdale argues that a theology of gender complementarity stands as the "issue under the issues" in ecclesiology today—frustrating a more adequate official response to the many contributions of women to the life of the church. Hinsdale suggests several ecclesial practices that can provide the kind of disciplining of power relations appropriate to a church with open doors.

In chapter 7, Susan Wood turns to the sacramental nature of the church. There she explores the possibilities for the future of Catholic ecclesiology drawn from liturgical theology. To do so, Wood engages in an appreciative, yet critical, ecumenical discussion of baptismal and eucharistic ecclesiologies found within the Orthodox and Anglican traditions. She concludes by developing the beginnings of her own liturgical ecclesiology grounded in the action of the worshiping assembly. In chapter 8, Edward Hahnenberg focuses on the Catholic theologies of ministry that emerged after Vatican II. He notes a basic shift from a deductive, neoscholastic methodology to more inductive approaches, highlighting the importance of both history and contemporary experience to Catholic theologians writing on ministry. However, the theological appeal to history and experience needs further methodological refinement in order to avoid overlooking the ministerial anomalies that have shaped the past, mark the present, and point toward the future. In the final chapter, chapter 9, Michael Fahey draws on his own long engagement in ecumenical work to highlight the great strides and the remaining challenges of ecumenism today. Noting the lack of reception of many ecumenical statements, Fahey offers a positive discussion of "receptive ecumenism" as a promising way forward for ecumenical dialogue.

What unites the essays in this volume is the shared conviction that Catholic ecclesiology cannot remain closed in on itself; it must engage the world beyond the walls of the church. This sense of openness can be found in the documents of the Second Vatican Council and in the example of Pope Francis. It can also be found in the lifework of the theologian this volume is meant to honor. Few of the topics treated here escaped the interest, study, and insightful commentary of Thomas F. O'Meara. From his early engagement with Midwestern Lutherans to his recent reflections on the cosmic expanse of God's grace, running throughout O'Meara's theological work is a deep appreciation for the interplay of church and culture, a recognition that all of human history is a story of salvation and that all of creation is a world of grace. Thanks to God's pervasive presence, nothing escapes theological reflection. No theology—and certainly no ecclesiology—can retreat into solipsistic solitude, or remain locked behind closed doors.

Part 1

A Church of Missionary Disciples

Beyond the New Evangelization: Toward a Missionary Ecclesiology for the Twenty-First Century

Stephen Bevans, SVD

Thomas O'Meara's theological autobiography, *A Theologian's Journey*, bristles with references to time. "I have written down these memories," he writes, "to be a witness to a time, to recall that I once stood on the edge of a change in history that still continues."[1] Roman Catholicism before Vatican II, the period in which he grew up and was formed as a Dominican, O'Meara describes as one of "bland timelessness."[2] Summers in the seminary were "summers without days." The timelessness of Dominican life was "the only world." "Little radio, rare newspapers, and no magazines entered this isolated world."[3] "In monastic life, and in Eisenhower's America, I expected all days to be the same."[4]

But when he travelled to Europe to begin doctoral studies at the Ludwig-Maximilian University in Munich in 1962, "experience and history, my new mentors, stepped forth to meet me, ready to show me Europe and ages past, but also worlds being born, worlds yet to come."[5] He had walked into history; he had walked into the modern world; he had encountered time, and with time, culture.[6] It was this encounter that

---

[1] Thomas F. O'Meara, *A Theologian's Journey* (Mahwah, NJ: Paulist Press, 2002), 314.

[2] Ibid., 29.

[3] Ibid., 33.

[4] Ibid., 38. See also 105.

[5] Ibid., 67.

[6] See ibid., 71 and the title of chapter 4, 105.

set the mark on his career as a theologian and a teacher and mentor to so many.

O'Meara's life is thus emblematic of a fundamental change in the last fifty years in the theology of the church. In the years before Vatican II, "the church too often was the schoolteacher of blind obedience and subservience to an ignorant, authoritarian will."[7] But now time "was setting us free from the prisons of the 1940s and 1950s, from the ruthless and mindless scholasticisms of Rome, Moscow, and Washington."[8] A century before, the church of Pius IX had refused to have anything to do with the "modern world" or "progress." Now the council had issued *Gaudium et Spes* (The Pastoral Constitution on the Church in the Modern World), expressing its solidarity with the "joys and hopes, the grief and anguish of the people of our time" (GS 1). A century before, the church spoke of its essence as institutional, hierarchical, and monarchical. The council did not reject that identity but emphasized the identity of the church as mystery and as God's pilgrim people. A century before, laity were encouraged to do little more than "to be led and to follow its pastors as a docile flock";[9] the council spoke of a fundamental equality shared by all Christians because of baptism, an idea that exploded, as O'Meara has described it, into a wide variety of lay ministries.[10] Thanks to the council, the church began fashioning a self-image for real time; time was leading the church into the modern world, and so into experience, history, and culture.

The Second Vatican Council was fundamentally a "missionary council."[11] This is not always seen clearly, but as one revisits the council after fifty years and in the light of present developments, its missionary spirit and style emerge quite sharply.[12] As John XXIII's articulation of his goals for the council gained precision in the years between 1959 and 1962, a

[7] Ibid., 29.

[8] Ibid., 212.

[9] Pius X, *Vehementer Nos* (To the Bishops of France), February 11, 1906, quoted in Michael A. Fahey, "Church," in *Systematic Theology: Roman Catholic Perspectives*, vol. 2, ed. Francis Schüssler Fiorenza and John Galvin (Minneapolis, MN: Fortress Press, 1991), 32.

[10] See Thomas F. O'Meara, *Theology of Ministry*, rev. ed. (Mahwah, NJ: Paulist Press, 1999), 6–12.

[11] Johannes Schütte, "Ce que la mission attendait du concile," in *Vatican II: l'activité missionaire de l'église* (Paris: Cerf, 1967), 120.

[12] See Stephen Bevans, "Revisiting Mission at Vatican II: Theology and Practice for Today's Missionary Church," *Theological Studies* 74, no. 2 (June 2013): 261–83.

vision emerged that the council "would mark a transition between two eras, that is, that would bring the Church out of the post-tridentine period and . . . into a new phase of witness and proclamation."[13] John XXIII called for *aggiornamento* in the church, but not for its own sake. Any renewal the council would bring was for the sake of a more intelligible and effective preaching of the Gospel.[14] The church, the council proclaimed, was "missionary by its very nature" (AG 2). Vatican II's missionary church was a church for real time.

The New Evangelization

Vatican II's document on mission outlined three areas or fields where the church carries out its missionary mandate. The major emphasis of mission is "missionary work among the nations," but "closely connected with the church's missionary endeavor" is "pastoral care of the faithful" and "efforts aimed at restoring Christian unity" (AG 6). As the years progressed after Vatican II, however, the ecumenical aspect of mission diminished (although this did not completely disappear).[15] What began to emerge in official church documents in place of this third area of mission activity was a greater emphasis on the need to evangelize within the context of growing secularity and indifference to the church among those peoples who made up traditionally Christian nations. This emerging emphasis was eventually named the "new evangelization."[16]

Ronald Witherup suggests that the roots of the new evangelization go back at least to Paul VI's 1975 apostolic exhortation, *Evangelii Nuntiandi*,

---

[13] Giuseppe Alberigo, "The Announcement of the Council: From the Security of the Fortress to the Lure of the Quest," in *History of Vatican II*, ed. Giuseppe Alberigo and Joseph A. Komonchak, vol. 1, *Announcing and Preparing Vatican Council II* (Maryknoll, NY: Orbis Books), 42.

[14] This is certainly the spirit of Pope John's opening speech. See the speech in Walter M. Abbott, ed., *The Documents of Vatican II* (New York: Association Press, 1966), 710–19.

[15] Paul VI, *Evangelii Nuntiandi*, 54, 64, http://www.vatican.va/holy_father/paul _vi/apost_exhortations/documents/hf_p-vi_exh_19751208_evangelii-nuntiandi _en.html, accessed September 23, 2014; John Paul II, *Redemptoris Missio*, 23, 49, http:// www.vatican.va/holy_father/john_paul_ii/encyclicals/documents/hf_jp-ii_enc _07121990_redemptoris-missio_en.html, accessed September 23, 2014.

[16] For a much more detailed history of the new evangelization than appears here, see Stephen Bevans, "New Evangelization or Missionary Church? *Evangelii Gaudium* and the Call for Missionary Discipleship," *Verbum SVD* 55, nos. 2–3 (2014): 158–76.

which speaks of the need for evangelization in the modern world.[17] It was John Paul II, however, who began to use the term in his speeches and documents, possibly influenced, as missiologist John Gorski suggests, by the 1979 statement issued by the Latin American bishops meeting at Puebla.[18] John Paul II's first use of the term was during his historic visit to Poland that same year, although he used it without any particular sense that this would be one of the hallmarks of his future teaching.[19] He used it again in a much more deliberate way in 1983 while addressing the bishops of Latin America and the Caribbean assembled in Haiti, and again in his opening address at Santo Domingo in 1992, explaining that what was needed in Latin America today was an evangelization "new in its ardour, methods and expression." [20] Subsequently the Latin American bishops picked up the term in their 1992 General Assembly in Santo Domingo in the Dominican Republic, recognizing the new evangelization as the "all-encompassing element" or "central idea" of the conference.[21]

In 2005 Joseph Ratzinger was elected pope and quite deliberately chose the name Benedict, the choice of which he explained in his first general audience. The name was to recall Benedict XV (1914–1922), who had worked to prevent World War I and worked afterward to promote reconciliation. Probably more significant, however, Benedict's name referred to Benedict of Nursia, "one of the patron saints of Europe who—

[17] Ronald D. Witherup, *Saint Paul and the New Evangelization* (Collegeville, MN: Liturgical Press, 2013), 10–11. Witherup does not give a reference to the apostolic exhortation, but the pope speaks of evangelization within the context of secularism in *Evangelii Nuntiandi* 54 and 56.

[18] See John F. Gorski, "From 'Mission' to 'New Evangelization': The Origin of a Concept that Challenges Our Institutes," 5, http://www.sedosmission.org/sedos articles/documents/jgorski_2013_en.pdf, accessed September 14, 2014.

[19] See John Paul II, "Homily at the Sanctuary of the Holy Cross, Mogila, Poland, June 9, 1979," *L'Osservatore Romano: Weekly Edition in English* (July 16, 1979): 11; *Acta Apostolicae Sedis* 71 (1979): 865. XIII Ordinary General Assembly of the Synod of Bishops, *Lineamenta* of The New Evangelization for the Transmission of the Christian Faith, 5, http://www.vatican.va/roman_curia/synod/documents/rc_synod_doc _20110202_lineamenta-xiii-assembly_en.html, accessed September 23, 2014.

[20] John Paul II, Discourse to the XIX Assembly of CELAM (March 9, 1983), 3; *L'Osservatore Romano: Weekly Edition in English* (April 18, 1983), 9; *AAS* 75 (1983): 778.

[21] Fourth General Conference of Latin American Bishops, "Conclusions: New Evangelization, Human Development, Christian Culture," in *Santo Domingo and Beyond: Documents and Commentaries from the Fourth General Conference of Latin American Bishops*, ed. Alfred T. Hennelly (Maryknoll, NY: Orbis Books, 1993), 80.

according to the pope—had exercised an enormous influence on Europe's Christian heritage"[22] and saved Europe from the ravages of the non-Christian or Arian migrating tribes of his time. As a cardinal, Ratzinger had repeatedly expressed his concern for Europe in the twentieth and twenty-first century. Especially since 1989, he had argued that "Europe has been deeply affected by the master narratives of progress and emancipation" and has embraced a relativism that has actually betrayed genuine truth and freedom. Because of this, the church has to witness to a truth which is not the result of subjective experience but is given in revelation. The church has to be a "minority that is often opposed to 'the spirit of the world.'"[23] As pope, Ratzinger committed himself to saving Europe from the ravages of postmodernism and unbelief. In this way Benedict, it could be said, was trying to move the church back into its timeless, pre–Vatican II existence through a number of policies that missiologist John Sivalon characterizes as "romantic conservatism."[24]

It is in this context that Pope Benedict created the Pontifical Council for Promoting the New Evangelization in September 2010. In the apostolic letter *Ubique et Semper* that established the new council, Benedict acknowledged that "to speak of a 'new evangelization' does not in fact mean that a single formula should be developed that would hold the same for all circumstances." Nevertheless, he says that churches in "traditionally Christian territories" require a "renewed missionary impulse."[25] Shortly afterward the pope announced that the theme of the upcoming Synod of Bishops in 2012 would be "the New Evangelization for the Transmission of the Faith,"[26] the *lineamenta* for which speaks of the new evangelization as "primarily addressed to those who have drifted from the Church in traditionally Christian countries."[27]

---

[22] Lieven Boeve, "Europe in Crisis: A Question of Belief or Unbelief? Perspectives from the Vatican," *Modern Theology* 23, no. 2 (April 2007): 209.

[23] Ibid., 208.

[24] See John Sivalon, *Mission in Postmodernity: The Gift of Uncertainty* (Maryknoll, NY: Orbis Books, 2012), 32.

[25] Benedict XVI, *Ubicumque et Semper*, http://www.vatican.va/holy_father/benedict_xvi/apost_letters/documents/hf_ben-xvi_apl_20100921_ubicumque-et-semper_en.html, accessed September 23, 2014.

[26] Benedict XVI, "Homily at the Conclusion of the Special Assembly for the Middle East of the Synod of Bishops," *L'Osservatore Romano: Weekly Edition in English*, October 27, 2010.

[27] XIII Ordinary General Assembly of the Synod, *Lineamenta*, preface.

Pope John Paul II had spoken several times of three aspects of the new evangelization: its newness in ardor, methods, and expression. Although all three are mentioned occasionally in the presynodal documents and in the talks of Pope Benedict, the impression these documents and talks give is that newness in *ardor* is the most important.[28] One of the key words in the *lineamenta* is "boldness," recurring thirteen times in the document, seven times in the text, and six times in the questions that follow. In the *instrumentum laboris* we read that "our institutions need to adopt a bold and even 'apologetic' approach and seek ways of publically affirming their faith, fearlessly and with a clear sense of pastoral urgency."[29] The *instrumentum laboris* quotes Pope Benedict's conviction that there is in the church an "educational emergency" due to the individualism and secularism of the age.[30]

The 2012 Synod:
Shifts in the Center of Gravity

While an emphasis on a new ardor or boldness in the church's evangelizing efforts was also expressed in the synod itself,[31] some of the more striking interventions of the bishops focused more on a new attitude of humility, gentleness, and listening that needed to be espoused by the church as it renews its efforts of evangelization in the world. Bishop Bernard Longley of Birmingham, England, for example, emphasized that the prerequisite for evangelization today is "profound listening." "There can be no effective proclamation of the faith, Longley said, 'without an attempt to understand how the message is likely to be heard, how it sounds to others.'"[32] Archbishop (now Cardinal) Luis Antonio Tagle

[28] XIII Ordinary General Assembly of the Synod, *Lineamenta*, 5; see also XIII Ordinary General Assembly of the Synod of Bishops, *Instrumentum Laboris* of The New Evangelization for the Transmission of the Christian Faith, preface, 23, 45, 62, http://www.vatican.va/roman_curia/synod/documents/rc_synod_doc_20120619 _instrumentum-xiii_en.html, accessed September 23, 2014.

[29] See XIII Ordinary General Assembly of the Synod, *Lineamenta*, 2–11. See also XIII Ordinary General Assembly of the Synod, *Instrumentum Laboris*, 138.

[30] XIII Ordinary General Assembly of the Synod, *Instrumentum Laboris*, 152.

[31] For example, the interventions of Cardinal Peter Erdő of Hungary, Archbishop John Dew of Wellington, New Zealand, and Cardinal Sodano. See http://www.vatican .va/news_services/press/sinodo/documents/bollettino_25_xiii-ordinaria-2012 /xx_plurilingue/b05_xx.html, accessed September 23, 2014.

[32] Intervention of Archbishop Bernard Longley, quoted in Noel Connolly, "New Evangelisation in Australia," *Sedos Bulletin*, 137, http://www.sedosmission.org/sedos articles/documents/nconnolly-2013-newev-en.pdf, accessed September 23, 2014.

of Manila also called for the church to listen first before speaking. "The Church must discover the power of silence," he said. "Confronted with the sorrows, doubts and uncertainties of people she cannot pretend to give easy solutions. In Jesus, silence becomes the way of attentive listening, compassion and prayer."[33] Another bishop from the Philippines, Socrates Villegas from Lingayen-Dagupan, emphasized the fact that "the new evangelization calls for new humility. . . . This humility will make us more credible new evangelizers. Our mission is to propose humbly, not to impose proudly."[34] To give one more example, Adolfo Nicolás, Jesuit Superior General and longtime Asian missionary, spoke of how humility, simplicity, generosity, and joy are the tried and true ways of best communicating the Gospel.[35] These interventions, though a minority voice at the synod, went beyond the impression often given that the new evangelization is simply evangelization "revved up,"[36] or as I have put it in several talks I have given, saying the same old thing but saying it more loudly. If other voices advocated a move back to the time before the council, these voices at the synod were advocating a real time dialogue of the church with today's world. Only a listening church could offer the conditions of the possibility of an evangelization adequate to the present day.

Ronald Witherup reflects on the fact that the synod pointed away from the new evangelization's rather exclusive emphasis on the secular West. Writing about the list of final propositions from the synod, he takes note of a "slight change in direction"[37] that developed as the synod progressed. As noted above, the original intention of the synod was to address issues arising particularly in the secularized West. Such a perspective was seen in many of the interventions as well, and also in the final propositions. Witherup says, however, that "a renewed emphasis on the mission *ad gentes* or *ad extra*, that is, an outreach to those who have

---

[33] Intervention of Luis Antonio Tagle, http://www.vatican.va/news_services/press/sinodo/documents/bollettino_25_xiii-ordinaria-2012/xx_plurilingue/b07_xx.html, accessed September 23, 2014.

[34] Intervention of Socrates B. Villegas, http://www.vatican.va/news_services/press/sinodo/documents/bollettino_25_xiii-ordinaria-2012/xx_plurilingue/b07_xx.html, accessed September 23, 2014.

[35] Intervention of Adolfo Nicolás Pachón, http://www.vatican.va/news_services/press/sinodo/documents/bollettino_25_xiii-ordinaria-2012/xx_plurilingue/b09_xx.html, accessed September 23, 2014.

[36] See Witherup, *Saint Paul*, 51.

[37] Ibid., 16.

not received the Gospel message, is now also prominent. It reinforces the notion that the church is always on mission, always outwardly oriented to proclaim the message of Jesus Christ."[38]

Pope Francis and *Evangelii Gaudium*: Beyond the New Evangelization

The calls at the synod for a more open, listening church, the shifts toward spirituality, structural reform, and dialogue, and the insistence on a renewed form of evangelization for the entire church, not just the West, are all features of the remarkable postsynodal apostolic exhortation of Pope Francis, *Evangelii Gaudium*. Since his election, Francis has astounded the world with one dramatic gesture after another—asking the crowds to pray for him when he first appeared on the balcony after his election, embracing a quadriplegic man at his inauguration, washing the feet of Muslim women on Holy Thursday, uttering his famous phrase, "Who am I to judge?" when asked about gay priests, releasing wide-ranging and frank interviews. Such gestures seemed to signal an entirely new, astonishingly fresh approach not only to the Petrine ministry but also to witnessing to the Gospel. The first pope ordained to the priesthood after the Second Vatican Council was signalling the validity of all that the council stood for. In his commentary on *Evangelii Gaudium*, Italian theologian Christian Albini expressed his conviction that the document "signals a new stage in the trajectory opened by Vatican II."[39]

Evangelii Gaudium seems to lead the church beyond the synod's theme of new evangelization toward a vision of the church as going forth as a "community of missionary disciples."[40] It is perhaps significant that the term "new evangelization" appears only twelve times in this very long

---

[38] Ibid.

[39] Christian Albini, *Guida alla lettura della* Evangelii Gaudium (n.p., n.d.), 72. This connection with the council has been noted as well by Richard R. Gaillardetz, "The 'Francis Moment': A New Kairos for Catholic Ecclesiology," *Proceedings of the Catholic Theological Society of America* 69 (2014): 63–64, http://ejournals.bc.edu/ojs/index.php /ctsa/article/view/5509/4988, accessed September 23, 2014. See also Richard R. Gaillardetz, "Francis: Pope of the Council," http://elephantsinthelivingroom.com, accessed September 23, 2014.

[40] Francis, *Evangelii Gaudium* (On the Joy of the Gospel), 24, https://w2.vatican.va /content/francesco/en/apost_exhortations/documents/papa-francesco_esortazione -ap_20131124_evangelii-gaudium.html, accessed December 11, 2014. See also Albini, *Guida*, 18.

document.[41] Equally significant are phrases like "new chapter," "new paths," "new phase," and "new processes" of evangelization.[42] The pope likewise speaks of a "new missionary going forth," a "new evangelical fervor," and "new challenges to evangelization."[43] The pope gives the strong impression that he is leading the church beyond the new evangelization toward an understanding of the church that is, in the words of Vatican II, "missionary by its very nature" (AG 2). As he introduces his apostolic exhortation, Francis notes that the topics on which he reflects in the document "help give shape to a definite style of evangelization which I ask you to adopt *in every activity you undertake*."[44]

"I dream of a 'missionary option,'" Francis writes, "that is a missionary impulse capable of transforming everything, so that the Church's customs, ways of doing things, times and schedules, language and structures can be suitably channeled for the evangelization of today's world rather than for her preservation."[45] Here in one sentence is Francis's vision for the church, one adequate for this time. The passage goes on to speak of a "pastoral conversion" that demands renewed structures that will make "ordinary pastoral activity on every level more inclusive and open," that will call pastoral workers to go forth to preach and witness to the gospel. As Martin Tuelan, National Director of Australia's Catholic Mission, observes, "rather than stressing new evangelization or overseas mission, Pope Francis sees that the whole Church needs to be 'permanently in a state of mission.'"[46] Francis echoed the 2012 synod's move to speak of new evangelization not only in terms of the secularized West but also as taking place in ordinary pastoral work, among people "whose lives do not reflect the demands of Baptism," and in situations of primary evangelization.[47] Thus, like the synod itself, he offers a wider

[41] Francis, *Evangelii Gaudium*, 73, 120, 126, 198, 239, 260, 284, 287, 288. A word count on the Vatican website yields a count of fourteen times, but two of these are in the introductory outline of the document, not in the document itself.

[42] Ibid., 1, 11, 17, 31, 69, 161, 287, 288.

[43] Ibid., 20, 29. I think it quite significant that the title given to the October 2014 Synod of Bishops is "The Pastoral Challenge of the Family in the Context of Evangelization"—not "the *New* Evangelization."

[44] Francis, *Evangelii Gaudium*, 18. Italics are in the original.

[45] Ibid., 27.

[46] Martin Tuelan, "Called to Be Missionary Disciples," in *The Francis Effect: Living the Joy of the Gospel*, ed. Danielle Achikian, Peter Gates, and Lana Turvey (Sydney: Catholic Mission and Catholic Religious Australia, 2013), 44.

[47] Francis, *Evangelii Gaudium*, 14. Here Francis is citing Benedict XVI's opening homily of the synod.

understanding of the new evangelization than the synod's preparatory documents, moving that understanding toward a consistent vision of a missionary church.[48]

This move from the new evangelization to a more comprehensive missionary church is a highly significant one, both ecclesiologically and missiologically. The new evangelization emerged out of the concern of two European popes in the context of a radically secularized Europe, on the one hand, and a church that, to their minds, had lost the clarity of its commitment to the content of the faith, on the other. Pope Francis's call for a truly missionary church comes out of a totally different context, and reflects not a European interest, but that of the majority world. Perhaps much of the missionary emphasis of the Aparecida document—a major source for *Evangelii Gaudium*, and the source of the term "missionary discipleship"—was occasioned by a need to respond to the growing exodus of Catholics to Evangelical and Pentecostal groups, and so very rooted in the Latin American context.[49] The tone of the apostolic exhortation, however, transcends that context and is motivated by a more universal missionary vision. It does not deny the vision of the new evangelization but takes the vision further to make it more comprehensive and more relevant for the entire church.

Moving Forward:
Toward A Missionary Ecclesiology

Pope Francis's call for the church to understand itself as a "community of missionary disciples" seems to require a thorough rethinking of ecclesiology in the light of missiology. The perspective favored by John Paul II and Benedict XVI was to reflect on and explain the church in terms of "communion," an understanding also favored by the Extraordinary Synod of Bishops of 1985.[50] Francis's preferred way of speaking about the church taps into a separate emphasis in Vatican II, evident in documents like the Pastoral Constitution on the Church in the Modern World and the Decree on the Church's Missionary Activity. This latter document

---

[48] For fuller reflections on *Evangelii Gaudium*, see Bevans, "New Evangelization," and Gaillardetz, "The 'Francis Moment,'" 67–72.

[49] Fifth General Conference of the Bishops of Latin America and the Caribbean, Concluding Document, 225–26 (Aparecida, 2007), http://www.aecrc.org/documents/Aparecida-Concluding%20Document.pdf, accessed September 23, 2014.

[50] See Gaillardetz, "The 'Francis Moment,'" 64–65.

speaks forcefully of the church, rooted in the missions of the Trinity, as "missionary by its very nature" (AG 2). It is this phrase, I suggest, that should be the starting point for a contemporary ecclesiological reflection that is adequate for our time. As Richard Gaillardetz describes Francis's ecclesiological agenda, "a missionary council has inspired a missionary pope to create a missionary church."[51]

Gaillardetz himself, of course, has gone a long way in developing a missionary ecclesiology in his *Ecclesiology for a Global Church*, especially in terms of dialogue with cultures beyond the West.[52] Neil Ormerod's recently published *Re-Visioning the Church* stresses the "operator" of mission as shaping the "integrator" of communal identity.[53] While more specifically missiological, Roger Schroeder's and my books *Constants in Context* and *Prophetic Dialogue* have been rooted in an implicit missionary ecclesiology.[54]

What I would like to sketch out in the final section of this chapter is the outline of a full missionary ecclesiology, one that contains the main issues and questions demanding scholarly attention from ecclesiologists today. Such an ecclesiology attempts to unpack the lapidary phrase in Vatican II's Decree on the Church's Missionary Activity regarding the church's essential missionary nature. It might also be described as the unpacking of Pope Francis's call for a "community of missionary disciples."[55]

This sketch of a missionary ecclesiology is divided into three parts, emphasizing varying aspects of the image of the church as a "community of missionary disciples." A first part reflects on "The Essence of the Church: A Community of *Missionary* Disciples." A second part probes "The Mystery of the Church: A *Community* of Missionary Disciples." A third and final part outlines "The Structure of the Church: A Community of Missionary

---

[51] Richard R. Gaillardetz, "Francis Wishes to Release Vatican II's Bold Vision from Captivity," *NCROnline* (September 25, 2013), http://ncronline.org/news/vatican /francis-wishes-release-vatican-iis-bold-vision-captivity, accessed September 25, 2014. See also Gaillardetz, "The 'Francis Moment,'" 67–71.

[52] Richard R. Gaillardetz, *Ecclesiology for a Global Church* (Maryknoll, NY: Orbis Books, 2008).

[53] Neil Ormerod, *Re-Visioning the Church: An Experiment in Systematic-Historical Ecclesiology* (Grand Rapids, MI: Eerdmans, 2014).

[54] Stephen B. Bevans and Roger P. Schroeder, *Constants in Context: A Theology of Mission for Today* (Maryknoll, NY: Orbis Books, 2004); Stephen B. Bevans and Roger P. Schroeder, *Prophetic Dialogue: Reflections on Christian Mission Today* (Maryknoll, NY: Orbis Books, 2011).

[55] Francis, *Evangelii Gaudium*, 24.

Disciples."[56] The challenge of a missionary ecclesiology is to keep a balance between the "centrifugal" nature of the church lived out in mission and a more "centripetal" aspect of the church expressed in the understanding of the church as communion. One might characterize the church, a community of missionary disciples, as a "communion-in-mission," a dynamic interplay of communion and mission.

In developing such a missionary ecclesiology, attention needs to be paid to sources available in the global church, not only Roman documents. These might be documents from official sources like the Conference of Latin American Bishops (CELAM), the Federation of Asian Bishops' Conferences (FABC), the Symposium of Episcopal Conferences of Africa and Madagascar (SECAM), the Commission of Bishops' Conferences of the European Community (COMECE), the Episcopal Conference of the Pacific (CEPAC), the United States Conference of Catholic Bishops (USCCB), or the Canadian Conference of Catholic Bishops (CCCB). Such an ecclesiology should be developed in dialogue with major Orthodox, Protestant, and Evangelical sources such as those issued by the World Council of Churches, the various Orthodox Churches, and the Lausanne Movement. Sources should also include major theologians from every region of the globe, especially the voices of various liberation and contextual theologies, such as feminist, African American, queer, Asian, and Latino/a theologies. Concerns from all these various perspectives, as Natalia Imperatori-Lee advocates in her chapter in this volume, should be "mainstreamed" into an ecclesiology that is in dialogue with all Christian and theological voices. Such an ecclesiology would be both contextual—rooted in particular contexts and cultures—and a product of dialogue *among* contextual theologies.

The Essence of the Church:
A Community of Missionary Disciples

What needs to be recognized first in the construction of a missionary ecclesiology is that the church is rooted in the overflowing life of the Trinity, which is itself a communion-in-mission. God's first act of mission is creation, and God has been present and active in creation from its first

---

[56] Readers will no doubt notice that this threefold structure is very much influenced by Hans Küng's classic ecclesiology *The Church* (New York: Sheed and Ward, 1967). While in many ways now outdated after fifty years, it still remains, in my mind, an articulation of Catholic ecclesiology of the utmost importance.

nanosecond. Such presence and activity is the work of the Spirit, who from the beginning persuades, encourages, cajoles, inspires—but never imposes on creation's freedom.[57] And so came to be the gasses, the molecules, the stars, the galaxies, and our earth with its abundant life. As human beings emerged on our planet, the Spirit was there and was present in humanity's first groping toward understanding the depth and breadth of life's meaning, gradually taking shape in the world's great religions.[58] One of these religions was that of Israel, who expressed God's presence and activity in the images of wind, fire, breath, water, oil, a soaring bird—all images that, while palpable, are nevertheless illusive and mysterious, images of God as Mystery "inside out" in creation and human history.[59] We read of God breathing life into "earth creature" (*ha Adam*, Gen 2:7),[60] anointing prophets to proclaim healing and justice (Isa 61:1-2), flowing like a river to bring freshness and life in the desert (Ezek 47), blowing over dry bones to bring them together and back to life (Ezek 37:1-14).

The history of the presence of the Holy Spirit in creation and especially in Israel is a prelude to understanding the foundation of the church, which begins with the mission and ministry of Jesus. In the "fullness of time," as Paul wrote (Gal 4:4), the ever-present saving activity of God took on flesh and a human face in the person of Jesus of Nazareth. As Elizabeth Johnson writes, "[T]hrough [Jesus'] human history the Spirit who pervades the universe becomes concretely present in a small bit of it."[61] Jesus' mission was, in the words of Neil Ormerod, the advancement of the reign of God[62]—the continuation of God's saving work from the beginning, but now imminent. "The time is fulfilled, and the kingdom of God has come near; repent, and believe in the good news" (Mark 1:15).

---

[57] Both Denis Edwards and, more recently, Elizabeth Johnson have written elegantly in this regard. See Denis Edwards, *How God Acts: Creation, Redemption, and Special Divine Acts* (Minneapolis, MN: Fortress Press, 2008); and Elizabeth A. Johnson, *Ask the Beasts: Darwin and the God of Love* (London: Bloomsbury, 2014).

[58] The inspiration for this sentence is Denis Edwards, *Breath of Life: A Theology of the Creator Spirit* (Maryknoll, NY: Orbis Books, 2004), 33, 171–72.

[59] See Stephen Bevans, "God Inside Out: Toward a Missionary Theology of the Holy Spirit," *International Bulletin of Missionary Research* 22, no. 3 (July 1998): 102–5.

[60] "Earth creature" is author's translation.

[61] Elizabeth A. Johnson, *She Who Is: The Mystery of God in Feminist Theological Discourse* (New York: Crossroad, 1992), 150.

[62] Ormerod, *Re-Visioning the Church*, 106–8.

Jesus witnessed to this coming fulfillment by his own personal behavior of welcoming and inclusion, as well as his freedom from the ritualistic and dehumanizing aspects of religious custom. He served his vision by his healings and exorcisms—signs of the wholeness of God's salvation and of God's liberating action in human life. And he preached God's nearness in parables that spoke of God's mercy, God's commitment to justice, God's inclusion, and God's tenderness. Jesus was a person filled with the Holy Spirit, anointed by the Spirit at his baptism to proclaim the good news and bring healing and hope to God's people (Luke 4:18-19).

Such behavior, however, got Jesus into trouble. What infuriated the religious leaders of his day, says Latino theologian Virgilio Elizondo, was "his willingness and ability to have a good time with anyone and everyone" and his refusal "to be scandalized by anyone."[63] And so they killed him. But, of course, three days later his disciples began to experience his living presence among them, and gradually, in the aftermath of Pentecost, they came to the amazing realization that the Spirit that had been lavished upon Jesus had also been lavished upon them. In this growing realization that *Jesus'* mission was *their* mission, the church was born. The church is indeed "missionary by its very nature" because it is missionary in its very origin.

The missionary nature of the church is further probed by a reflection on its complex relation to the reign of God. As Jesus' mission and ministry were defined by the reign of God, so are those of the church. The church exists as subordinate to and servant of the reign of God, although God's reign is not entirely a separate reality from it. Indeed, the church is a community of sinners, God's people imperfectly assembled, who nevertheless pray for the reign's arrival as they "wait in joyful hope." It is to the reign of God—and not necessarily to the church—that all are called by God's all-inclusive salvific will (see LG 16). Nevertheless, the church must never cease from inviting women and men to join its ranks, but not out of a motivation to join an exclusive group whose members alone are saved. Rather, the church must be envisioned as a life-giving community that finds the fullness of life in the joyful sharing in God's saving work and service. Salvation is found in such kenotic free giving of self. Understanding the church's relationship to the reign of God re-

---

[63] Virgilio Elizondo, "The Miracle of Conversion," *Give Us This Day* 3, no. 1 (January 2013): 205.

veals the church as "not of ultimate importance."[64] Although opinions vary here,[65] a fair consensus among ecclesiologists is that the church as such will cease to exist when the reign of God is finally established. This is the essence of the church: to give itself in service to God's reign, just as Jesus, anointed by the Spirit, gave *him*self. The church—sign, foretaste, and witness to God's reign—continues Jesus' mission in a trinitarian practice of "prophetic dialogue," boldly yet humbly witnessing to the Gospel with which it is entrusted.[66]

The Mystery of the Church: A Community of Missionary Disciples

Having established the missionary nature of the church, ecclesiology turns to the reality of the church as mystery. The church is not simply a visible, fallible society. It is, in its deepest core, a society "imbued with the presence of God," a communion of "people made one with the unity of the Father, Son, and Holy Spirit."[67]

Here we reflect on the missionary nature of three scripturally based images of the church: the people of God, the Body of Christ, and the creation/temple of the Holy Spirit. The image of the church as God's special people, grafted onto the original olive tree of Israel (see Rom 11:17-24), is that of a people chosen not for privilege but for service, a people in which all nations will find a blessing (see Gen 12:3).[68] Paul's image of the Body of Christ appears in 1 Corinthians and Romans, and on closer reading, we discover that it is a missionary image. Baptism identifies us with Christ, whom we have put on as a garment, in whom we live, and with whom we become one in our participation in the Eucharist (see Rom 6:1-11; Col 3:10-11; Gal 2:20; 1 Cor 10:16-17). In this image, the church is the way that Christ continues to be present and active in the world. The third image is that of the creation/temple of the

---

[64] Bevans and Schroeder, *Constants in Context*, 7.

[65] E.g., Avery Dulles, *Models of the Church* (New York: Image Books, 1978), 109–27.

[66] See Bevans and Schroeder, *Prophetic Dialogue*; and David J. Bosch, *Transforming Mission: Paradigm Shifts in Theology of Mission* (Maryknoll, NY: Orbis Books, 1991), 489.

[67] Paul VI, Opening Address of the Second Session of Vatican II, in *Enchiridion Vaticanum* (Bologna: Edizioni Dehoniane, 1968), 97; LG 4.

[68] See also Christopher J. H. Wright, *The Mission of God: Unlocking the Bible's Grand Narrative* (Downers Grove, IL: IVP Academic, 2006), 190–264; Lesslie Newbigin, *The Gospel in a Pluralist Society* (Grand Rapids, MI: Eerdmans, 1989), 80–88.

Holy Spirit. In the previous section, we saw that it is the Spirit who creates the church as she pushes the early community beyond the boundaries of Israel to the Gentiles, who continues to push the church to new and surprising realizations and practices.[69] The temple is the place of God's mysterious yet palpable presence in the world (1 Kgs 9:1-9; Ezek 10:18-23; 1 Cor 3:16). As God's temple, the church is called to be a witness to God's saving presence in the world.

The four traditional "marks" of the church—one, holy, catholic, and apostolic—are, in evangelical theologian Charles van Engen's words, dynamic "distinctives" of the church's mission.[70] In a missionary ecclesiology, the mark of "apostolicity" comes first, since it roots the church in the apostolic commission of "teaching all nations" (Matt 28:19; cf. Acts 1:8; 1 Pet 3:15).

Each dimension of the church has a threefold identity. Thus the church *is* apostolic as a gift; it is *called* to be apostolic in fidelity; and it is to *act* apostolically in mission. In the following chapter, Paul Lakeland will develop this dynamic notion of the mark of apostolicity. Similarly, the church *is* catholic but *called* to be catholic in its appreciation of local identity and diversity-in-unity, and commissioned to *work* for the catholicity of the world by protecting and fostering diversity (as regards culture, theology, gender, and generational identity) in a constant dialogue for unity. Such unity *is* already a gift and yet *calls* the church to *work* for unity among all Christians and to work as well for unity among all religions and peoples. Finally, the church *is* holy as God's special people and therefore *called* to be holy as a sign of God's presence in the world. The church is called as well to *point out* the holiness beyond its boundaries and invite people into the explicit relationship with God that it already enjoys.

In sum, "communion and mission enrich each other." As Pope Francis has written, "we no longer say that we are 'disciples' and 'missionaries,' but rather that we are always 'missionary disciples.' "[71]

---

[69] See Commission on World Mission and Evangelism, *Together Towards Life: Mission and Evangelism in Changing Landscapes*, http://www.oikoumene.org/en/resources /documents/commissions/mission-and-evangelism/together-towards-life-mission -and-evangelism-in-changing-landscapes, 25. See also Stephen B. Bevans, "The Church as Creation of the Spirit: Unpacking a Missionary Image," *Missiology: An International Review* 35, no. 1 (January 2007): 5–21.

[70] Charles van Engen, *God's Missionary People* (Grand Rapids, MI: Baker Academic, 1991), 59–71.

[71] Francis, *Evangelii Gaudium*, 120.

The Structure of the Church:
A Community of Missionary Disciples

The structure of the church should serve the church's mission. As Reformed theologian Craig van Gelder put it tersely, the church "organizes what it does."[72] Pope Francis writes that, in light of the "missionary option" about which he dreams, everything in the church "can be suitably channeled for the evangelization of today's world rather than for her self-preservation. The renewal of structures demanded by pastoral conversion can only be understood in this light: as part of an effort to make them more mission-oriented."[73]

An initial point that needs to be made is that, in the light of mission, the primary structure of the church is no structure. Rather, first and foremost there is a "structure" of fundamental equality in virtue of baptism. We are first of all *disciples*—in particular, *missionary* disciples (see LG 32).[74] As Hans Küng insists, distinction of any kind in the church "is of secondary if not tertiary importance."[75] Kathleen Cahalan argues that disciples are *followers* of Jesus, as well as worshippers, witnesses, neighbors, forgivers, prophets, and stewards.[76] All participate in the mission of God, as God's people.

Thomas O'Meara writes that, in terms of the reality of grace, "ultimately, there are only two theological perspectives: the dividing line or the circle of circles."[77] The same is true of the church's structure. While some disciples are called to ministry within the church, ministry does not so much *divide* ministers from "ordinary disciples" as it marks a particular presence of baptismal grace that all share equally. Rather than distinguishing sharply between "laity" and "clergy," a missionary ecclesiology should focus on the various ways that Christian women and men share in the one mission of the church in its witness, service, and proclamation of the reign of God.[78]

---

[72] Craig van Gelder, *The Essence of the Church* (Grand Rapids, MI: Baker Books, 2000), 37.

[73] Francis, *Evangelii Gaudium*, 27.

[74] See also Kathleen Cahalan, *Introducing the Practice of Ministry* (Collegeville, MN: Liturgical Press, 2010), 24–47; and Francis, *Evangelii Gaudium*, 24.

[75] Küng, *The Church*, 363.

[76] Cahalan, *Introducing the Practice of Ministry*, 3–23.

[77] O'Meara, *A Theologian's Journey*, 301.

[78] On this, see the very helpful reflections of Richard R. Gaillardetz, *The Church in the Making: Lumen Gentium, Christus Dominus, Orientalium Ecclesiarum* (Mahwah,

That being said, there does exist in the church a certain order that is not so much hierarchical as ministerial. As Edward Hahnenberg points out, various kinds of ministries are shaped by various factors. First, there is the degree of commitment that a minister evidences. Is it occasional? For a particular period of time? A lifetime commitment? Second, ministry is characterized by the kind of ministry in which the minister is engaged. Is the person working under someone else's leadership or assuming a distinct role of leadership in a particular area? Third, a particular ministry is distinguished by the type of recognition it is given in the church and by the church's leadership.[79] Some ministries are public roles of service in the church yet are taken up occasionally and require a relatively minimal level of training and formation. Lectors and choir members are certainly examples of these important ministers. Others are responsible for a particular area of leadership in the church—for example, the director of religious education in a parish or the director of music or liturgy or social justice ministries. For this task a particular expertise is required, a theological degree is necessary, and the minister might be a salaried member of a parish or diocesan staff and receive a special commission from a local bishop. Still others are called to be more widely responsible for the general order of their community, coordinating, forming, and leading the various ministries of a parish or diocesan faith community. Such a ministry ordinarily demands a lifetime commitment and a high level of theological and pastoral competence.

These various kinds of ministries are traditionally spoken of as lay ministry, the newly emerging reality of lay ecclesial ministry, and ordained ministry. Richard Gaillardetz has proposed that we speak instead of commissioned ministries (e.g., lectors), installed ministries (e.g., directors of liturgy), and ordained ministries (bishops, presbyters/priests, and deacons).[80] However we speak of them, their purpose is to serve and order the church's mission.

In the Roman Catholic Church we speak of the Petrine ministry, or the ministry of the pope. In the light of a missionary ecclesiology, the pope is the "servant of the servants of God," the one who exercises the

---

NJ: Paulist Press, 2006), 52–55; see also Edward P. Hahnenberg, *Theology for Ministry: An Introduction for Lay Ministers* (Collegeville, MN: Liturgical Press, 2014), 107–27.

[79] Hahnenberg, *Theology for Ministry*, 120.

[80] Richard R. Gaillardetz, "Ecclesiological Foundations of Ministry within an Ordered Communion," in *Ordering the Baptismal Priesthood*, ed. Susan Wood (Collegeville, MN: Liturgical Press, 2003), 26–51, esp. 36–47.

care of all the churches and serves as a sign of unity and the possibility of dialogue for the entire communion of local churches that make up the universal, global church of today. While the pope is indeed, in the preferred idiom of Pope Francis, the "Bishop of Rome," nevertheless, in light of the fact that the last three popes have not been Italian, the papacy has taken on a rather new role in the church as a global leader in a globalized church. In this role, the pope is not a "super bishop," but one whose primacy is to oversee the entire church as it engages in its mission of witness, service, and proclamation of the reign of God.

The title of David Power's important book, *Mission, Ministry, Order,* is instructive. First there is *mission,* in which every Christian shares as a baptized disciple. Then there is *ministry,* in which some Christians share with varying levels of responsibility—although these do not correspond to differences in importance or dignity (as Pope Francis insists, our dignity "derives from Baptism, which is accessible to all"[81]). In the third place comes *order* "for the sake of the particular church and the sake of communion between churches."[82] The church is shaped to serve its participation in the mission of God.

Conclusion

This chapter has been a reflection on how today's church, under the leadership of Pope Francis, is once more discovering its time, and with time, history and culture. Today's church is a missionary church. The "fields" of mission described by *Ad Gentes* are present in virtually every instantiation of the local church. In almost every church there are people to whom the Gospel needs to be preached or re-presented, people whose Christian life needs to be nourished and equipped for service, and Christian communities that need to be healed of the scars of 1054 and 1517. This is as true in suburban Boston as it is in inner city Chicago, the Kibera slum in Nairobi, the favelas of Rio, or the barrios of Ilocos Sur in the Philippines. The new ardor, methods, and expressions called for by Pope John Paul II need to be operative in every field of mission, not just in situations of Western secularism. Our time calls forth a church that moves beyond what has been called the new evangelization to the formation of a community of missionary disciples, and ecclesiology for our

---

[81] Francis, *Evangelii Gaudium,* 104.
[82] David Noel Power, *Mission, Ministry, Order: Reading the Tradition in the Present Context* (New York: Continuum, 2008), 2.

time has to reflect that community's life and practice as it participates in the mission of God.

For Further Reading

Bevans, Stephen B. "Revisiting Mission at Vatican II: Theology and Practice for Today's Missionary Church." *Theological Studies* 74, no. 2 (June 2013): 261–83.

Bevans, Stephen B., and Roger P. Schroeder. *Constants in Context: A Theology of Mission for Today*. Maryknoll, NY: Orbis Books, 2004.

———. *Prophetic Dialogue: Reflections on Christian Mission Today*. Maryknoll, NY: Orbis Books, 2011.

Bosch, David J. *Transforming Mission: Paradigm Shifts in Theology of Mission*. Maryknoll, NY: Orbis Books, 1991.

Gaillardetz, Richard R. *Ecclesiology for a Global Church: A People Called and Sent*. Maryknoll, NY: Orbis Books, 2008.

Ormerod, Neil. *Re-Visioning the Church: An Experiment in Systematic-Historical Ecclesiology*. Grand Rapids, MI: Eerdmans, 2014.

Paul VI, *Evangelii Nuntiandi*, http://www.vatican.va/holy_father/paul_vi /apost_exhortations/documents/hf_p-vi_exh_19751208_evangelii -nuntiandi_en.html. Accessed September 23, 2014.

Power, David Noel. *Mission, Ministry, Order: Reading the Tradition in the Present Context*. New York: Continuum, 2008.

Sivalon, John. *Mission in Postmodernity: The Gift of Uncertainty*. Maryknoll, NY: Orbis Books, 2012.

Witherup, Ronald D. *Saint Paul and the New Evangelization*. Collegeville, MN: Liturgical Press, 2013.

CHAPTER 2

Ecclesiology and the Use of Demography: Three Models of Apostolicity

Paul Lakeland

Things Jesus Never Said: "My target demographic is . . ."

—Don Miller

I am not sure that today theologians can risk saying anything valid for people in general and especially for their own Church, if they refuse to accept the fact that the world around them is tottering.

—Ghislain Lafont

Grace draws forth human striving to all that is good.

—Thomas O'Meara

The science of demography is driven by human curiosity to know more than we do about the world we live in, the church we love or the company we keep, and to know it better. It begins with statistics, but it is in the analysis of the numbers that demography has its true purpose. If statistics are the starting point, analysis is the consequence and understanding is the result. If numbers are where we begin, comprehension is where we hope to end up.

Ecclesiology in today's world is also the product of a desire to know more and to know better, though it was perhaps not always so. Indeed, for most of Christian history reflection on the church has been a largely deductive activity, mirroring theology in general. But with the advent of a more inductive approach to theological method, the starting point for ecclesiological reflection has moved from abstractions to the actual living community itself.[1] And with that has come the need for statistical and demographic information, lest our ecclesiology be simply anecdotal. Ecclesially, demography provides us with facts. Interpretation provides us with conclusions.[2]

Most striking about the way we respond to demographics is what that response reveals about our ecclesial self-understanding, and more particularly, what it reveals about the shortcomings of our self-understanding. In particular, it is instructive to examine the relationship between centripetal and centrifugal approaches to ecclesiology as they variously digest the findings of demography. The "centripetal" approach suggests both the necessary attention to the internal health of the church as well as more introspective or even solipsistic inclinations. "Centrifugal" suggests all movement outward from the church, both evangelization and dialogue with the secular world. The relationship between the two directions is most easily expressed in the conviction that the church does not exist for its own sake but for the sake of the world to which it is sent. Both movements are of course necessary, but getting the balance between the two correct is important and instructive. The centripetal impulse, necessary though it is to some degree, has to be at the service of the centrifugal. Unfortunately, not all ecclesiology looks at things this way or recognizes the urgency to do so that flows from the results of demographic analysis of today's church. Too often, ecclesiology is introspective and the centrifugal dimension is, if anything, an add-on to ecclesial existence, rather than its *raison d'être*. It is this serious ecclesiological misunderstanding that will be explored in what follows.

The balance between centripetal and centrifugal impulses in ecclesiology reflects convictions about the relationship between the church as the community of faith and the church as an evangelical body of believers. What is at stake here is how the church understands its apostolic mission,

---

[1] Precisely because contemporary ecclesiological reflection needs to be inductive, it is therefore contextual. The context of these remarks is that of North America and, to a lesser degree, Europe. An additional consideration here is that, while the church of the southern hemisphere is by most estimates much more vibrant than that of the north, serious demographic studies of African, Latin American, and Asian Catholics and their communities have not yet been accomplished.

[2] As we shall see later, demography is by no means an exact science and its conclusions inevitably reflect the way in which its questions are asked, the choice of questions to ask, and the means of access to its data.

and so it will be instructive to examine three types of apostolicity, reflecting on the ecclesial self-understanding that accompanies them and the ways in which they use the findings of demography. They are an apostolicity of maintenance, an apostolicity of the new evangelization, and an apostolicity of *kenosis*. The intention is to show that the ways in which the faith community absorbs the findings of demographic analysis both reflect and stimulate how the church understands itself internally and how it sees its apostolic mission. While there is some value to the first and second of these three types, it is in the third, kenotic form of apostolicity that a vigorous postmodern ecclesiological posture can be discerned. This may be the only one of the three that demonstrates realistic hope rather than muted despair and, perhaps, the only one that follows the christic paradigm of death to self for the sake of new life.

Apostolicity is much more than a slavish conformity to the distant past, as if we could exempt ourselves from history. The term "apostolicity" is most often associated simply with the continuity between the ancient church and that of the present day, in much the way that "apostolic succession" is often understood as an almost literal continuity between the ministry of the apostles and that of today's bishops. Apostolicity goes way beyond this kind of faithfulness, as Ormond Rush has reminded us. "Genuine continuity demands ongoing reinterpretation," he writes, and he points out that this can be seen as early as in the New Testament itself, where we find "a process of reception and traditioning within the apostolic era that shows creative and innovative adaptation of the Gospel as the early church expanded into new cultures." Indeed, Rush calls to his aid here no less an authority than Yves Congar, whose eschatological interpretation of apostolicity supports his position. In Congar's words, "Apostolicity is the mark that for the church is both a gift of grace and a task. It makes the church fill the space between the Alpha and the Omega by ensuring that there is a continuity between the two and a substantial identity between the end and the beginning."[3] As Rush comments, "a static traditioning of the faith endangers the continuity of the church."[4]

---

[3] Yves Congar, "The Spirit Keeps the Church Apostolic," in *I Believe in the Holy Spirit* (New York: Crossroad, 1997), 2:39.

[4] Ormond Rush, *The Eyes of Faith: The Sense of the Faithful and the Church's Reception of Revelation* (Baltimore, MD: Catholic University of America, 2009), 53. This richer understanding of apostolicity as the ongoing apostolic activity of the church is worked out in detail by Yves Congar in his *Lay People in the Church* (Westminster, MD: Christian

Type One:
"Build It and They Will Come"

The first type of apostolicity is almost wholly centripetal. Evidently, apostolicity that is focused solely on promoting the preservation of the existing ecclesial community is a form that is at best muted, at worst not apostolic at all. Understanding the primary role of the church to be self-maintenance fetishizes the current form of the church, inevitably reducing apostolic activity to a sign of a well-ordered community. Apostolic purpose, if it exists at all in this picture, is the open invitation to conversion. More likely, apostolicity is subsumed in the conviction that if the church is maintained faithful to its apostolic roots, it is true to God and itself, and there the matter rests. And, indeed, for much of the twentieth century in the English-speaking world the church successfully presented itself as a bastion of certitude in a changing world and, in consequence, attracted a not inconsiderable number of converts.[5]

Without explicitly pursuing the trope of apostolicity, a number of significant post–Vatican II studies have identified this particular form of church, the "build it and they will come" community of faith, in a variety of interesting ways. Reaching back a half-century, this would be the church that Avery Dulles described under the model of "institution," at least if institution is understood as *the* definition of the church and not as one important model in the ecclesiological balancing act he so superbly described in his classic work, *Models of the Church*.[6] The clarity of Bellarmine's definition of the church as a visible society, wrote Dulles, "was bought at a price." The "innermost reality of the Church," he added, "is the divine self-gift," and definitions do not work where models might, because "at the heart of the Church one finds mystery."[7] Crucially, in his discussion of the institutional model, Dulles quoted Yves Congar's remark that the accompanying ecclesiology sees the church "as machinery of hierarchical mediation" in which the Holy Spirit and the faithful

---

Classics, 1965), 349–99. See also Paul Lakeland, *Church: Living Communion* (Collegeville, MN: Liturgical Press, 2009), 51–59.

[5] This fundamentally neoscholastic model is outlined in John Burkhard's discussion of the work of Joaquin Salaverri (1892–1979), who defines apostolicity as "the permanent identity of the Church's mission as entrusted to the apostles when Christ instituted the Church." See John Burkhard, *Apostolicity Then and Now: An Ecumenical Church in a Postmodern World* (Collegeville, MN: Liturgical Press, 2004), 200, 113.

[6] Avery Dulles, *Models of the Church* (Garden City, NY: Image Books, 1974).

[7] Ibid., 20–21.

people "were kept out of ecclesiological consideration."[8] So, says Dulles, the institutionalist ecclesiology is "operating in terms of a world view in which everything remains essentially the same as it was when it began, and in which origins are therefore all-important."[9] One might reasonably suggest, though Dulles himself does not, that the working understanding of apostolicity in this ecclesiology is that of faithfulness to the apostolic tradition understood entirely retrospectively. Retrospectively and, inevitably, centripetally.

Useful, even seminal, as Dulles's analysis was, it will be instructive to amplify it with two more recent discussions, those of Ghislain Lafont[10] and Staf Hellemans.[11] What Lafont names as "the Gregorian form of the Church," Hellemans identifies in its modern guise as "ultramontane mass Catholicism." Both are describing the church whose death knell was sounded by Vatican II, even if it remains for many still to hear that tolling bell. One of the symptoms of the complacency that marks this church, as Congar implies in the quote above, appears to be deafness to the call of the Spirit, to the clamor of the signs of the times.

Ghislain Lafont's book calls us to reimagine the church in the world after the collapse of modernity. Because the church failed to find within its own resources a response to modernity and instead turned against it, neither church nor culture could influence the other for good. The collapse of modernity is matched by the bankruptcy of "the Gregorian form of the Church." If the church is to survive the crisis of our world, which Lafont sees is also its own crisis, then it must reimagine itself. The danger is that we "give in to the reassuring thought that the current crisis is of no import for the Church but only for the world."[12] The opportunity to imagine the church anew arrives with Vatican II, whose meaning, he thinks, is by no means exhausted by its internal concerns but "assumes greater significance when it is considered in relation to the human

---

[8] Congar, *Lay People in the Church*, 45, quoted in Dulles, *Models of the Church*, 41.

[9] Dulles, *Models of the Church*, 44.

[10] Ghislain Lafont, *Imagining the Catholic Church: Structured Communion in the Spirit* (Collegeville, MN: Liturgical Press, 2000).

[11] Staf Hellemans, "Tracking the New Shape of the Catholic Church in the West," in *Tilburg Theological Studies*, vol. 5, *Towards a New Catholic Church in Advanced Modernity: Transformations, Vision, Tensions*, ed. Staf Hellemans and Jozef Wissink (Zürich: LIT Verlag, 2012), 19–50. While I will be focused on the lengthy opening essay by Hellemans, this entire collection is valuable.

[12] Lafont, *Imagining the Catholic Church*, 30.

predicament out of which it was born."[13] Vatican II ends in principle the trifold pillars of the Gregorian form: the epistemological doctrine of illumination by which the church and its bishops guard "the quasi-identity of revealed truth and the formulas expressing the truth,"[14] the glorification of the papacy, and the holiness of the priesthood. The challenge of Vatican II, not yet fully taken up, is that "the Church must find a way of articulating exactly what is human . . . but without the Church trying to fully disclose the times or trying to supplant their human, immanent capacity to understand the world and act on it."[15]

Staf Hellemans opens his essay, "Tracking the New Shape of the Catholic Church in the West," with a question that places him alongside Lafont, namely, "How will the Catholic Church remain a major church in the West?"[16] Like Lafont, Hellemans sees the earlier forms of the church—Gregorian, early modern, and ultramontane mass Catholicism—as appropriate modernizing steps in their own time. Unlike Lafont, Hellemans interprets Vatican II as an unsuccessful attempt to bring this ultramontane church "into an open church that would cooperate with other churches and with secular movements to bring about a prosperous and just society for all." The 1968 of *Humanae Vitae* rather than the 1968 of the student revolts was "the first signal that the Catholic Church was returning to a conservative stance," but it turned out to be impossible to go back, even for the conservatives.

Dulles, Lafont, and Hellemans all in their different ways ascribe to the pre–Vatican II church a predilection for retrospection that has as its theological motif a profound introspection. Nowhere more clearly can we see this than in phenomena like Pope Benedict's nostalgia for the alliance of Catholic theology and Greek thought,[17] or in the efforts to restore the Tridentine liturgy to a place of greater honor and more fre-

---

[13] Ibid., 30. Lafont's understanding of Vatican II has much in common with the discussion of the council as an event proclaimed most forcefully by Joseph Komonchak and John O'Malley. In his concern to link the council to cultural events, in particular to the student uprisings of 1968, Lafont's approach also shares much with that of Stephen Schloesser. For key essays from all three, see David Schultenover, ed., *Vatican II: Did Anything Happen?* (London and New York: Bloomsbury, 2007).

[14] Lafont, *Imagining the Church*, 39.

[15] Ibid., 45.

[16] Hellemans, "Tracking the New Shape of the Catholic Church," 19.

[17] See Benedict XVI, "Faith, Reason and the University: Memories and Reflections," available at http://www.vatican.va/holy_father/benedict_xvi/speeches/2006/september/documents/hf_ben-xvi_spe_20060912_university-regensburg_en.html, accessed November 26, 2014.

quent celebration. What, one has to ask, does the world in which the church exists and to which it is sent care about a renewed Platonism, a return to Latin, or a back view of the priest celebrating the liturgy? What is there enticing or inspiring to modern Europeans and North Americans about the interpretation of their honest efforts to negotiate a complex world as sheer relativism? Though postmodern human beings would not put it in these words, what does a church have to offer that reprioritizes Law over Gospel? Of course there are many Catholics with good and bad reasons to favor the priestly posture *ad orientem*, to love Plato, and to oppose relativism. But does this mean that the Gospel should not and could not demonstrate historical flexibility occasioned by the needs of the human race as a whole? These seem to be the questions that Lafont and Hellemans would like to press in the context of their sober if not equally gloomy assessment of the post–Vatican II church.

What comfort can the church of Bellarmine, of ultramontanism, and of Pope Gregory draw from the results of demographic studies of church life and belief? How will the demographics support the hope that it is this church and not another which is the one that will survive? To what will one pay attention, and what will one ignore? For the most part, demographic analysis of the Catholic Church is conducted responsibly with no perceptible ideological or theological bias.[18] But that does not mean that individuals or institutions cannot read the statistics, however unconsciously, in ways that reveal their biases.

The remnants of the Gregorian form of the church or of ultramontane mass Catholicism have a hard time with the findings of demographic analysis. Today these remnants are found mainly in fringe groups like sedevacantists and, less eccentrically, among those who read publications like the *National Catholic Register*, *Crisis*, and, even at times, *First Things*. Their distinctive mix of anxiety and nostalgia is not well-served by statistics that show that about half of "highly-committed Catholics"[19]

---

[18] See William V. D'Antonio, Michelle Dillon, and Mary L. Gauthier, *American Catholics in Transition* (Lanham, MD: Rowman and Littlefield, 2013); Christian Smith, Kyle Longest, Jonathan Hill, and Kari Christoffersen, *Young Catholic America: Emerging Adults In, Out of, and Gone from the Church* (Oxford: Oxford University Press, 2014); and *The CARA Report*, Center for Applied Research in the Apostolate, Georgetown University, various issues.

[19] This category is defined in the D'Antonio volume as those who believe that the church is the most important or one of the most important aspects of their life, who go to church at least once a week, and who are least likely ever to consider leaving the church. This group comprises 19 percent of US Catholics, down from 27 percent in 1987.

believe that one can be a good Catholic while being in an irregular marriage or not attending weekly Mass,[20] or that 79 percent of the pre–Vatican II generation believe that Catholics should have the right to determine whether priests should be allowed to marry (up from 35 percent in 1987),[21] or that on questions of church authority there is little discernible difference between the generations. They will take comfort, however, from the conclusion that highly committed Catholics are more likely to find major theological doctrines like the bodily resurrection of Christ or Mary as the Mother of God to be important, and, by a two-to-one margin, are more likely than less-committed Catholics to endorse church teachings prohibiting abortion, birth control, and same-sex marriage.[22] They may also find support in statistics that show that younger Catholics are more likely to remain faithful, churchgoing people if they attended Catholic school or have parents who fall into the highly committed category.[23]

Although the demographics are challenging to more conservative elements in the Roman Catholic Church, there is a way to see them as heartening, even to find them confirming the traditionalist position. It is obviously true that Catholics are not attending church (and not attending to the church) in the numbers they once did. There are many ways to interpret this change: some theological, some cultural, some political, and some frankly paranoid. But it is not evidently unreasonable to assign some measure of responsibility for the shift to the growing climate of secularization in the Northern Hemisphere. And it is possible to cling to a vision of the church that remains faithful to the old ways, that understands episcopal authority in the way that it used to be seen by the laity as a whole, and that takes comfort from the more conservative mien of younger ordinands today.[24] Moreover, conservatives have

---

[20] D'Antonio, *American Catholics in Transition*, 59.

[21] Ibid., 27.

[22] Ibid., 47–68.

[23] Smith, *Young Catholic America*, 76–87.

[24] See the blog by "The Jacobite" on January 28, 2013, http://hotair.com/greenroom /archives/2013/01/27/next-generation-of-catholic-clergy-more-conservative/: "I know a fair number of seminarians or priests ordained in the last few years—call it 15–20— and every single one of them is highly orthodox. More stunning, to pick a more specific indicator: Almost every single one is interested in celebrating the traditional mass. 10 or 20 years ago, that would have been unthinkable—absolutely unthinkable. The priests coming in now are a world away from those being ordained back in the 80's or early 90's. When you will really see the change unfold is in the 2020's, when

a legitimate gripe about the ways in which some demographics identify Catholics. In many surveys, Catholics are those who simply self-identify as Catholic. This may skew statistics on many issues away from how they would look if "real" Catholics were the only ones answering the questions.[25] Of course, this begs the question of who counts as a "real" Catholic. In any case, the difference might not be as dramatic as conservatives think, since the D'Antonio volume is clear that even highly committed Catholics have moved in a more progressive direction over the years on many issues.[26] There is, however, absolutely no demographic support for the belief that this particular understanding of the church will cease to decline. All the statistics point in the other direction. Demographics suggest continuing decline for the Gregorian form of the church. But which form of church, if any, will replace it?

Type Two: The Church of the New Evangelization

With the end of the traditional Gregorian form of the church came a transition to what Staf Hellemans calls "choice Catholicism."[27] In his view, the distinguishing characteristic of this form is that it exists in a new world in which "commitment to an institutional religion is being considered as a non-evident act of choice."[28] The power relations have been reversed so that the church becomes "a service organization that has to cater to a clientele that is conscious that it can always turn its head away."[29] So the church has had to become "delocalized" (less dependent on a parish structure) and more flexible, meaning that "every decision has become contingent," on both organizational and more substantive questions.[30] But the single greatest contrast to ultramontane mass Catholicism is that the church has become "religionized," that is, reduced

---

these men start becoming rectors and bishops. If you think recent appointments of bishops have been more conservative, you haven't seen anything yet."

[25] One should note that the term "real Catholics"—as meaning those who are "highly committed"—itself evidences a particular understanding of the church.

[26] There is something to the claim that there should be more discrimination about who exactly is Catholic. This point is made quite forcefully in Smith, *Young Catholic America*, 126–54.

[27] Hellemans, "Tracking the Shape of the Catholic Church," 24–36.

[28] Ibid., 26.

[29] Ibid., 28.

[30] Ibid., 32.

to the core business of religion and no longer functioning as a "total institution." In other words, while the church's appeal to its members is a religious one, their relations to the secular world, to political society and so on are largely matters of individual choice. Of course, phenomena like the current concerns of the US bishops over what they see as the erosion of religious freedom indicate not only a nostalgia for an age in which this could not happen but also a recognition that the church as a primarily spiritual entity must now negotiate its freedoms within political society. The degree to which American Catholics seem not to be interested in the bishops' call to arms in the cause of "religious freedom" seems to confirm Hellemans's point of view.

Although Hellemans's work is primarily focused on the European church, so that, for example, his gloominess about the decline of parish life may be inapplicable or at least premature in the North American context, it has some pertinence to the US situation. In fact, on the central question of religious choice it may be more informative about the United States, where some 30 percent of people switch religions during their lifetimes. Overall, however, Hellemans's prognostications about the European church match those current in North America, where everyone knows the statistic that ex-Catholics are the second largest religious group in the United States. One third of people born Catholic no longer declare themselves Catholic, which means that 10 percent of all Americans are ex-Catholics. Sixteen percent of Americans claim no religious affiliation at all, and this number rises to around 25 percent for those in the eighteen-to-twenty-five age group, many of them raised Catholic.[31]

The findings of demographers in the D'Antonio volume and the work in general of both CARA and Pew substantiate the picture of the changing church described by Hellemans and anticipated by a considerable number of years by Johann Baptist Metz in his notion of the "supply services church" typical, he thought, of bourgeois Catholicism.[32] Broadly speaking, the US church is shifting away from a non-Hispanic toward an

---

[31] Pew Research Center, "America's Former Catholics," June 13, 2008, http://www.pewresearch.org/daily-number/americas-former-catholics/, accessed November 26, 2014.

[32] In 1980 Metz saw this as the church that had displaced the "paternalistic" church of the past but also believed that it "had passed its historical zenith" and would need to make space for the growth of a post-bourgeois people's church. See his *The Emergent Church: The Future of Christianity in a Postbourgeois World* (London: SCM, 1981), 86–88.

increasingly Hispanic church, with its Anglo character showing serious displacement, either into the category of the nonaffiliated (the well-known but unpronounceable category of "Nones") or, less frequently, into liberal or even evangelical Protestant communities. Choice Catholicism is also well-illustrated in the statistics that show decreasing levels of familiarity with basic church doctrines, accompanied sometimes by frankly bizarre convictions and commitments. Bearing in mind that most demographics allow for self-selection, that is, anyone who says he or she is Catholic is classified as Catholic, it is quite amazing that the four aspects of Catholicism rated as most important continue to be belief in the bodily resurrection of Jesus Christ, helping the poor, the importance of Mary, and the centrality of sacramental life. What do we make of a church where 63 percent of people classify the sacraments as of high importance but a far smaller percentage participates in them? What does it mean when 78 percent of people consider that one can be a good Catholic without accepting church teaching on the importance of attending Mass, or 60 percent think one can dissent from church teaching on abortion and remain in good standing, while only 40 percent grant the same freedom to those who do not "get" transubstantiation, and a mere 31 percent allow that one can be a good Catholic and have problems believing in the resurrection?

These statistics are the kind of information that has led the global church and especially the church north of the equator to promote what is usually known as "the new evangelization." Unlike the Gregorian form of the church, this form of church life definitely sees apostolicity as more than a backward-looking faithfulness to the apostolic witness of the early church. But to a high degree the outreach of the new evangelization is also in-reach. It is a species of what used to be called "internal mission," proclaiming the Gospel to those who remain within the church in a more or less ignorant and more or less half-hearted fashion, or who have relatively recently departed and are perhaps ripe for reclamation. The United States Conference of Catholic Bishops defines the new evangelization as calling "each of us to deepen our faith, believe in the Gospel message and go forth to proclaim the Gospel" and adds that its focus is "in a special way . . . on 're-proposing' the Gospel to those who have experienced a crisis of faith."[33] There can be no doubt, of

---

[33] United States Conference of Catholic Bishops, "The New Evangelization," http://www.usccb.org/beliefs-and-teachings/how-we-teach/new-evangelization/index.cfm, accessed November 26, 2014.

course, that a healthy community of faith is needed for a healthy sense of mission to the wider world. But the new evangelization movement seems to have little sense that its message need be any different from that of the old evangelization. "New" seems largely to mean a new attempt, rather than an attempt to do anything new.

There is an interesting and very telling essay on the USCCB website describing the characteristics of the new evangelization. In this piece Fr. James Wehner, president of the Pontifical College Josephinum, explains the initiative as a response to the call of Vatican II. He helpfully avoids limiting it to internal mission only, quoting Pope John Paul II's warning that "the program of a new evangelization cannot be restricted to revitalizing the faith of regular believers, but must strive as well to proclaim Christ where he is not known."[34] Throughout Fr. Wehner's piece, however, it seems that what is envisaged is an exclusively one-way approach to the objects of evangelization, be they indifferent or lapsed Catholics, other religious bodies, or national and international cultures. Seeing Vatican II as setting the scene for the new evangelization, he seems to overlook its emphasis on dialogue. The problem shows up particularly clearly in the final paragraph. Quoting or paraphrasing Benedict XVI (which, is not entirely clear), he points out that while the church is a missionary body that wants to spread the Gospel and "transmit the gift of truth," it also wants to assure "people and their Governments that she does not wish to destroy their identity and culture by doing so." Rather, the church wants to "give them . . . a response which, in their innermost depths, they are waiting for."[35] So much for *Gaudium et Spes*, where the church "is not unaware how much it has profited from the history and development of humankind," and "also recognizes that it has benefited and is still benefiting from the opposition of its enemies and persecutors" (GS 44). And here is a telling passage from John O'Malley's great work on the council. Having mentioned the uneasiness of the German bishops about the draft of *Gaudium et Spes*, he continues:

[34] James A. Wehner, "What Is 'New' About the New Evangelization?" *Catechetical Sunday* (September 16, 2012), http://www.usccb.org/beliefs-and-teachings/how-we-teach/catechesis/catechetical-sunday/new-evangelization/upload/What-is-New-About-Evangelization-2.pdf, accessed November 26, 2014. It has to be noted, nevertheless, that the same pope stressed the importance of the essentially remedial role that the new evangelization plays with less-than-fervent current Catholics.

[35] Benedict XVI, "Discourse to the Roman Curia," December 22, 2005, www.vatican.va/holy_father/benedict_xvi/speeches/2005/december/documents/hf_ben-xvi_spe_20051222_roman-curia_en.html, accessed December 11, 2014.

Their misgivings about the text were shared by a young, relatively unknown Polish archbishop, Karol Wojtyla, who criticized the document for being too optimistic in its assessment of modern society. . . . Meanwhile the pope [Paul VI] let the commission know that he wanted dialogue to be the inspiring principle of the text.[36]

In summary, the church of the new evangelization utilizes demographic information to identify the scope of the challenge it must meet and the scale of the problems that afflict those who claim to be Catholic but who are either not noticeably so or who participate but suffer from a serious lack of religious literacy. Though it is not unaware of the responsibility for evangelizing beyond the boundaries of the Catholic community, its primary concern is centripetal. It utilizes demographics in the service of a predominantly remedial evangelization. Its understanding of apostolicity is more than simply retrospective, but its ambit is largely internal to the community. When this church contemplates evangelization of the world beyond the church, it tends to default to a pre–Vatican II conception of the secular as inherently problematic. The "little-known Polish archbishop" who went on to become Pope John Paul II and his German successor were representative of this ecclesiology, and the US bishops—or perhaps only the most vocal of them—were faithful to this view, at least until the election of Pope Francis. The tone set by Francis is different, faithful but humble: "In her dialogue with the State and with society, the Church does not have solutions for every particular issue."[37] It remains to be seen how smoothly the US bishops can make the shift of emphasis.

Type Three:
Kenotic Ecclesiology

A third ecclesiology understands concern for the world beyond the church to be the primary if not the exclusive meaning of apostolicity. Taking the account of the first Pentecost in Acts as its inspiration, in this view the church is from the first moved by the Spirit to proclaim the

[36] John W. O'Malley, *What Happened at Vatican II* (Cambridge, MA: Harvard University Press, 2008), 250.

[37] Francis, *Evangelii Gaudium* (On the Joy of the Gospel), 241, http://w2.vatican.va /content/francesco/en/apost_exhortations/documents/papa-francesco_esortazione -ap_20131124_evangelii-gaudium.html, accessed November 26, 2014.

Gospel to the whole world, but to do so in such a way that everyone, whatever their language, can understand the message. So the central question here is one of reception. How can the secular world be engaged by the church in such a way that what the church exists to proclaim, the good news of the Gospel, can be heard by those who do not or cannot appreciate the language in which the same message is proclaimed to those who belong to the church? Unlike the two previous models, this one is unfazed by the idea of secularity (if not secularism), thoroughly centrifugal, and marked by a theology of grace that does not restrict divine activity and presence to the ranks of Christians but rather sees divine grace permeating the entire world. This ecclesiology is inspired above all by Vatican II's *Gaudium et Spes* (The Pastoral Constitution on the Church in the Modern World), which saw so clearly that what we might call an evangelical dialogue is one in which the church does not simply bring the grace of God to the secular world, but also finds it there waiting for us.

It is appropriate to designate this ecclesiology as "kenotic" for two principal reasons. In the first place, kenosis denotes the self-emptying of the church in discipleship to Christ in whom God emptied the self of God in the world. The church, like Christ before it, will be filled with the Spirit to the degree that it empties itself of all that is a hindrance to true apostolicity. A kenotic ecclesiology is the theological commitment of a humble, de-centered church. The second and less obvious reason to call this ecclesiology kenotic is in recognition of the relationship between culture and the church. A postmodern Western culture which does not appreciate essentialist thinking and notions of transcendence exhibits a symbiotic relationship to a church which takes seriously the death of the God of the philosophers on the one hand, and a Christ in whom the biblical God has "emptied himself," on the other. To develop this second characteristic in a little more detail would show how a kenotic church can be enriched by its encounter with the secular world, how indeed it can perform an ecclesiology of self-forgetfulness.

In a slim volume of autobiographical reflections, the Italian philosopher Gianni Vattimo lays out how he was drawn away from secularism into a kind of religion (again) by studying the work of Friedrich Nietzsche and Martin Heidegger.[38] In Vattimo's view, the "nihilism" of both men amounts to the rejection of transcendence, the end of metaphysics, and

---

[38] Gianni Vattimo, *Belief* (Stanford, CA: Stanford University Press, 1999).

"the weakening of Being." The long-term and trickle-down cultural influences are evident in postmodern culture's distaste for big ideas, for absolutes, for institutional religions proclaiming the transcendent God as Lord of the universe (the prime example of this last category, of course, being Catholicism). But Vattimo is equally persuaded that the premodern understanding of God espoused by the Catholic Church up until the recent past (and still in many quarters today) was more a product of onto-theology than of the Gospel. Vattimo asks rhetorically if it makes sense "to conceive of the Christian doctrine concerning the incarnation of the Son of God as an announcement of an ontology of weakening?"[39] Is God's self-emptying, in other words, a signal to humanity that its salvation lies in historical concreteness, not in a yearning for transcendence? In answering his own question in a positive vein, he suggests that the kenosis of God in the incarnation should be "interpreted as the sign that the non-violent and non-absolute God of the post-metaphysical epoch has as its distinctive trait the very vocation for weakening of which Heideggerian philosophy speaks."[40] There is a "parallelism between a theology of secularization and an ontology of weakening,"[41] such that the inability of philosophy today to think in terms of foundations may be traced to its education by the theology of incarnation, perhaps unconsciously and certainly over the long term, to recognize "the implicit violence of every finality, of every principle that would silence all questioning."[42] The Christian Gospel has thus schooled our world to be suspicious of all efforts to say the last word, to close off further searching.

It is unlikely that the Christian churches in general or the Roman Catholic Church in particular could receive Vattimo's interpretation of Christianity in its entirety. It is simply offered here as an example of a secular voice espousing Nietzschean nihilism and Heidegger's "weakening of Being" that articulates the challenge of the secular world to institutional religion in a manner which may indeed be calling the church to renew itself in the light of exactly these "secular" insights. Vattimo's conclusions represent a profound act of gratitude to theology for critical philosophical insights while at the same time challenging the church to greater humility and a deeper appreciation of history as the place of

[39] Ibid., 36.
[40] Ibid., 39.
[41] Ibid., 63.
[42] Ibid., 65.

salvation. There is much to be said for Vattimo's identification of institutional religion's resistance to a more kenotic approach—let us say,
finally, to a more humble church—with its ties to metaphysical concep-
tualizations of the God of philosophy. On the other hand, God's tri-unity
is established in Scripture and does not depend on philosophy. Vattimo's
lack of interest in "the Father" is deeply problematic from a Christian
perspective and exegetically represents a kind of undialectical reduction
of the doctrine of kenosis in Philippians. Nevertheless, there is great food
for thought here; theology would benefit from extended dialogue with
Vattimo on this matter.

Whatever we make of Vattimo's version of the theology of incarnation,
his thinking represents exactly the kind of position to which a kenotic
ecclesiology has to respond because of its particular understanding of
apostolicity. Like any coherent understanding of apostolicity, it begins
from the sense of faithfulness to the witness of the ancient church;
however, here faithfulness is more a matter of proclaiming the Gospel
in the world than of anxious concern to replicate orthodoxy. If "tradition
is the living faith of the dead,"[43] then in the words of Ormond Rush,
"the principle of reception enables effective traditioning."[44] It is because
the process of traditioning is the dynamic work of the Spirit, whom the
Catechism of the Catholic Church refers to as "the Church's living memory,"
that apostolicity is always seeking a way to proclaim the Gospel in such
a manner that it can be heard. Vattimo's secular world is ripe for the
reception of the message from a kenotic church. One might think here
of the theology of grace that inspires the quote from Thomas O'Meara
at the head of this paper: "Grace draws forth human striving to all that
is good."[45] One could also invoke Ghislain Lafont's conviction that
"evangelization absolutely presupposes that the Church regain the confidence of men and women."[46] And, indeed, his remark quoted earlier
that "the Church must find a way of articulating exactly what is human
. . . but without the Church trying to fully disclose the times or trying

---

[43] This phrase, together with what follows, "while traditionalism is the dead faith
of the living," has been ascribed to many originators, including among others, Jaroslav
Pelikan. I first heard it, however, on the lips of the wonderfully maverick retired
archbishop of Bombay, Thomas Roberts, many moons ago.

[44] Rush, *Eyes of Faith*, 53.

[45] Thomas F. O'Meara, *Thomas Aquinas, Theologian* (Notre Dame, IN: University of
Notre Dame Press, 1997), 242.

[46] Lafont, *Imagining the Church*, 4.

to supplant their human, immanent capacity to understand the world and act on it," sounds like an elegant first foray into the kind of dialogue that the church ought to be eager to conduct.

This brings us back to the subject of demographics, and to the question of how a kenotic ecclesiology employs their results. The work of Catholic demographers certainly paints a picture of a church that is weaker than it was, though demographics cannot of its nature comment on whether this weakening does or does not does not produce more humility.[47] We saw that the ecclesiology of "build it and they will come" makes use of demographics largely to identify the faithful minority and to draw comfort from the continuity of more traditional perspectives, even if they too seem to be waning rather than growing. We found that the ecclesiology of the new evangelization reaches out to try to draw back into the fold those whom demographic analysis identifies as challenged by religious illiteracy and little enthusiasm for the doctrinal and moral teaching of the contemporary church. From the perspective of a kenotic ecclesiology, demographic analysis needs to be approached with greater subtlety. In the first place, precisely because the kenotic understanding of apostolicity is a matter of evangelical dialogue with those who are distinctly not part of the church, demography that takes church membership as its subject necessarily leaves them out of account. At the same time, however, in the picture that demography paints of the shifts in perspective among Catholics, especially among those who are more marginal (but not entirely so), there are hints about possible directions that an apostolicity of dialogue might be well-advised to consider. From this perspective, the less-committed Catholics may have an almost priestly role, standing with one foot firmly in their Catholic identity and one equally firmly planted in the secular world.

Kenotic ecclesiology should be able to see in demographic analysis just how many of the so-called "fringe" Catholics who motivate the new evangelization would warm to a catechesis inspired, if not by Vattimo himself, then by someone like him able to give shape to their reservations or indifference about the church in language that resonates with their postmodern experience but still recalls the central Christian doctrine of the incarnation. So the continuing attachment even of the less-committed Catholics to fundamental doctrines of the church need not be seen as

---

[47] The lessons of history suggest the contrary, namely, that when the church is weak the tendency is to become more rather than less resistant to self-analysis. The nineteenth-century Roman Catholic Church is a perfect example.

eccentric or nostalgic inconsistencies, while their growing independence of judgment on moral issues does not have to be classified as relativism. There are hints here to the whole church that its future can be better assured by sticking to preaching the Gospel and by turning away from the kind of absolutes that not only do not compel the assent even of many highly committed Catholics any longer but also are hard to justify from the Gospel faith. From the perspective of a theology of grace, the Spirit is speaking loudly and clearly to correct the errors of a church turned inward on itself. Moreover, there is more than a little evidence that to the degree that the church can show a more open and less judgmental face to the world, the world in its turn will soften its attitude toward the church. While this is not conversion, it is most certainly a step in the direction of the kind of open dialogue that perhaps constitutes the only kind of "preparation for the Gospel" that is appropriate to a world of free human beings.

Karl Rahner seems to have come to much the same conclusion several decades ago. In "Theological Reflections on the Problem of Secularization," Rahner calls for "a special theological discipline" made necessary by "the relationship of the Church to the secular world as it exists today." This "practical ecclesiological cosmology"[48] genuinely seems to be the kind of ecclesial outreach that can be inspired by a more kenotic ecclesiology. Stemming from the theological vision of *Gaudium et Spes*, this new branch of theology does not yet exist, thinks Rahner, and cannot until the church comes to know "man as he exists today."[49] In Rahner's view, which Vattimo would surely relish, apostolicity must await better knowledge of those who are its objects. The fact that very few are listening to the church, he thinks, is evidence of its ignorance of secular human beings, who cannot simply be the church's "objects," since "the secular world is a free partner in an open dialogue."[50] The church itself must recognize that it is "a genuine part of this secular world which collaborates as an element within history in the history of the world of which God alone is the autonomous controller. . . . And in this history she herself is not simply the representative of God."[51] To extemporize just a little on Rahner's view, one might be moving from the traditional sense that offering a helping hand to a world in need can be justified as "a

---

[48] Karl Rahner, *Theological Investigations*, vol. 10, *Writings of 1965–67* (New York: Seabury, 1977), 318–48.

[49] Rahner, *Theological Investigations*, 10:340.

[50] This is exactly the point made by Lafont above.

[51] Rahner, *Theological Investigations*, 10:341.

preparation for the Gospel," to a more challenging consideration that coming to know better the secular world and to see the grace of God at work in it independently of the church may be an indispensable preparation of the church itself, by which it may be conditioned to be able to proclaim the good news in a manner in which it can be heard.

Finally, then, if this picture is fair, we can see that the dialectic of the centripetal and the centrifugal is critical to apostolicity, though the relationship of the two must be reversed from that usually imagined. We are not ready to be a healing presence in the world simply because we are faithful to the apostolic witness or because we have restored the church community to a level of religious literacy and faithful sacramental practice, or because we have become better able to articulate an ethical perspective that is credible and persuasive. On the contrary, our faithfulness to the apostolic church that sought to preach the Gospel to all nations and our health as a faith community await our ability to appreciate the grace of God at work in the world, in all its holiness and sinfulness, and our own sharing in the dialectic of sin and grace that is an inescapable element of what it is to be incarnated in the world, to be a kenotic church, to be a humbler partner in the dialogue with secularity by which we are indelibly marked. To the degree that the Spirit can lead us into this kind of new relationship with all of God's people, we will be capable of the kind of prophetic instruction Rahner imagined to follow from practical ecclesiological cosmology. And then, perhaps, the evidence of demographic analysis will begin to look up.

For Further Reading

Baggett, Jerome P. *Sense of the Faithful: How American Catholics Live Their Faith*. Oxford: Oxford University Press, 2009.

Burkhard, John. *Apostolicity Then and Now: An Ecumenical Church in a Postmodern World*. Collegeville, MN: Liturgical Press, 2004.

D'Antonio, William V., Michelle Dillon, and Mary L. Gauthier. *American Catholics in Transition*. Lanham, MD: Rowman and Littlefield, 2013.

Hellemans, Staf. "Tracking the New Shape of the Catholic Church in the West." In *Tilburg Theological Studies*, vol. 5, *Towards a New Catholic Church in Advanced Modernity: Transformations, Vision, Tensions*, edited by Staf Hellemans and Jozef Wissink, 19–50. Zürich: LIT Verlag, 2012.

Lafont, Ghislain. *Imagining the Catholic Church: Structured Communion in the Spirit*. Collegeville, MN: Liturgical Press, 2000.

Matovina, Timothy. *Latino Catholicism: Transformation in America's Largest Church*. Princeton: Princeton University Press, 2014.

Rahner, Karl. "Theological Reflections on the Problem of Secularization." In *Theological Investigations*, vol. 10, *Writings of 1965–67*, 318–48. New York: Seabury, 1977.

Smith, Christian, Kyle Longest, Jonathan Hill, and Kari Christoffersen. *Young Catholic America: Emerging Adults In, Out of, and Gone from the Church*. Oxford: Oxford University Press, 2014.

Weigel, George. *Evangelical Catholicism: Deep Reform in the 21st-Century Church*. New York: Basic Books, 2014.

Part 2

Church and Culture

CHAPTER 3

Unsettled Accounts: Latino/a Theology and the Church in the Third Millennium

Natalia M. Imperatori-Lee

Canadian author Margaret Atwood wisely observes, "There's the story, then there's the real story, then there's the story of how the story came to be told. Then there's what you leave out of the story. Which is part of the story, too."[1] Fifty years ago the Second Vatican Council changed the way ecclesiologists tell the story of the Catholic Church. The *aggiornamento* program of Pope John XXIII freed the bishops at the council to open the church to the world. In doing this, the council moved away from "static, idealized notions of perfection"[2] and toward the messiness of history; it acknowledged the church's role in human events, including politics; and it professed to have a stake in the future of the world—a hope for, and a role in, its salvation. Vatican II broadened and complexified the church's story, moving it toward a more genuinely global narrative. Nevertheless, elements that continue to be left out of the church's story, as Atwood reminds us, are part of the story too. Ecclesiology, especially in its Euro-American formulations, omits crucial contributions from marginalized communities, such as the insights that can be gleaned from Latino/a Catholic theology and praxis. This chapter seeks to highlight some of these omissions and to put them forth as unsettling accounts that disrupt ecclesiology and provoke a reframing of the church's story for the third millennium.

[1] Margaret Atwood, *MaddAddam* (New York: Bloomsbury, 2013), 56.
[2] Anne Carr, "Mary in the Mystery of the Church," in *Mary According to Women*, ed. Carol Frances Jegen (Kansas City, MO: Leaven Press, 1985), 25.

Irish theologian John O'Brien asserts that "ecclesiology has always taken the form of a narrative, or more precisely, a conversation between narratives."[3] Narrative and storytelling may even constitute the bedrock of Christianity, grounded as it is in the gospel narratives, which themselves tell the stories of Jesus' own storytelling. Ecclesiology seeks to thematize and theorize the story of the church, a daunting task that involves the intertwining of historical research, philosophical analysis, and attention to the complexity of the human experience of salvation. Fifty years after the Second Vatican Council, the church's story has expanded to reflect its global reality, but the narrative remains a work in progress.

If narrative is the proper form of ecclesiology, then understanding the historical narrative of the church seems essential to grasping the whole story of salvation history and, ultimately, to constructing an ecclesiology that takes seriously the genuine varieties of Christian experience. Recent ecclesiologies have indicated the importance of the experience of particular, local churches in accounting for the genuine diversity and legitimate variety within global Catholicism.[4] In contrast to totalizing metanarratives that erase differences in favor of a unifying story, an emphasis on narratives of particularity allows ecclesiology to avoid the marginalization of nondominant voices, and reveals, in some sense, the invariable core of the Christian message in all its various cultural, historical, and linguistic expressions.

Nevertheless, even particular narratives have the potential to marginalize some accounts in favor of others. In the context of the United States, the experience of Latino/a Catholics has been made to fit, uncomfortably at times, into a particular historical narrative that emphasizes the arc of immigration and eventual assimilation, or Americanization. In addition, the Hispanic presence in American Catholicism, viewed through the lens of immigration, is frequently referred to as the "future" of the church, the "emerging" church, the "coming" reality. The features of Latino/a Catholicism, its popular religious practices, devotions, and worship style, are often treated as if they were recent developments, only now arriving at American shores. Even more worrisome is the scholarly treatment of the so-called contextual theologies, often regarded as a group and frequently relegated to the margins of theological discussion

---

[3] John O'Brien, "Ecclesiology as Narrative," *Ecclesiology* 4, no. 2 (2008): 149.

[4] As one prominent example, see Richard R. Gaillardetz, *Ecclesiology for a Global Church: A People Called and Sent* (Maryknoll, NY: Orbis Books, 2010).

(sometimes literally, when they are explored in the final chapters of books). When these theological voices are not marginalized, they can be treated as exotic or viewed as enhancements to theology. Rarely do the insights of so-called contextual theologies serve to uproot the mainstream theological narrative (which also, of course, emerges from a particular context) and reorient discussion. Latino/a theologies, Black theologies, Asian theologies, and others are in danger of being reduced to scholarly sidebars or miscellaneous adornments. In a globalized world, telling the story of the world church demands more than an "add diverse voices and stir" methodology.

The thesis of this chapter is that the insights of Latino/a theology fundamentally disrupt the narrative of Catholic ecclesiology and prompt a historical, methodological, and thematic recalibration of the discipline that corrects the trajectory of ecclesiology as we enter Christianity's third millennium. Latino/a theology preserves a dangerous memory that reframes the story of American Catholicism and in so doing nuances our understanding of both New and Old World forms of being church. Through its methodological focus on intercultural identity and dialogue, as well as on the ties between the pastoral and systematic, Latino/a theology helps diagnose the reality of an increasingly globalized church, and it presses the goals of the Second Vatican Council forward. Lastly, the themes taken up by Latino/a theologians, in particular the sacredness of everyday life, the theological nature of popular Catholicism, and the importance of forms of Christian praxis outside the parish structure, provide guideposts for ecclesiology in the third millennium.

Dangerous Historical Memory

Central to the *aggiornamento* paradigm set out by the Second Vatican Council was the desire to self-consciously immerse the church in human history, or rather, to put an end to ecclesial understandings that maintained that the church somehow existed in some ethereal holy sphere above or outside the vicissitudes of earthly existence. The bishops expressed the church's desire to share in the joys, hopes, and anxieties of the world—indeed to remind the world that the Body of Christ shared in these experiences all along. In promulgating this attitude of openness toward the world and the wish to participate fully in it, the bishops "horizontalized" ecclesiology. Many theologians hoped, with Karl Rahner, that the Catholic Church was embarking on a new global phase, a "world church," over and against the dominant European Catholicism that had reigned for nearly two thousand years.[5] Without a doubt, the global makeup of the bishops at the council, including and especially the presence of bishops indigenous to the colonial lands they were representing, changed the course of the council and upended the preparatory agenda dramatically. The polyphony of global voices yielded a reorientation of the church's trajectory: away from anathemas and toward the complexity of history, away from truncated ideals of perfection and toward human experience in all its messiness. In a sense, one could view the council as stepping away from notions of a pristine Catholicism, recognizing the eschatological nature of the church's perfection, and seeing the people of God as inevitably enmeshed in human history. *Lumen Gentium* (The Dogmatic Constitution on the Church), *Gaudium et Spes* (The Pastoral Constitution on the Church in the Modern World), and indeed the entire ethos of the council seemed to take an initial step away from purity narratives about the church and toward a more complex appreciation of the ways in which the fate of the church and that of human history remain inextricably intertwined.

Despite the horizontalizing steps taken by the council, narratives about the relationship of Catholicism and human history still tend to overlook aspects arising from the church's complicity in racial, colonial, and patriarchal tensions. In his recent book, *Latino Catholicism*, historian Timothy Matovina makes a case against the prevailing paradigm for understanding US Catholicism. In particular, Matovina identifies in the dominant discourse a pattern he calls the "Americanization paradigm" and calls for replacing this with a "hemispheric paradigm" that accounts for the longstanding historical, cultural, and racial overlapping of communities in the United States and the rest of the Western Hemisphere. He does this to critique what he deems to be a bias among religious historians in general, and historians of US Catholicism in particular, who tend to "focus on the Eastern seaboard and European settlers and immigrants" while ignoring significant portions of the population, including Black Catholics, women, Asian American Catholics, and of course, the inhabitants of the frontier lands in the West and Southwest.[6] While

---

[5] Karl Rahner, "A Basic Theological Interpretation of the Second Vatican Council," in *Theological Investigations*, vol. 20, *Concern for the Church* (New York: Crossroad, 1981), 77–89.

[6] Timothy Matovina, *Latino Catholicism: Transformation in America's Largest Church* (Princeton, NJ: Princeton University Press, 2012), 2. This point has been made by many other US Latino/a theologians, including Allan Figueroa Deck, who in 1992 wrote

the US church is certainly undergoing a demographic shift toward a Hispanic majority, and many of these Catholics are immigrants, "Spanish-speaking Catholics have lived in what is now the U.S. for twice as long as the nation has existed."[7] These nonimmigrant Catholics in the Southern and Western parts of the country were incorporated into the United States in the process of westward expansion without migrating at all. Thus, Matovina contends, Hispanic Catholicism represents an integral part of the story of the US church and challenges the paradigm of immigration and slow assimilation that characterizes the experience of most European immigrant Catholic communities in the Northeast and Midwest. The reality of nonimmigrant Catholic communities continually existing in parts of the South and Southwest complicates our narrative of US Catholic history, to be sure. If history is to be true to reality, however, it must include these nonconforming, disruptive narratives.

Surfacing the historical narratives of the Hispanic roots of American Catholicism allows these to function as dangerous memories in the sense put forth by Johann Baptist Metz: they "illuminate for a few moments and with harsh and steady light the questionable nature of things we have apparently come to terms with."[8] The legacy of nonimmigrant Hispanic Catholicism in the United States disrupts our ideas of the history of American Catholicism and of an American identity based solely on the immigrant experience. But it does not just disrupt our understanding of the past. When we acknowledge the constant presence of Hispanic Catholic communities in the United States, we temper the narrative of Hispanicization as an "emerging" reality, never before seen in the country. To be sure, the demographic trends show that the ethnic makeup of the US Catholic Church is trending toward becoming majority-Hispanic in the very near future. But the emerging majority status of Hispanic Catholicism should be contextualized within the broader reality of what Matovina calls the "multiple origins of Catholicism in the United States."[9] By reconstructing the past in a more hemispheric way, we contextualize the church's present demographic reality.

---

that "these [Hispanic] roots [of North American Catholicism] have consistently been obscured by views of US Catholic history which incorrectly place its origins in Maryland, and narrowly conceive of it as a movement westward." Introduction to *Frontiers of Hispanic Theology in the United States* (Maryknoll, NY: Orbis Books, 1992), x.

[7] Matovina, *Latino Catholicism*, 7.

[8] Johann Baptist Metz, *Faith in History and Society* (New York: Seabury, 1980), 109.

[9] Matovina, *Latino Catholicism*, 36.

Ultimately a historical reframing of the kind suggested by Matovina acknowledges the dangerous memory of US Latino/a experience in all its varied forms. Ecclesiologically, this dangerous memory guards against naïve understandings not only of American Catholicism as an immigrant, primarily northern European, reality but also against caricatures of a uniform European Catholicism that simply never existed. Latino historian David Badillo, noting the Iberian roots of Latino/a Catholicism, describes this Iberian Catholicism as somewhat pre-Tridentine, noting that the Tridentine reforms were not as rigorously applied in southern Europe (i.e., Spain) as they were in northern Europe. Thus, Hispanic Catholicism reflects a "blend [of] pre- and post-Tridentine influences."[10]

For Badillo and others, the "Catholicism preserved in Latin America reflected the popular faith lived in rural Spain."[11] It largely escaped Trent's organization of church life into the parish structure, the regularization of sacramental practices, and the centralization of power in Rome. Instead, Iberian Catholicism retained a focus on local clergy (not the Roman Church which was associated with religious orders in Spain) and popular religious devotions, home-based practices like *altarcitos*, and dramatic public events such as processions and *posadas*.[12]

The reforms of the Council of Trent only slowly took hold across Europe and did so to differing degrees. Consequently, the Catholicism that was exported to the Americas from different parts of Europe varies. The stories and practices we emphasize when we talk about "immigrant Catholicism" reveals much about our assumptions not only about what we are trying to define as "American" Catholicism but also about the complexity of what Rahner (and many others) have called "European" Catholicism. Neither is a fixed, uniform reality, and a close examination of either phenomenon reveals the genuine variety that has always existed in Catholic religious expression. Catholicism in Europe was and remains as mixed and diverse a reality as American Catholicism, and indeed this unity-in-diversity produced by Christianity's (now global) inculturation can be considered a historical mark of the church.

The dangerous memory of the roots of Hispanic Catholicism in America brings to light the complexity of Catholic belief and practice not only in the New World but also in Europe. Even European Catholi-

---

[10] David Badillo, *Latinos and the New Immigrant Church* (Baltimore, MD: Johns Hopkins University Press, 2006), xiv.

[11] Ibid., xiii.

[12] Ibid., xiv.

cism can be said to be of mixed heritage, or *mestizo,* to use a term employed in Latino/a theology. Likewise, there surely exist American and Latin American Catholicisms, Asian Catholicisms, and African Catholicisms in the present day. Both Badillo and Matovina make the point that any presumption of a uniform "Hispanic" Catholicism is, at best, unfounded.[13] How, then, are ecclesiologists to interpret the unity of the church? What sort of unity can coexist within the genuine diversity of authentic Catholic expressions worldwide? The answer to these questions may be methodological, process based, and communal in nature.

Latino/a Theology's Interculturality

Since its inception in the 1970s and 1980s, Latino/a theology has endeavored to make sense of the experience of a wide variety of cultures grouped together demographically in the term "Hispanic" or "Latino/a." Though the terms used to refer to Latinos encompass cultures from the Andes to the Antilles, Latino/a theologians have elaborated key categories that underscore the commonalities present in the multicultural reality that is *latinidad* or Latino/a identity. These categories include the notion of *mestizaje,* a distinctive methodological interculturality, and a dialogical method of collaboration, or *conjunto.* Taken together, they point a way forward for constructing ecclesiology that is suitable for the third millennium.

A historical reframing of the origins of Hispanic Catholicism in the United States complicates any narrative of Latinos/as as the emerging church, while simultaneously shedding light not only on the complexity of American Catholicism but also on the genuine variety that exists throughout global Catholicism. Given this authentic diversity of religious expression, one might call into question the unity of the church, a foundation of Christian ecclesiological doctrine. It can be difficult to see unity, for example, if different constituencies within the church celebrate the liturgy in different ways or with seemingly different emphases, like the emphasis on Marian devotion in Latino/a Catholicism, to cite one example. But this need not be the case. One source of ecclesial unity can be found in intercultural dialogue. US Latino/a theology is uniquely suited to this methodology in part because of the amount of reflection it has undertaken on the intercultural nature of *latinidad* itself. In

---

[13] Matovina, *Latino Catholicism,* 15.

considering the nature of Hispanic identity, theologians like Virgilio Elizondo have pointed out the singular importance of *mestizaje*—the (often violent) process of intermixing of cultures, races, and religious beliefs that occurred during the conquest and brought forth a new race in Latin America. Later thinkers incorporated into this analysis the idea of *mulatez*—the mixing of African and Spanish blood—an addition that allows scholars to speak more fully to the reality of colonial life throughout Latin America. To describe *latinidad* or Latino/a identity without reference to the reality of racial and cultural intermixing is impossible. The encounter between the Old and New World constitutes a defining event of the second millennium and it must inform our thinking as we move into the third. To that end, the categories of *mestizaje* and *mulatez* represent dangerous memories of their own, and with these memories, an end to purity narratives about the origins of the cultures that came to be known as Hispanic.

In his work, Elizondo describes a second *mestizaje* occurring in the encounter between mestizo Mexican culture and northern European culture in Texas[14] as well as other mission territories in the West. Roberto Goizueta has described a third *mestizaje* emerging in the United States with the intermarriage of Hispanics from different cultures.[15] Oddly then, "Hispanic," a term adopted by the US government during the Nixon administration to simplify census forms by grouping together a set of hispanophone "others" from any and all Latin American cultures, has increasingly become a reality. The use of the term Hispanic in the United States might be described as a colonial move, since it was originally imposed by the government on groups that would never refer to themselves as "Hispanic" but rather as Cuban-American, Mexican-American or Chicano/a, Peruvian-American, etc. More recently, however, because of continuing intermarriage among Latinos/as, along with ongoing migration and lasting ties to home countries, what was once an artificial moniker has come to describe the real lives of Hispanics in the United States—and this reality is intercultural.[16] As a result, in forging academic

[14] Virgilio Elizondo, *Galilean Journey: The Mexican-American Promise* (Maryknoll, NY: Orbis Books, 1983), 13–17.

[15] Roberto Goizueta, *Caminemos Con Jesus: Toward a Hispanic/Latino Theology of Accompaniment* (Maryknoll, NY: Orbis Books, 1995), 8.

[16] Of course, Latino/a theologians did not develop the idea of interculturality, but I want to distinguish the sort of intercultural dialogue and method undertaken in Latino/a theology from, for example, that set forth by Benedict XVI, who argued that

links in solidarity, Latino/a theology has always been an intercultural endeavor, in part because of who Latino/a theologians are themselves, as individuals and as an intercultural community of scholars with roots all over the Americas.

The legacy of colonialism does not allow for Latino/a theologians to enter naïvely into intercultural dialogue, however. As María Pilar Aquino claims, "The reality of *mestizaje* also implies a conscious option for intellectual, cultural and theological *mestizaje*. Incorporated as a fundamental principle of the intelligence of the faith and as a methodological axis, this option constitutes the basis on which to articulate an intercultural vision of Christian identity."[17] *Mestizaje*, as Elizondo explains it, has been historically treated as a basis for rejection and exclusion. As a cornerstone of Hispanic identity, *mestizaje* attunes Latino/a theology to the need to recognize power differentials between cultures, constituencies, and individuals—prompting these theologians to make an option for the poor and excluded. Because of this, we can say that Latino/a theology approaches methodology not only interculturally but also with a decidedly liberative intent.

To approach ecclesiological method with such an intercultural, liberative purpose would mean to attend to the historical factors involved in erasing narratives of difference from the Catholic story, and then to reorient the story in order to take these narratives into account. Correcting, or retrieving, is not enough. The American example in the previous section is merely one case of this phenomenon, and the critique of purity narratives proves insufficient. Aquino notes that an essential part of Latino/a theological methodology grounded in *mestizaje* is the accompaniment of the poor and marginalized and the constant attention to the sacredness of the (culturally plural) daily lives of Catholics.[18] It is in this fidelity to reality that the intercultural method highlights the unity of

---

Catholicism (in its necessarily Western European/Hellenic inculturation) engaged in intercultural dialogue with "others" who were culturally different. The sort of intercultural dialogue embraced by Latino and Latina theologians acknowledges the problematic power dynamics in play when cultures meet and strives to maintain a liberative perspective with regard to these power differentials. María Pilar Aquino traces the roots of Latino/a intercultural method, from Metz through Raul Fornet-Betancourt to the present, in her essay "Theological Method in U.S. Latino/a Theology: Toward an Intercultural Theology for the Third Millennium," in *From the Heart of Our People*, ed. Orlando Espín and Miguel Diaz (Maryknoll, NY: Orbis Books, 1999), 6–48.

[17] Aquino, "Theological Method in U.S. Latino/a Theology," 37.

[18] Ibid., 40–41.

the church. In exploring the complexities of Hispanic identity, Latino/a theology sets forth *mestizaje* as a conceptual and methodological key for understanding the church as an intercultural reality that retains unity in diversity.

In addition to their rootedness in *mestizaje* and intercultural method, Latino/a systematic theologians have a history of close collaboration with pastoral theology. A central goal of Vatican II, this sort of collaboration was most clearly embodied in the processes leading up to and including the Encuentro gatherings, sponsored by the US bishops' conference, which brought together theologians, pastors, and lay leaders in an effort to work out a pastoral plan for Hispanic Catholics across the country.[19] The history of the Encuentros has been documented by a variety of scholars, but for our purposes it is important to note that the gatherings exemplified how a collaborative process that includes divergent voices can foster unity in a diverse church. John O'Brien claims that in the Second Vatican Council, the "pastoral had regained its proper standing as something far more than the mere application of doctrine but as the very context from which doctrines emerge, the very condition of the possibility of doctrine, the touchstone for the validity of doctrine and the always prior and posterior praxis which doctrine at most, attempts to sum up, safeguard, and transmit."[20] The Encuentro processes exemplified this crucial collaboration between pastoral work, ecclesiological insight, and doctrine. This methodology of accompaniment appears throughout the work of Latino theologians such as Goizueta and Elizondo, as well as in the language of "midwifery" adopted by Ada María Isasi-Díaz.[21] From its inception, Latino/a theology professed a commitment to accompany the communities that brought it forth, in order to systematize the faith experience of the people of God, and to advocate for justice on behalf of Latino/a communities.[22] Building bridges between

---

[19] For histories of the Encuentros, see Matovina, *Latino Catholicism*, 67–97; Jorge Presmanes and Alicia Marill, "Hispanic Ministry and Theology," in *Hispanic Ministry in the 21st Century: Present and Future*, ed. Hosffman Ospino (Miami, FL: Convivium Press, 2010), 83–97. See also Luis Tempe, "Encuentro Nacional Hispano de Pastoral (1972–1985): An Historical and Ecclesiological Analysis" (PhD diss., The Catholic University of America, 2014).

[20] O'Brien, "Ecclesiology as Narrative," 150.

[21] See Ada María Isasi-Díaz, *En la Lucha, In the Struggle: Elaborating a Mujerista Theology* (Minneapolis, MN: Fortress Press, 2004).

[22] The Mission Statement of the Academy of Catholic Hispanic Theologians of the United States (ACHTUS) states that the academy seeks to "accompany the Hispanic

pastoral experience and systematic theology is a cornerstone of Latino/a theology, which is why these theologians have espoused terms like accompaniment, midwifery, or "teología en conjunto"—akin to communal theology, these can best be described as a collaborative interdisciplinary process aimed at achieving both fidelity to people's faith experience and academic precision—to describe their theological methods.

Here again, I must stress that Latino/a theology serves not only as an interesting supplement to mainstream systematic theology or ecclesiology but rather as a cornerstone of the reframing that must take place if we are to posit a credible ecclesiology for an increasingly globalized, interconnected world. Just as the silenced historical narrative of the Hispanic roots of some US Catholicism invites a complete retelling of the history of American Catholicism and elucidates the hybrid nature of American and European Catholicism, this methodological exposition should impel us to recalibrate the way ecclesiology interacts with nondominant cultural insights, with pastoral theology, and with the faith lives of the people of God.

Thematic Guideposts

If Latino/a theology can be said to have an essential achievement, a singular decisive contribution to ecclesiology, it would be its relentless emphasis on popular religious expressions, the study of the faith as it is lived in local communities. Through their attentiveness to popular piety, popular Catholicism, religious devotion, and public and private expressions of faith, Latino/a theologians have lifted up the sacredness of everyday life (termed *lo cotidiano*) as a locus of theology. We have seen that Latino/a theology calls ecclesial history to conversion with its dangerous memory of the variegated roots of Catholicism in the New World. It benefits ecclesiology through its intercultural and bridge-building methodology. In addition and perhaps most importantly, Latino/a theology has consistently emphasized the lived experience of faith as a

communities of the United States, helping to critically discern the movement of the Spirit in their historical journey; thematize the faith experience of the people within their historical, socio-economic, political and cultural contexts; encourage interdisciplinary scholarly collaboration; create resources, instruments and a professional network to develop a U.S. Hispanic *teología de conjunto*; support Hispanics currently engaged in theological research and studies." See http://www.achtus.us/mission/, accessed July 28, 2014.

source for theological reflection, including popular Catholicism, aesthetic expressions of faith, and everyday life. In doing this, Latino/a theologians carry out the charge of *Lumen Gentium* to affirm the holiness of the entire people of God.

Numerous factors have contributed to the flourishing of popular religious practices in Latino/a communities in the United States and all over Latin America. The Iberian Catholicism imported to the New World during the conquest, with its pre-Tridentine emphasis on local pious devotions and relative de-emphasis on doctrinal purity and magisterial authority, is only one critical source of this phenomenon. Catholicism in the New World interacted with indigenous and slave traditions, resulting in a truly variegated phenomenon over which the relatively small number of clerics had limited control. The colonial mindset, with its inherent racism, and the worldview of many missionaries precluded the ordination of indigenous clergy. This limited the number of priests available in the mission territories, allowing local lay leadership to flourish and local customs, sometimes derived from the towns from which the *criollos* hailed in Spain, to take root in the Americas as well. Synergy developed between, on the one hand, a Catholicism that embraced popular piety and dramatic, public displays of faith like processions and religious plays and, on the other hand, myriad *mestizo/mulato* communities melding European, indigenous, and African cultures who, stripped of their cultural patrimony and religious identity, were forging hybrid expressions of religiosity. Out of this matrix developed the rich devotional expressions of Catholicism in the New World. Aspects of Latin American and Latino/a popular Catholicism evoked by turns the Catholicism of medieval Spain, the musical traditions of West Africa, and the reverence for the dead of some Mesoamerican cultures. Though Latinos/as are not the only community with a tradition of Catholic popular piety composed of the hybridization and inculturation of indigenous and missionary cultures, Latino/a popular religious practices have been objects of study for Latino/a theologians for at least thirty years.

The emphasis Latino/a theology places on popular religious devotions, daily life, and the connection between pastoral and systematic theology addresses lacunae left in the wake of the council about how to theologize the experience of the laity, how to speak truthfully about women's experience of leadership in the church, and what ecclesiology should look like as we move forward. Theologians reflecting on the experience of Latino/a communities emphasize the theological significance of popular Catholicism and the complex but fundamentally graced nature of daily life. These insights carry the work of the council forward into the twenty-first century and might help to alleviate some unresolved questions about the *sensus fidelium*, women's roles, and the role of the parish in the church of the future.

Though *Lumen Gentium* states that the people of God possess a super-natural intuition about the faith and that the people of God participate in the church's infallibility through their faithful intuition (LG 12), the church has no clear mechanism for discerning the *sensus fidelium* or ascertaining where or when it is operating. Ecclesiologists invoke the *sensus fidelium* and the inerrancy of the whole people of God, rightly, as a corrective to theologies that rely too much on clerical or magisterial under-standings of the faith. Most recently, the attention of the magisterium turned toward the subject of the *sensus fidei* and *sensus fidelium* when the International Theological Commission (ITC) published a study of the matter in early 2014.[23] In it, the ITC affirms that the *sensus fidelium* differs from theology in that it is "akin rather to a natural, immediate and spontaneous reaction, comparable to a vital instinct or 'flair'" through which a believer (or group of believers) determines both what constitutes part of the faith and what runs contrary to the Gospel.[24] Further, the ITC notes that the intuition of faith is "infallible with respect to the true faith but can err in opinions or errors linked to its cultural context."[25] Thus the findings of the commission support Orlando Espín's notion that the sense of the faith is an intuitive grasp of the truth about the divine, always in need of interpretation.

The ITC document claims that the *sensus fidelium* is not only reactive but also proactive in that it "gives an intuition as to the right way forward amid the uncertainties and ambiguities of history."[26] Immediately after this statement, however, the document claims that the discernment of the *sensus fidelium* can be a lengthy process. The commission carefully analyzes the role of theologians in accompanying communities and helping to establish criteria for discerning the *sensus fidelium*, including an examination of the process of reception.[27] Nevertheless, given the gap

---

[23] International Theological Commission, "*Sensus Fidei* in the Life of the Church," http://www.vatican.va/roman_curia/congregations/cfaith/cti_documents/rc_cti _20140610_sensus-fidei_en.html, accessed September 30, 2014.

[24] Ibid., 54.

[25] Ibid., 55.

[26] Ibid., 70.

[27] Ibid., 78–80.

of time between the expression of the *sensus fidelium* and its discernment, even this understanding of the *sensus fidelium* operates only in retrospect. That is, the notion of reception allows us to claim somewhat reliably that a teaching is or is not part of the *sensus fidelium* only after decades (or more) of lag time, after waiting to see if the teaching is received and put into practice. While this use of the *sensus fidelium* is beneficial from the perspective of wanting clarity or certainty about the sense of the faithful on a particular topic, it remains largely reactive, relegating the laity once again to a passive role. But how can theologians, pastors, and others play a more active role in discerning the *sensus fidelium*? How do we know what the church is thinking? Is the system of doctrinal trial-and-error (to put it crudely) the sole methodology for conducting the teaching function of the church?

Latino/a theologians offer an alternate path that prioritizes the experiences of the majority of the church, the lay poor. From its inception, Latino/a theology has accentuated its connection to the people, its desire to theorize the lived faith experience of its communities. The primary way in which Latino/a theology has done this is through its rigorous and relentless study of popular Catholicism, pioneered by Orlando Espín and taken up by many others, including María Pilar Aquino and other Latina theologians. For Aquino, "what Latino/a theology emphasizes is that the faith of the people is the faith lived and expressed primarily and fundamentally within the concrete reality of popular Catholicism."[28] The devotions and prayers, the symbols and processions that make up the piety of the majority of the church cannot be relegated to insignificance if we take seriously the doctrine of the *sensus fidei/sensus fidelium*. Indeed, if popular Catholicism includes the praxis of faith-filled persons and communities, it necessarily reveals something of how God works in history.

In theological terms, the contents of theology cannot be determined from preestablished discourses but only from the lived and reflected historical expressions of the faith of the people. That is, Latino/a popular Catholicism offers us the material to discover and name the present and always challenging mystery of God and, on this foundation, to redo and rewrite every other central topic in systematic theology.[29]

---

[28] Aquino, "Theological Method in U.S. Latino/a Theology," 28.

[29] Ibid., 35. The ITC seems to affirm this when it points to the "authenticity of the symbolic or mystical language often found in liturgy and popular religiosity." ITC, "*Sensus Fidei*," 82.

This rewriting necessarily includes ecclesiology, which I fear has not fully divested from the deductive methodologies Aquino describes above. Popular Catholicism, which Espín has called "the real faith of the real church," provides fertile ground for discerning the *sensus fidelium*.[30] Espín claims that popular Catholicism—rather than being ignored by theologians as a slightly embarrassing remnant of superstitious beliefs, or horizontalized to the point of being relegated solely to the domain of social scientists—is an alternate form of tradition, a form that is significant though it differs from the more accepted textual forms understood to make up the tradition.[31] Popular religion as a manifestation of the *sensus fidelium* must be interpreted, and this interpretation cannot be undertaken naïvely.[32] Espín stresses that popular Catholicism should not be understood as equivalent to the *sensus fidelium*, but that criteria for authenticity and appropriateness based in Scripture, tradition, and praxis should be brought to bear by theologians and the magisterium.[33] One important criterion crucial to evaluating popular religiosity as a manifestation of the *sensus fidelium* is a reminder echoed throughout Latino/a theology: there is no a-cultural Catholicism, no a-cultural evangelization, no a-cultural doctrine or religious expression.[34] Theologians must be careful, then, to judge the validity and appropriateness of popular religious practices not on the basis of what (northern) European epistemologies and practices would dictate but instead on whether they are congruent with Scripture and tradition and whether they promote the liberative praxis at the heart of the gospels.

Two additional aspects of Latino/a popular Catholicism can fruitfully inform ecclesiology: the centrality of women in Latino/a popular religious practices and the extraparochial character of many of these practices.

[30] Orlando Espín, "Introduction," in *The Faith of the People: Theological Reflections on Popular Catholicism* (Maryknoll, NY: Orbis Books, 1997), 3.

[31] Orlando Espín, "Tradition and Popular Religion: An Understanding of the *Sensus Fidelium*," in *The Faith of the People: Theological Reflections on Popular Catholicism* (Maryknoll, NY: Orbis Books, 1997), 64–65. The entirety of Espín's essay holds profound insights for ecclesiological studies of popular Catholicism.

[32] "*Sensus Fidei*" recognizes this complexity and addresses it by listing the following criteria for evaluating the intuitions of the faithful: participation in the life of the church, listening to the Word of God, openness to reason, adherence to the magisterium, holiness, and seeking the edification of the church. ITC, "*Sensus Fidei*," 89–104.

[33] Espín, "Tradition and Popular Religion," 66–68.

[34] This insight is at the bedrock of Latino/a theology, first declared by Fernando Segovia and echoed by Espín and virtually every Latino/a theologian since.

Latino/a theologians' treatment of popular religiosity almost always dovetails with a discussion of *lo cotidiano* or the category of "everyday, ordinary life" as a locus of theology. This insight, pioneered by feminist theorists (and not by "androcentric liberation theology," as Aquino emphatically notes) before the birth of Latino/a theology, has nevertheless proven vital to understanding the role of Latinas as pastoral leaders in their communities. Aquino states, "It is in everyday life where revelation occurs. We have no other place but *lo cotidiano* to welcome the living Word of God or to respond to it in faith. The faith of the people as lived and expressed in popular Catholicism happens within the dynamics of everyday life."[35] Feminist insights about the import of everyday existence, quickly summarized in the conviction that "the personal is political," help other subjugated communities retrieve aspects of their experience deemed secondary or irrelevant. Inevitably, studying daily life brings women's work to the fore, since it is primarily women who take part in the daily routines of housework, childrearing, and the "stuff" of everyday life. The interesting shift when we talk about Latino/a communities is that, given the prevalence of home-based popular devotions, religious instruction and leadership, the care and transmission of these religious traditions was and remains largely "women's work." This leads theologians and sociologists of religion like Ana María Díaz-Stevens to posit that Latino/a religiosity is characterized by a "matriarchal core."[36]

Lo cotidiano is not a solely feminine sphere, but it is central for Latina theologians, as well as other feminist theologians. For example, *lo cotidiano* represents a cornerstone of Ada María Isasi-Diaz's *mujerista* theology—she invokes it as a source of struggle, the locus of revelation, the arena for liberation-salvation.[37] Undoubtedly, the everyday life of the diverse Latino/a communities includes popular religious practices that are led, promoted, or supported by women. This points to a long, possibly continuous narrative of women's roles in Catholic praxis: the real faith of the real church. Biblical scholars and historians have retrieved examples of women's leadership in the early Christian church, and Latino/a

---

[35] Aquino, "Theological Method in US Latino/a Theology," 39. Other theologians have stressed the importance and significance of ordinary life to the theological task. See especially Edward Schillebeeckx's *The Church with a Human Face*, trans. John Bowden (New York: Crossroad, 1985). The emphasis on everyday life also lends credence to O'Brien's claim that ecclesiology and narrative are inseparable.

[36] Ana María Díaz-Stevens, "The Matriarchal Core of Latino Catholicism," *Latino Studies Journal* 4, no. 3 (September 1993): 60–78.

[37] Ada María Isasi-Diaz, "Creating a Liberating Culture," in *La Lucha Continues: Mujerista Theology* (Maryknoll, NY: Orbis Books, 2004), 47–48.

theology traces a long tradition of women's religious leadership and their indispensability to the passing on of the faith into the present. This is true despite the deep-rooted patriarchal system that prevails in many parts of the world, identified in Latin American circles as "machismo." The seminal role of women of faith, especially older women of faith,[38] in Latino/a communities has been a constant, and continues to be a sign of the times in the present. As ecclesiologists and social scientists remind us that women do the majority of parish work and religious education, we must ask what is preventing this *de facto* leadership from evolving into more formal, recognized positions of authority for women.

One answer might be that popular religious practices tend to occur outside the purview of the parish. Whether because they are home based, like the use of home altars, or because they are unwelcome in parishes unaccustomed or unfriendly to Latino/a religious expressions, or because of the historical legacy of Iberian Catholicism with its tendency to operate outside parish structures, Hispanic popular Catholicism pushes past the borders of parish life. Historian David Badillo hears echoes of Iberian and New World nonparochial ecclesial groups like *cofradias* in the relatively low attachment to the parish he perceives among Hispanic Catholics in urban centers.[39] Movements like Cursillo and the Charismatic Renewal, which have had great success in Latino/a communities, also operate outside strict parish boundaries. The rich extraparochial devotional life enjoyed by many Latino/a Catholics distinguishes their approach to faith from that of many northern European coreligionists. For example, Badillo contends that Latino/a Catholics tend to deemphasize regular eucharistic reception without thinking themselves less observant.[40] This marginality with respect to parish life also has roots in the countries of origin of many Hispanic immigrants, where parish life was reserved for the wealthy in urban centers, and the relative paucity of priests and parishes meant that Catholics in rural areas had limited access to what Vatican II termed "the summit and source of the Christian life," the Eucharist (SC 10).

Today, new ecclesial movements have emerged that resonate with this extraparochial existence lived out in Hispanic communities.[41] Young

---

[38] Orlando Espín, "An Exploration into the Theology of Grace and Sin," in *From the Heart of Our People*, ed. Orlando Espín and Miguel Diaz (Maryknoll, NY: Orbis Books, 1999), 121–52.

[39] Badillo, *Latinos and the New Immigrant Church*, 204–5.

[40] Ibid., 205.

[41] Ibid., xix.

people especially are drawn to these groups, some of which are lay based and lay run. Might the Latino/a experience provide a historical and theoretical framework for incorporating groups such as Communion and Liberation or Focolare or Regnum Christi into the day-to-day life of the church? In recent years there have been massive restructuring initiatives in the US church, with parishes merging or closing and a general shift in North American ecclesial geography. Many Catholics are no longer bound by their territorial parishes and seek out groups of like-minded people, either in far-flung parishes or in small Christian communities that may or may not be affiliated with a particular parish. The experience of Latino/a Catholics on the margins of parish life helps ecclesiology stretch its notions of the church *ad intra*, demanding a more nuanced categorization of the ways in which the people of God partake in the ecclesial reality. This parallel of Latino/a religious experience with new ecclesial movements remains underexplored but could prove worthwhile in theologizing a postparochial future for the church.

Conclusion

Hispanics do not merely represent the emerging church—they have played crucial roles in its past, their theology helps accurately diagnose the present, and they are the cornerstone of the future of the US church demographically and theologically. Systematic theology, especially reflection on the church, should engage Latino/a theologians not as a supplement or remedy, nor as a corrective, but indeed as a foundational component of any ecclesiology in the third millennium. The theological reframing that becomes possible when we take seriously the challenges and insights of Latino/a theology includes a restructuring of the way we understand the relationship of Catholicism and culture, as well as a methodological recalibration where, by incorporating intercultural dialogue and *conjunto*-style theologizing, we can more accurately assess the needs and experience of the people of God in the present moment. The faith experience of diverse Latino/a communities, particularly the popular Catholicism practiced by Latinos/as, stokes new insights about the *sensus fidelium*, the nature of tradition, and the transmission of that tradition. Latinas play a critical role in the church of the present and the future, and the theologizing of their faith experience, particularly their position of religious authority, points toward an avenue for women's leadership in the church at large. Finally, the "with, without, or despite the clergy" aspect of popular religious practices may provide inroads as to how to incorporate other nonparish groups, including the rapidly growing contingent of new lay ecclesial movements that appear to be a sign of the times.

Ultimately, Latino/a theology and Latino/a Catholics are not a panacea to cure the church of its very real problems, nor are we merely to be regarded as a novelty or enhancement to American Catholicism. While demographic research indicates that Latino/a Catholics will soon be the majority of Roman Catholics in the United States, the American church remains the most ethnically and racially diverse ecclesial body in the world.[42] What ecclesiology makes of the dangerous memory of Latino/a Catholicism, and how seriously it incorporates the insights and the challenges posed by theology from colonialized and marginalized groups, will largely determine the fate of Catholicism in the third millennium.

For Further Reading

Badillo, David. *Latinos and the New Immigrant Church*. Baltimore, MD: Johns Hopkins University Press, 2006.

Espín, Orlando, and Miguel Diaz, eds. *From the Heart of Our People*. Maryknoll, NY: Orbis Books, 1999.

Gaillardetz, Richard. *Ecclesiology for a Global Church: A People Called and Sent*. Maryknoll, NY: Orbis Books, 2010.

Goizueta, Roberto. *Caminemos Con Jesus: Toward a Hispanic/Latino Theology of Accompaniment*. Maryknoll, NY: Orbis Books, 1995.

Isasi-Díaz, Ada María. *En la Lucha, In the Struggle: Elaborating a Mujerista Theology*. Minneapolis, MN: Fortress Press, 2004.

Matovina, Timothy. *Latino Catholicism: Transformation in America's Largest Church*. Princeton, NJ: Princeton University Press, 2012.

Ospino, Hosffman, ed. *Hispanic Ministry in the 21st Century: Present and Future*. Miami, FL: Convivium Press, 2010.

---

[42] Matovina, *Latino Catholicism*, 38.

CHAPTER 4

Ecclesiology, Cultural Change, and the Changing Nature of Culture

Vincent Miller

The relationship of religion and culture is unavoidable for Catholicism because of its understanding of the communal, ecclesial nature of salvation. Catholicism does not conceive of Christian salvation as something that comes to individuals apart from their social and cultural relationships. The salvation God works in Christ draws us into the communion of the divine life through a historical communion on earth. The Second Vatican Council conceived of the church as the gathered people of God called to a living communion so profound that it is the Body of Christ. This communion is not something the church possesses for itself. The church is ultimately a sacrament of God's salvation in the world. The Gospel proclaims God's gracious kingdom coming to be in the world. The church is called not only to proclaim this way of being together but also to embody and to share it in history. Thus, the church must engage the collective, social dimensions of human existence: politics, economics, and culture.

This essay will explore the meaning of the word "culture" as it has been understood in secular and theological scholarship in the modern period. It will then outline two of the most important magisterial discussions of the church and culture in the past fifty years: Vatican II's *Gaudium et Spes* (The Pastoral Constitution on the Church in the Modern World) and Pope John Paul II's encyclical letter *Evangelium Vitae* (The Gospel of Life). These examples of the church's understanding of and engagement with culture will be analyzed in terms of their own cultural contexts with special attention given to the media structures of each time.

Gaudium et Spes faced the promise and challenge of the postwar, national-scale mass media. These media tended to homogenize culture—eliminating difference by broadcasting majority voices and constructing a popular culture aimed at the lowest common denominator. John Paul II's understanding of culture can be seen as a strategic response to the challenge that this cultural ecology posed to Christian identity and formation. This response however, took place within a changed cultural ecology in which new forms of media enabled diverse voices to speak to ever purer and differentiated audiences. This context poses the opposite challenge. It threatens to separate and isolate cultural groups—including the church—from one another. It preserves and even elicits difference, locking groups into their own niches, thus hindering the kind of engagement that the Gospel demands. This essay will conclude with a reflection on the church's mark of catholicity as a principle for responding to this challenge.

Meanings of "Culture"

As is often the case with a frequently used term, the meaning of "culture" seems at first glance to be self-evident. On closer examination, it becomes quite complex. Raymond Williams famously described culture as "one of the two or three most complicated words in the English language."[1] Originating as a noun of process referring to the tending of crops or animals, its meaning was gradually extended to the intellectual, moral, and spiritual cultivation of persons. This meaning was, in turn, extended to describe the universal cultivation of humankind. In this sense it functioned as a synonym for "civilization." During the period of colonization, Europeans extended this sense of culture from social elites to describe Western civilization as a whole—over against the supposedly "primitive" peoples they were conquering. Combined with historical consciousness, this notion gave rise to the idea of the ongoing development of culture implicit in the modern notion of "progress." This developmental meaning came to apply to matters of high culture as well, whether the fine arts or all of the intellectual and scientific production offered by cultural elites. In this sense, culture is understood to comprise the shared questions, insights, and aspirations of a given society or age.

[1] Raymond Williams, *Keywords: A Vocabulary of Culture and Society* (New York: Oxford University Press, 1976), 76.

In the late eighteenth century, Johann Gottfried Herder challenged the universalizing and rationalistic presumptions of this understanding of culture and proposed the plural meaning which now forms an essential part of our understanding. Culture in this sense designates the "specific and variable cultures of different nations and periods."[2] This plural sense of culture attends to the particular intellectual, symbolic, and narrative traditions of different peoples and also provides the basis for considering the various class, ethnic, and regional subcultures within national cultures. Herder's definition long informed anthropological understandings of culture. These understandings treated cultures as self-enclosed and self-contained worlds marked by internal coherence and social consensus. Such understandings of culture were often wed to national assumptions—that the human race is composed of discrete nations who are ideally mapped to a system of separate, territorially contiguous nation-states. These assumptions have been called into question by contemporary anthropology in light of the dynamism, conflict, and hybridity that seem to be present in all human cultures.[3]

Culture is intrinsically bound up with technology. This connection is clearest with the artistic aspects of culture—from the Neolithic Venus of Willendorf or the cave paintings at Lascaux to the stained glass windows of Chartres or the frescos of the Sistine Chapel. Art depends literally on the media in which it is expressed. Media also influence culture in a less direct, but no less important, way. In addition to serving as the means of expression, media technologies also provide differing means of sharing human cultural production. The very nature of culture as a shared dimension of human existence is inextricably bound to the means at our disposal to share with others, and it is dependent on the scale and intensity of sharing that given media allow. The history of human culture is intertwined with communication technologies. These include: the emergence of written language, the printing press, salons and artistic gatherings, publishing and news industries, the rise of radio and television broadcasting, and the latest "new" media of computer and internet technologies. This connection between technology and culture is evident in the use of the term "popular culture" to describe the consumer cultural products distributed through mass media.

---

[2] Ibid., 79.

[3] See Robert J. Schreiter, *The New Catholicity: Theology between the Global and the Local* (Maryknoll, NY: Orbis Books, 1997), 46–53; and Kathryn Tanner, *Theories of Culture: A New Agenda for Theology* (Minneapolis, MN: Fortress Press, 1997), 1–60.

From this complex, but interrelated, set of concerns, we can catalogue a range of meanings of culture. Culture concerns formation in the shared, moral dimension of human existence. Culture is a historical reality that changes over time. Culture also differs across different human communities, both between and within nations. Culture is marked by a tension between elite and popular production. Culture is bound up with communication technologies that enable its dissemination.

The relationship of church to culture has been an important theme in Catholic ecclesiology since the Second Vatican Council. The topic appeared in the aftermath of the council in a variety of contexts: the attention to the diversity of cultures at a moment when the legacies of colonialism were being challenged, the relationship of the church to the increasingly secular societies of Europe and North America, the enormously formative power of modern media, and the need to preserve the distinctive character of the Gospel as the church engages these various dimensions of culture.

Culture in *Gaudium et Spes*

Vatican II's Pastoral Constitution on the Church in the Modern World offers one of the most extended reflections on culture that can be found in any magisterial text. In a chapter devoted entirely to the topic, *Gaudium et Spes* defines culture in a manner that unites the developmental understanding of culture with Catholic theological notions of creation, nature, and grace. Humankind "can achieve true and full humanity only by means of culture, that is through the cultivations of the goods and values of nature" understood here both as human nature and the broader natural world in which we live. Culture is thus described as the process whereby humankind develops and perfects its "diverse mental and physical endowments." Culture is essentially social. It renders social life more human through "the improvement of customs and institutions" (GS 53). Because it is a process whereby humans strive to live life fully and hand their wisdom on to following generations, it is also intrinsically historical.

In addition to embracing historical change, *Gaudium et Spes* also speaks explicitly of the "ethnological" sense of culture which addresses the "plurality of cultures." Each human community and nation has its own cultural traditions. These manifest a diverse manner of labor, expression, religion, customs, laws, sciences, and the arts. This attention to the diversity of cultures fits well with the times. *Gaudium et Spes* echoed

Pope John XXIII's description of the global quest for political independence among the nations colonized by the West (GS 9).[4] These concerns
were present in contemporary secular anthropology. Clifford Geertz's
influential anthropological work embodied this sensibility to the nuances
of local culture. He would publish his seminal essay "Religion as Cultural
System" in 1966.[5]

The use of the terminology "human communities" or "human communities and nations" is noteworthy in light of the European national
model of culture which was dominant at the time.[6] This presumes that
culture is best understood on the scale of the nation-state; that a nation
is a unified, homogenous culture embodied within a state structure. Such
a view of culture marginalizes minority social groups, many of whom
are the victims of colonization, slavery, and other violent forms of ex-
propriation and repression. The council's terminology avoids conflating
the biblical notion of "the nations" (e.g., Matt 28:19ff.) with the modern
nation-state. Thus, it refuses to baptize the cartography of victors, which
had displaced and marginalized so many peoples.

This embrace of the plurality of cultures is theologically important
because it separated the church's proclamation of the universality of
God's saving offer from the universalizing pretentions of Western cultural imperialism. The council declared that the church "is not tied exclusively and indissolubly to any race or nation. . . . The church is
faithful to its traditions and is at the same time conscious of its universal
mission; it can, then, enter into communion with different forms of culture, thereby enriching both itself and the cultures themselves" (GS 58).

Throughout all of these dimensions, *Gaudium et Spes* speaks of the
rise of cultural agency made possible by twentieth-century technology
and prosperity. "Now for the first time in history people are not afraid
to think that cultural benefits are for all and should be available to everybody" (GS 9). What were once the reserve of elites, cultural formation
and participation should be open to all who were previously excluded—
including women, minorities, and the poor (GS 55).

---

[4] See John XXIII, *Pacem in Terris* (On Establishing Universal Peace in Truth, Justice,
Charity, and Liberty), 42, http://www.vatican.va/holy_father/john_xxiii/encyclicals
/documents/hf_j-xxiii_enc_11041963_pacem_en.html, accessed August 31, 2014.

[5] Clifford Geertz, "Religion as Cultural System," in *The Interpretation of Cultures:
Selected Essays* (New York: Basic Books, 1973), 87–126.

[6] *hominum communitates et nations* (GS 42).

Cultural Challenges in *Gaudium et Spes*

The concerns about culture expressed by the council are consistent with its view of culture. *Gaudium et Spes* described three major cultural struggles that dominated the postwar period through the 1980s, and that, along with other challenges, continue today. They are: the challenge to synthesis posed by the rise of science and technology, the threat of cultural homogenization to traditional and especially minority cultures, and the need to grant everyone, especially the marginalized, access to culture.

A Challenge to Synthesis

The massive discoveries of the natural and human sciences that define the modern period pose a more extreme challenge to synthesis than any previous moment in history. Earlier eras knew the disruption that divergent systems of thought could pose to faith. Thomas Aquinas's great contribution in the Middle Ages was to synthesize the newly recovered philosophy of Aristotle with an Augustinian theological tradition wedded to the very different sensibilities of Plato. Aquinas's achievement was, without question, enormous. The task of integrating Aristotle into theology, however, pales in comparison with the challenge posed by the scope and diversity of contemporary scholarship and science. Although competence might take a lifetime, the entirety of the extant works of Aristotle can be read in a few months. Today, a lifetime of disciplined reading would not be enough time to keep up even with one academic discipline, let alone the breadth of contemporary knowledge.

The council celebrated discovery in the academic disciplines as opportunities to be "more fully enlightened by the marvelous wisdom, which was with God from eternity, fashioning all things with God, rejoicing in God's inhabited world, and delighting in humanity's sons and daughters" (GS 57). The difficulty of synthesizing the conclusions of modern science, however, decreases our ability to integrate them into an understanding of the whole human person (GS 61). This threatens to separate faith from everyday life as theological and ethical judgment struggle to engage the modern explosion of knowledge and the world being built around it.

The council judged that such difficulties were only circumstantial. The profound difficulties raised by new knowledge do not defeat the reconciliation of faith and reason, rather, they "demand new scrutiny by theologians" in order to address them (GS 62). Such investigations require knowledge of and engagement with contemporary culture. This is the task of the entire church.

> Therefore, the faithful ought to work closely with their contemporaries and ought to try to understand their ways of thinking and feeling, as these find expression in current culture. Let the faithful incorporate the findings of new sciences and teachings and the understanding of the most recent discoveries into christian morality and thought, so that their practice of religion and their moral behavior may keep abreast of their acquaintance with science and of the relentless progress of technology: in this way they will succeed in evaluating and interpreting everything with an authentically christian sense of values. (GS 62)

Thus, the council called for deep and sustained engagement between the church and contemporary culture. Such engagement demands presence—Christians living in close union with scientists, scholars, and cultural leaders so that the church could understand and "evaluate" contemporary discoveries from a Christian perspective. More than simple evaluation, the council called for synthesis, to "blend" contemporary discoveries with Christian doctrine and morality so that religious culture and morality may themselves "keep abreast." This imperative for critical engagement and synthesis resembles the theological project of correlation which seeks to bring the Gospel message into dialogue with contemporary questions and concerns.[7]

This vision of engagement with culture is grounded in the bedrock dogmatic principles of creation, incarnation, and soteriology. Although humankind is fallen, the development of human culture is not a random or nihilistic exercise in human self-construction. Whatever its flaws, human cultural endeavor remains the development and discovery of the potential given to humankind by the creating God. *Gaudium et Spes's* christological anthropology—which sees "the incarnate Word" as revealing the mystery of human nature (GS 22)—is also important in this engagement with culture. The Gospel of Christ "continually renews the life and culture of fallen humanity." It corrects errors resulting from sin. It purifies what is good in moral traditions, taking "the spiritual qualities

---

[7] For a discussion of the method of correlation, see David Tracy, "The Uneasy Alliance Reconceived: Catholic Theological Method, Modernity, and Postmodernity," *Theological Studies* 50, no. 3 (1989): 548–70.

and endowments of every age and nation," elevating them, and causing them "to bear fruit . . . from within." This is the "very fulfillment" of the church's function, including its liturgical action; it "stimulates and advances human and civic culture" (GS 58).

The council is confident that the challenge to synthesis posed by the modern proliferation of knowledge can be met through a deeper engagement with culture. This confidence is not simply an expression of optimism concerning modern science or human intellectual capacity. It is ultimately rooted in faith that God's saving presence is at work in human history in a way that makes the historical and ethnographic diversity of culture both intelligible and redeemable.

The Threat of Homogenization

Homogenization refers to the loss of cultural diversity—a monotone form of unity that doesn't respect diversity but instead reduces it to the same. This can take place through the suppression of vulnerable cultures, the imposition of a dominant culture (as in colonialism), or through cultural change where traditional cultures are replaced with scientific, commercial, and popular forms of culture. In all cases the richness of human culture is threatened as both the breadth of diversity and the depth of various forms of wisdom are lost.

Gaudium et Spes links scientific developments to the challenge of homogenization. By challenging earlier cosmologies and anthropologies, science threatens to supplant traditional beliefs and cultures. Their connection with new technologies, including human technologies, may swamp more complex worldviews with a materialistic understanding of human existence. The successes of technical rationality—from electricity and airplanes to penicillin and antidepressants—are so evident that they supplant the spiritual and moral concerns of more traditional forms of knowledge.

This challenge to traditional cultures is reinforced by the homogenizing tendencies of the postwar era. "Customs and patterns of life tend to become more uniform from day to day; industrialization, urbanization, and other factors which promote community living create new mass-cultures which give birth to new patterns of thinking, of acting, and of the use of leisure." Commerce increases contact between cultures and can give rise to a "more universal form of culture" (GS 54).

In the postwar era, the rise of national-scale mass media distributed a new form of homogenized, consumerist popular culture that reinforced the hegemony of majority cultures over national minorities. This was not simply the result of prejudice against minority cultures. The technological structure of mass media is itself homogenizing. Media such as national news magazines, radio, film, and television enabled a very limited number of voices to reach a broad audience. The expensive infrastructure these media required tied them to national-scale systems of distribution and led them to seek to appeal to the lowest cultural denominator in order to attract a sufficient audience. For that reason, they tended to strengthen and deepen the cultural hegemony of majority national cultures. The global distribution of Western popular culture also threatened a new form of cultural imperialism that continued, with glitz and gloss, the colonial domination of the Two-Thirds World.[8]

The council exhorted political authorities to respect the autonomy of culture (GS 59), warning both against the absorption of culture as an ideological tool of political power (as in totalitarian states) and against the reduction of culture to an instrument of economic power (as in the consumer cultures of capitalist societies).

The council hoped that cultural exchange could also bring a positive outcome, to the degree that "the particular characteristics of each culture are preserved" (GS 54). This vision of cosmopolitan diversity and a "new humanism" (GS 55) embodies the optimistic internationalism of the 1960s. It is, however, rooted in a deeper vision of the church's catholicity that forms the basis for a critical challenge to an overly optimistic internationalism. Because the church is not bound to any particular culture or system, it "can be a very close bond between the various communities of people and nations" (GS 42).

The vision of the church as independent from any particular culture, the sacrament of unity and artisan of bonds between diverse peoples, is of course an expression of an ideal rather than a statement of accomplished fact. But this theological principle, along with this understanding of culture, enabled the church on many levels to participate in the struggles for independence, political recognition, and cultural identity that took place in the second half of the twentieth century. This is apparent in the struggle of liberation theology with various forms of colonialism, as well as in the projects of African, Asian, Latino/a, feminist, Mujerista, Womanist, and other contextual theological projects which

---

[8] See Schreiter, *The New Catholicity*, 10–12; and Vincent Miller, *Consuming Religion: Christian Faith and Practice in a Consumer Culture* (New York: Continuum, 2004).

aim to give voice to the Gospel as it unfolds in diverse cultures and contexts.

The Challenge of Cultural Agency and Participation

The final challenge posed by culture is in fact a new opportunity: participation. Economic prosperity and technology have made access to, formation in, and the ability to contribute to culture possible for everyone. This challenges traditional distinctions between the cultured classes who participate in culture and the laboring classes who do not. "Now for the first time in history people are not afraid to think that cultural benefits are for all and should be available to everybody" (GS 9). The mass media have the positive potential to provide the resources for increased literacy, education, and cultural and social communication (GS 61). This possibility envisions the moral formation of culture as a universal right and obligation. The council speaks of "everyone's right to human and civil culture in harmony with personal dignity, without distinction of race, sex, nation, religion, or social circumstances," so that they may contribute "in an authentically human way to the common good" (GS 60). Here the council unites traditional notions of culture as moral formation with a recognition of the diversity of cultures and the need for all to bring their cultural riches to the quest for the universal common good.

True to its aims, *Gaudium et Spes* displays well the church's engagement with the cultural issues of its day. The national-scale mass media held the promise of bringing literacy and culture to the masses. The rising levels of literacy and the technologies that made them possible also enabled religious traditions to deepen their formation of believers in a historically unprecedented manner. Religious traditions could feel confident in the stable identity of their faithful and focus instead on the demanding work of engagement with broader culture. The concerns the document expressed regarding culture do not support portraying this as an instance of the so-called "optimism" of the document. Indeed, *Gaudium et Spes* clearly articulated the overwhelming challenge of this media structure for culture: its homogenizing power. This threatened to swamp the voices and traditions of minorities and traditional cultures and to reduce the diversity of the world's myriad perspectives to a shallow consensus or empty consumer mass culture. *Gaudium et Spes* held out hope that, if the proper principles were respected, the moment could bring forth a true cosmopolitanism in which people could be formed for the responsible moral engagement that respected the difference of cultures and enabled cooperation between them in advancing the universal common good. This Catholic hope was not simply an optimistic wish—it inspired the demanding project of sympathetic yet critical Christian engagement with the depth and diversity of modern cultures.

Postconciliar Evaluations of Culture

The next moment in the church's relationship to culture does not represent as much a fundamental break in the understanding of culture as a change in the evaluation of the church's fortunes amid modern cultures. The primarily positive assessment of modern culture found in *Gaudium et Spes* was replaced with a more negative appraisal. While this can be legitimately portrayed as a contrast between theological orientations (e.g., progressive vs. conservative, *Concilium* vs. *Communio*, Thomist vs. Augustinian), the reevaluation transcends these particular divides. The French Jesuit Michel de Certeau serves as an example of a theological progressive (and *Concilium* author) who judged that the negative outcomes warned of in *Gaudium et Spes* were already established realities even as the text was being debated. De Certeau, who came of age during World War II, grew up in a world where Catholicism was no longer excluded from French culture. This resulted not in influence but indifference and the dissipation of Christian identity. His generation experienced secular civil society as a massive consensus in which traditional Christian belief, commitment, and practice were increasingly implausible.[9] Whatever potential the media promised for widespread Christian formation, mass media also challenged this formation by offering a powerful alternative to traditional communal and intergenerational formation.

The project of engagement and correlation became increasingly difficult in the decades that followed the council. As a new generation of scholars attempted to carry out the "in principle" transcendental engagements exemplified in different ways by Karl Rahner and Bernard Lonergan, they found it difficult to sustain an engagement with the vast particularity and radical diversity of academic theology and contemporary culture. This cultural context profoundly handicaps constructive synthetic theological engagements. That is not to say that constructive,

---

[9] Michel de Certeau, "The Weakness of Believing: From the Body to Writing, a Christian Transit," in *The Certeau Reader*, ed. Graham Ward (London: Blackwell, 2000).

engaged theology is no longer produced, but that our context makes it difficult. Systematic theological work is more easily undertaken in the dialectical mode of Karl Barth, which can conceive of no cooperation with the fallen world, or historical retrievals that seek to recover a past synthesis without any consideration of dialogue with the changed present. In some circles, there is active animus against any form of contextual theological undertaking. David Tracy notes the irony that rejections of the correlationist method were often justified by a decidedly contextualized historical assumption "that the loss of identity by all traditions in modernity is the central situational question facing all theologians who can see our present situation clearly."[10] What remains of the theological project of correlation is shunted into engagements with various critical and genealogical theories that do not provide the infrastructure for grand visions that can inspire an age but rather facilitate partial critiques and limited, tactical engagements.

The 1980s were marked by the emergence of a "postliberal" family of theological projects which fit well with this atmosphere. These sought to employ the thought of Wittgenstein, narrative literary analysis, and cultural anthropology to do theology in a manner that focused on speaking from the particular logic of Christianity more than engaging concerns of those outside of a given theological tradition. George Lindbeck's proposal for a "cultural-linguistic" theological method exemplifies this project.[11] Such an approach often ends up portraying Christianity itself in cultural terms. As Tracy observed, "[A]nticorrelational theologians appeal to Geertz-like understandings of theology as, in effect, a kind of descriptive religious anthropology."[12]

This more pessimistic interpretation of the cultural context sees little opportunity for synthesis. Rather, modernity and the cultural formation fostered by modern media are at best indifferent to the Gospel, at worst they are profound counterformations that threaten to dilute and confuse Christian belief and identity. Thus the context elicits theological and ecclesial projects that emphasize the particular logic and identity of Christianity over against secular society. This contrast is frequently expressed in terms of culture.

---

[10] Tracy, "The Uneasy Alliance Reconceived," 557.

[11] George A. Lindbeck, *The Nature of Doctrine: Religion and Theology in a Postliberal Age* (Philadelphia, PA: Westminster, 1984).

[12] Tracy, "The Uneasy Alliance Reconceived," 557. See Tanner's critique of such equation of Christian social practices with anthropological notions of culture in *Theories of Culture*, 61–120.

Pope John Paul II's Use of Culture

Pope John Paul II's papal magisterium is noteworthy for its frequent use of the terminology of culture. On the one hand, his understanding of the term is largely in continuity with *Gaudium et Spes*. It preserves that document's confidence in the reconciliation of faith and reason and it fully embraces the theological imperative for Christians to work for the transformation of culture.

On the other hand, John Paul offers a much more pessimistic evaluation of the state of modern or "contemporary culture."[13] It is arguable that John Paul II's use of the word "culture" in his encyclical *Evangelium Vitae* is the single most significant word in his vast papal magisterium. The conceptual change it represents both expressed and inspired the ecclesiological revolution undertaken by his papacy. John Paul subtly shifted the meaning of culture in a manner that emphasized the particularity and distinctiveness of Christianity. John Paul's engagement with culture emphasizes the contrast between the perspectives and values of modern culture and those of the church. He did not abandon the project of cultural engagement, but in his account this was transformed from a matter of maintaining closeness with the men and women of the age to a more contrastive but still constructive practice of witness.

Evangelium Vitae is one of the most influential and dense loci of John Paul II's use of the term "culture." The term appears eighty-two times in one form or another, most famously in the formulae "culture of death" and "culture of life." John Paul does not offer a definition of his understanding of the term in the text. There are several passages that clearly use the term in its plural, ethnological sense in a relatively straightforward manner, e.g., "the peoples of different nations and cultures."[14]

John Paul's use of the singular form of the term is, however, much harder to define. This can be clarified by considering his use of the adjectival form "cultural." It is generally used to designate a sphere of human social existence. In such cases it is categorized in a series with other adjectives such as "economical," "legislative," "political," or

---

[13] During the council, Bishop Karol Wojtyla—the future John Paul II—was critical of the optimism of the early drafts of *Gaudium et Spes*. Similar criticisms were made by the German bishops and their theological experts, including Karl Rahner. See John O'Malley, *What Happened at Vatican II* (Cambridge, MA: Belknap, 2008), 250, 258–59.

[14] John Paul II, *Evangelium Vitae* (On the Value and Inviolability of Human Life), 85, http://www.vatican.va/holy_father/john_paul_ii/encyclicals/documents/hf_jp-ii_enc _25031995_evangelium-vitae_en.html, accessed August 31, 2014.

"social," which modify nouns such as "climate," "conditions," or "level" (EV 18, 21, 66, 91). In this usage, culture designates a particular dimension or sphere of human social existence distinct from—but influenced by and capable of influencing—the other spheres.

"Cultural" is also paired with "moral" and "religious" in a more complimentary way. The text pursues an "assessment of a cultural and moral nature" (EV 21) that examines various "mentalities." Here John Paul's conception of culture begins to emerge. It designates the shared ontologies and anthropologies of a society. He speaks of "contemporary" and "present-day" culture as being marked by two pernicious mentalities. The first is a "completely individualistic concept of freedom" which leaves no room for solidarity and concern for the weak (EV 19). The second is secularism, which, by eclipsing the sense of the divine creator, ends up eclipsing a sense of the dignity of human life and a morality that honors it (EV 21). These mentalities are manifest in shared assumptions in civil society and popular media; they are also concretized in and given formative power by economic structures, law, and professional policy. These mentalities form the "moral conscience of society" which gives rise to a "culture of death" by "creating and consolidating actual 'structures of sin' which go against life" (EV 22). This dialectical relationship between ideology and structure is particularly evident in his many references to the ways in which economic structures and political policies influence decisions regarding abortion (e.g., EV 59). These mentalities are concretized both in the use of contraception and in the liberal capitalist economic principle of efficiency.

John Paul's understanding of culture combines two elements of the modern use of the term employed in *Gaudium et Spes*: the formation of individual and social character and the plural notion of multiple cultures. These two dimensions exist in tension in John Paul's use of the term.

On the one hand, culture designates distinct mentalities insofar as these mentalities form the collective and individual moral conscience. Thus there can be multiple "cultures" within a single nation or society— in this case the "culture of death" and the "culture of life." These are not, however, comprehensive "cultures" in the ethnological sense. They resemble the subcultures analyzed by cultural studies that coexist in a shared society with other class and ethnic subcultures.

On the other hand, John Paul's notion of the "culture of death" describes an enlightenment mentality deeply woven into the worldview, ethos, and practice of modern societies. Culture designates the broad horizon of beliefs, values, and structures that contribute to acceptance of abortion in society. The tension between these two scales remains unresolved. John Paul's use of the comprehensive categories of "death" and "life," however, do shift the rhetorical weight of his analysis to the larger scale.

Another aspect of the understanding of culture as formation is evident in John Paul's juxtaposition of the "culture of life" to the "culture of death." This juxtaposition is often described as apocalyptic. It should be noted, however, that the term "culture of death" did not originate with John Paul. It appeared publically a year earlier in the neoconservative political manifesto "Evangelicals and Catholics Together."[15] John Paul's addition of the positive cultural project of the "culture of life" displays a Catholic sacramental, ecclesial optimism that moderates its apocalyptic dualism. Christians are not simply forced to choose between the Gospel and a "culture of death" in a time of judgment. Rather, they are called to the positive project of cultivating a culture of life in history.

John Paul draws a much sharper contrast between the church and world than *Gaudium et Spes*, and he does so precisely in cultural terms. While the church works "in" the world, it does so more by offering its own distinct truth than by cooperating with the dominant culture. *Evangelium Vitae* does not speak of "synthesis" as either a problem or a task.[16] The separation between the two dimensions of his understanding

---

[15] Paul Lauritzen, "Holy Alliance? The Danger of Mixing Politics and Religion," *Commonweal* 133, no. 6 (March 24, 2006): 14–17.

[16] John Paul II did not frequently use the language of "synthesis" in the sense employed by *Gaudium et Spes*. He employed the term in his discussion of Augustine and Aquinas in *Fides et Ratio* (On the Relationship Between Faith and Reason), 40, 78, http://w2.vatican.va/content/john-paul-ii/en/encyclicals/documents/hf_jp-ii_enc_14091998_fides-et-ratio.html, accessed August 7, 2014. But there the term seems to refer more to their respective harmonizing of philosophical and theological reflection than to their engaging their contemporary context. The term also appears in a similar sense in *Christifideles Laici* (On the Vocation and Mission of the Lay Faithful in the Church and in the World), 34 and 60, http://w2.vatican.va/content/john-paul-ii/en/apost_exhortations/documents/hf_jp-ii_exh_30121988_christifideles-laici.html, accessed August 7, 2014. There, however, it functions in the mode of witness in a manner consistent with the use of culture present in *Evangelium Vitae*. John Paul did use the term in a manner identical with *Gaudium et Spes* in an address on Galileo to the Pontifical Academy of Sciences: "Contemporary culture demands a constant effort to synthesize knowledge and to integrate learning. Of course, the successes which we see are due to the specialization of research. But unless this is balanced by a reflection concerned with articulating the various branches of knowledge, there is a great risk that we shall have a 'shattered culture,' which would in fact be the negation of true culture. A true culture cannot be conceived of without humanism and wisdom."

of culture is at work here. On the one hand, the church must contend with a cultural civilizational horizon dominated by an opposing world-view and ethos. On the other hand, it can cultivate a "culture of life" that contributes to broader society.

I have argued that while John Paul II's papacy can be evaluated from the perspective of his more pessimistic evaluation of the state of con-temporary culture than *Gaudium et Spes*, he pointedly did not abandon the council's understanding of culture and its positive cultural project. That said, John Paul's thought marks a very important turning point in the church's understanding of culture. The church engages culture not through critical synthesis but by contrastive witness to the truth it has received.

John Paul's use of the terminology of culture in *Evangelium Vitae* trans-poses debates about doctrine and morals into manifestations of cultural difference. This has profound consequences for ecclesiology and the-ology. Dissenting judgments on matters of contraception or abortion, which often continued long-standing methodological debates within Catholic moral theology, were refigured as manifestations of an incom-patible culture—a failure not in doctrine but in cultural identity. As a result, Christian discipleship and ecclesial life were refigured in terms of cultural identity.

Although it was not apocalyptic, John Paul's cultural turn neverthe-less had a similarly polarizing effect. In more traditional perspectives, fidelity is measured by adherence to central doctrines and practices, leaving a wide degree of latitude—or at least the acceptance of sinfully falling short—in other matters. *Evangelium Vitae*'s model of culture portrays fidelity at stake in a much wider range of beliefs, practices, and structures.

As a result, orthodoxy and orthopraxis were refigured from commit-ment to the core to the maintenance of boundaries. This is particularly apparent in the decline of traditional forms of moral casuistry which sought to attend to the complexities of circumstance in the realization of moral norms. What were once essential tools for enacting core com-mitments in a fallen world are now often seen as methods of shirking responsibility and confusing others about the requirements of religious identity.

John Paul II, "Faith Can Never Conflict with Reason," *L'Osservatore Romano*, Novem-ber 4, 1992, http://www.its.caltech.edu/~nmcenter/sci-cp/sci-9211.html, accessed September 5, 2014. I thank Matthew Ashley for the reference.

A Changed Cultural Context, a Different Challenge

Both *Gaudium et Spes* and *Evangelium Vitae* viewed cultural homogenization as a fundamental challenge. We noted that the former was written at a time when national-scale mass media were dominant. While this problem continues, the ongoing development of media technology in the past fifty years has significantly changed the cultural impact of media. The rapid expansion of media bandwidth (e.g., cable and satellite television, the internet) ended the restrictions on access that characterized the mid-twentieth-century mass media. Cultural gatekeepers lost much of their power to exclude. It is no longer necessary to cater to the lowest common cultural denominator to gain an audience. Indeed, the most effective way to attract an audience in a crowded media field is to cater to a well-defined niche. As a result, the contemporary media climate tends to heterogenize culture rather than homogenize it. That is to say, contemporary culture is marked by a tendency to elicit difference rather than suppress it. Rather than reducing everything to the lowest common denominator or defaulting to the dominant culture, the contemporary cultural ecology sorts different subcultures into ever smaller and purer niches. The result is a cultural ecology in which sectarianism is the default stance.[17]

Thus, while John Paul II's reconception of the church along the lines of a threatened subculture would indeed be countercultural in a mass-media context, it was deployed in a new media context where it swims along with the dominant cultural tide. That is to say, being countercultural has, surprisingly, become the cultural default. Far from suppressing distinctive identities, our age elicits them. In so doing, it disciplines subcultures to define themselves not by their fundamental commitments but by contrastive difference. This cultural context reinforces and rewards the focus on boundary maintenance implicit in John Paul's cultural turn and presumed by postliberal approaches to theology.

This new ecology poses its own set of challenges quite distinct from that of the mass-media era. This ecology is not so much a specific culture

---

[17] For a more extended analysis of this context, see Vincent Miller, "When Mediating Structures Change: The Magisterium, the Media, and the Culture Wars," in *When the Magisterium Intervenes: The Magisterium and Theologians in Today's Church*, ed. Richard R. Gaillardetz (Collegeville, MN: Liturgical Press, 2012), 154–74; and Vincent Miller, "Media Constructions of Space, the Disciplining of Religious Traditions and the Hidden Threat of the Post-Secular," in *(Post)Secularity, Religion and the Public Sphere*, ed. William Barbieri (Grand Rapids, MI: Eerdmans, 2014), 62–196.

itself but a context that disciplines any culture. This new context presumes that social life will be organized into subcultures, each with their own particular worldviews, values, and practices. It welcomes distinctive religious and moral commitments. At the same time, it constrains the influence of their wisdom to a limited subculture. It constructs such commitments as a matter of choice between cultures. It is hard to conceive the meaning of "countercultural" in a context that presumes all cultural identities are defined by their distinction from others. Thus a context where the positive project of a "culture of life" and analogous projects such as the fight for recognition and agency among marginalized cultural groups find themselves both welcome and fatally restricted. Dialogue, evangelization, and engagement cannot easily escape a subcultural niche. If to use the terminology of "culture" in the mass-media era was to risk homogenization and the loss of the distinctiveness of the Christian message, in this context, to think of the church in cultural terms runs the risk of accepting this disciplining of truth into sectarian niches that fundamentally compromises the church's catholic mission.

Responding to This New Context

This brief review has shown that the term "culture" is a key concept in the theological conception of the nature and mission of the church. Although the examples considered share the same complex of meanings that the modern use of the term connotes, we have seen that emphasizing different dimensions of its meaning (e.g., universal human development, individual and social moral formation, ethnographic particularity, smaller subcultures) yield very different practical ecclesiologies. The term "culture" is never ecclesiologically neutral. Not only is the content of human culture historically varied, the nature of the category itself changes.

The church has faced cultural revolutions caused by economic, political, and technological changes in the past. This point is particularly important. Although this chapter has considered the views of culture operative in the ecclesiologies of *Gaudium et Spes* and *Evangelium Vitae*, it is important to distinguish that these ecclesiological projects responded to their broader cultural ecologies—they did not create them.

Gaudium et Spes called for an engagement with the challenges posed by the cultural context of the postwar era. To shirk the tasks of engagement and synthesis would be to ignore the demands of the church's sacramental mission. Although this task was never presumed to be easy, the power of the mass media to homogenize culture became increasingly clear. The church faced a double threat to its apostolicity: the challenge of handing on the Gospel in a radically different context and an erosion of its own identity in the face of the competing formation offered to its members by the mass media.

John Paul II's cultural project and allied postliberal theological projects are justified in response to this challenge. Unfortunately, these very responses leave the church vulnerable in the changed cultural ecology that has emerged in the new media context. They risk the strategic error of "generals fighting the last war."

This new media ecology threatens the unity of the church, as it replaces Catholic ecclesial notions of communion with an imported secular model of cultural identity that reduces ritual and doctrine to tools to mark difference. At its extreme, unity is reduced to the mere internal result of the external marking of difference. Communion is tragically compromised by being reimagined as the fruit of excommunication. This focus on contrastive identity undermines *Lumen Gentium*'s description of the church's sacramental nature as a "sign and instrument" of "communion with God and of the unity of the entire human race" (LG 1). This cultural ecology threatens to cut off that sacramental work, relegating the church to a subcultural niche, pure in itself, but unable either to engage other niches or to call the logic of the system itself into question.

Pope Francis's brief papacy has been noteworthy for its attention to this new challenge. Francis has adopted John Paul's use of the term culture as a framework of formation in *Evangelii Gaudium*.[18] His emphasis on the "culture of encounter" is noteworthy because it is not simply an articulation of a positive cultural formation that the church has to offer the world. Rather it is a formulation that runs directly against the disciplining power of our sectarian ecology. Encounter in *Evangelii Gaudium* has the dual character of *Lumen Gentium*'s vision of the church as sacrament: union with God and among all men and women.

---

[18] See, for example, the following phrases: "throwaway culture," "individualistic culture," "culture of prosperity," "globalized culture," and "media culture" in *Evangelii Gaudium* (On the Joy of the Gospel), 53, 54, 63, 76, 78, 220, http://w2.vatican.va /content/francesco/en/apost_exhortations/documents/papa-francesco_esortazione -ap_20131124_evangelii-gaudium.html, accessed August 31, 2014.

Francis has also explicitly retrieved the notion of "synthesis" as it was used in *Gaudium et Spes*.[19] Synthesis describes not only the public witness and promotion of values lacking in broader culture but also something "new" that arises from the effective preaching of the Gospel in a particular culture. Francis warns that if we "allow doubts and fears to dampen our courage" to undertake this task, the church may "remain comfortable," but "we will not take an active part in historical processes." Christians will become "mere onlookers as the Church gradually stagnates" (EG 128).

Francis describes synthesis as the work of the Spirit that "can harmonize every diversity" and "overcome every conflict" (EG 230). This points to the mark of the church that is both the most threatened by the contemporary context and the most promising for guiding a response: the mark of catholicity.[20] Catholicity describes both the fullness of salvation and full communion of all in that salvation. It points beyond sectarianism in two ways. Regarding doctrine, it demands that we attend to the full range of doctrine, sacrament, and community in our understanding of the church, rather than focus only on those aspects that stand in contrast with other groups. Regarding unity, catholicity challenges simplistic homogeneity and calls for a much more demanding communion of difference. Johann Adam Möhler described catholicity using the analogy of a choir where harmony is the fruit of different voices singing together. Like harmony, catholic unity cannot be achieved through "wearying monotone" or "antagonistic discord."[21]

As noted above, *Gaudium et Spes* taught that the church could provide "a very close bond between the various communities of people and nations" precisely because it was not bound to any particular culture or nation (GS 42). Here the council expressed a vision of catholicity that transcended the default forms of the national structuring of culture. In our different cultural ecology, the church is likewise called to transcend the default secular structuring of culture. This requires of us both a

---

[19] See Dennis Doyle, "The Heart of Pope Francis Put Forth in His New Synthesis," *Origins* 43, no. 45 (April 2014): 735–36. Francis explicitly applies the term to the dialogue between faith and science (*Evangelii Gaudium*, 242).

[20] For a more extended discussion of catholicity as a resource in this context, see Vincent Miller, "Where Is the Church? Globalization and Catholicity," *Theological Studies* 69, no. 2 (2008): 412–32.

[21] Johann Adam Möhler, *Unity in the Church or the Principle of Catholicism*, trans. Peter Erb (Washington, DC: The Catholic University of America Press, 1996), 194–98.

critical awareness of how this context disciplines us and the shared ecclesial work to develop theologies, spiritualties, virtues, practices, and structures that enact the "task" of catholicity in this new age. The latter is the work of our age, which we take up in the footsteps of those before us, who responded in their own ways to the cultural challenges of their own times.

For Further Reading

Chenu, M. D. *Nature, Man, and Society in the Twelfth Century*. Chicago: University of Chicago Press, 1968.

Goizueta, Roberto S. *Caminemos con Jesús: Toward a Hispanic/Latino Theology of Accompaniment*. Maryknoll, NY: Orbis Books, 1995.

Lindbeck, George A. *The Nature of Doctrine: Religion and Theology in a Postliberal Age*. Philadelphia, PA: Westminster, 1984.

Miller, Vincent J. *Consuming Religion: Christian Faith and Practice in a Consumer Culture*. New York: Continuum, 2004.

O'Meara, Thomas F. *Romantic Idealism and Roman Catholicism: Schelling and the Theologians*. Notre Dame, IN: University of Notre Dame Press, 1982.

Rowland, Tracey. *Culture and the Thomist Tradition after Vatican II*. London: Routledge, 2003.

Saracino, Michele. *Being about Borders: A Christian Anthropology of Difference*. Collegeville, MN: Liturgical Press, 2011.

Schreiter, Robert J. *The New Catholicity: Theology between the Global and the Local*. Maryknoll, NY: Orbis Books, 1997.

Shorter, Aylward. *Toward a Theology of Inculturation*. Maryknoll, NY: Orbis Books, 1988.

Tanner, Kathryn. *Theories of Culture: A New Agenda for Theology*. Minneapolis, MN: Fortress Press, 1997.

Part 3

Ecclesiological Openings

CHAPTER 5

Power and Authority in the Church: Emerging Issues

Richard R. Gaillardetz

The Second Vatican Council did not dedicate a single document to the themes of power and authority. Yet the council's reformist program was in good part a response to the forms of ecclesiastical authority that had dominated Roman Catholicism since the French Revolution. The council's vision was marked by a decisive shift away from the church understood as an "unequal society" constituted by two ranks, clergy and laity.[1] Instead the bishops gave priority to faith, baptism, and Christian discipleship (LG 9–17) for establishing our ecclesial identity. They affirmed the necessary equality of all believers (LG 32) and distanced themselves from monarchical conceptions of church office (e.g., the pope as a quasi-imperial figure, cardinals as "princes of the church," and prelates who "rule" over their flock) in favor of power and authority exercised as Christian service (CD 16). The council affirmed the eschatological orientation of the church as pilgrim (LG 48), an orientation that provided the foundations for the reform of authority structures (UR 6). Its recovery of pneumatology (LG 4) allowed it, albeit inconsistently, to break free of a juridical conception of the exercise of power in the church and its consequent zero-sum framework (clergy have power, therefore the laity do not). Vatican I's dogmatic pronouncements regarding papal primacy and infallibility were acknowledged even as they were recontextualized

---

[1] See Pius X, *Vehementer Nos* (On the French Law of Separation), 8, http://www
.vatican.va/holy_father/pius_x/encyclicals/documents/hf_p-x_enc_11021906
_vehementer-nos_en.html, accessed November 8, 2014.

within a fuller theological consideration of episcopal collegiality (LG 21–25). The council encouraged the development of synods (CD 5, 36) and episcopal conferences (LG 23, CD 36–38), granting the latter considerable authority in liturgical matters (SC 22, 36). It restored the role of the bishop as pastor of the local church (SC 41, CD 11, LG 23) and rejected the view that the bishop was a mere vicar of the pope (LG 27).

Taken together, these contributions constitute a remarkable reorientation of the church's understanding of power and authority. Where do we stand now, five decades removed from such promising ecclesial developments? To be sure, the conciliar rhetoric of service, dialogue, and consultation now roll easily off the tongues of theologians and church leaders across the ideological spectrum. Yet the concrete exercise of power and authority, in many corners of our church, belies that rhetoric. We see the failure of authentic dialogue in the practices of both the most conservative hierarchs, on the one hand, and the most liberal theologians, on the other. In order to speak to this reality, the following chapter will sketch the outlines of a constructive account of power and authority, one that is faithful to the reformist vision of the council while addressing enduring obstacles to the authentic exercise of power and authority in our church today. This account will employ a more biblically and pneumatologically informed theology of power and a conception of authority that does not constrain but rather enables the exercise of freedom in service of authentic Christian discipleship.

Within the field of theology, the terms "power" and "authority" have overlapping semantic ranges such that it is difficult to consider one without the other. In this chapter I consider "power" as simply the capacity for effective action. Authentic ecclesial power, then, is the capacity to engage in effective action in service of the church's life and mission. "Authority" qualifies a set of ecclesial relationships in which individuals or communities freely consent to participate in the exercise of power as both agents and recipients. While acknowledging the semantic overlap, my reflections will be structured according to respective considerations of power and authority.

Ecclesial Power and Empowerment

Contemporary theological reflection on power has benefited from social scientific contributions. For example, Max Weber's sociological analysis provided a baseline for much subsequent work on power and authority.[2] Weber associated power with the ability of an actor or group of actors to carry out their will within a given set of social relationships.[3] Power is attached to the individual or group. Authority, however, is concerned with the social positions or roles through which power may be exercised. For Weber the exercise of power, in itself, does not rely on consent, whereas authority presupposes it. A tyrant, for example, can exercise power without authority. Authority is the legitimate exercise of power. Although much of his work has been subject to stringent critique,[4] Weber's framework has served as an important reference point for subsequent theological reflection on the nature and exercise of power and authority in the church.

One of the serious shortcomings of Weber's sociological analysis, from the perspective of ecclesiology, is that it presumes a predominantly zero-sum understanding of power such that, within any given society, the exercise of power is inherently dominating and coercive—some have power and others do not. This has led some Christians to accept Weber's account of power but then to call for a Christian repudiation of that power in imitation of the powerlessness of Christ. Although the call to a radical renunciation of power in keeping with the demands of the Gospel has considerable rhetorical force, it presents serious theological difficulties by identifying power only with its negative, coercive, and dominating forms. James Davison Hunter rightly punctures the Christian myth of powerlessness: "Only by narrowing an understanding of power to political or economic power can one imagine giving up power and becoming 'powerless.'"[5] Any form of authentic human existence will require the exercise of power in relation to others, and this is no less true within the church.

The human exercise of power has certainly been distorted by sin, hence Lord Acton's famous dictum, "Power tends to corrupt, absolute power

---

[2] For his most developed exposition of the topic, see Max Weber, *Economy and Society*, ed. Günther Roth and Claus Wittich, 3 vols. (Berkeley: University of California Press, 1978), originally published as *Wirtschaft und Gesellschaft* (Tübingen: Mohr, 1922).

[3] Weber, *Economy and Society*, 1:53.

[4] For a helpful summary of the sociological debates regarding Weber's work, see John A. Coleman, "Authority, Power, Leadership: Sociological Understandings," *New Theology Review* 10 (August 1997): 31–44.

[5] James Davison Hunter, *To Change the World: The Irony, Tragedy and Possibility of Christianity in the Late Modern World* (New York: Oxford University Press, 2010), 181.

corrupts absolutely."[6] Our God-given power to sustain life-giving relations with others can devolve into a submission to the "powers and
principalities" about which the writer of Ephesians warned (Eph 6:12).
Here we are dealing with power that feeds on the distortion of human
desire and is bent on domination, manipulation, and control. Jesus
understood his own ministry as one of combating the "powers" of this
world. His ministry, however, represented not the renunciation of power
but its radical transformation.

One of the most distinctive features of Jesus' ministry concerned his
exercise of power as a manifestation of the love of God (the key Greek
terms here are *dynamis* and *exousia,* which are often translated as "power"
and "authority," respectively). His exercise of power was vulnerable and
liberating. Jesus healed the sick and forgave sinners, rendering tangible
the profligate mercy of God (Matt 9:20-22; Mark 2:1-12). He promised
his followers that they too would receive a power that comes from the
Holy Spirit (Acts 1:8). That power is now made effective for believers
through Christian initiation. The life and teaching of Jesus displays its
essential logic as a subversion of the habits of worldly power and domination in favor of power exercised as humble service (Mark 10:42-45).
That distinctive logic was enacted in Jesus' washing the feet of his disciples and his command that they do likewise (John 13). As Neil Ormerod
notes, "God's power and authority are different from those of worldly
powers, but they are still power and authority, and Christians must come
to grips with the issues of power and authority if they are to be faithful
to the mission of the Church."[7]

The Disciplining of Power in Service of Christian Discipleship

Christians are both recipients of God's saving action and agents of
God's reconciling power. St. Paul reminds us that God "who reconciled
us to himself through Christ . . . has given us the ministry of reconciliation" (1 Cor 5:18). The work of reconciliation accomplished in Jesus of
Nazareth, through the power of the Spirit, is to continue in the mission
of the church. In service of this mission, the church must become a school
of discipleship in which dominating power and a preoccupation with

---

[6] Lord Acton to Bishop Mandell Creighton, April 5, 1887, in *Historical Essays and
Studies,* ed. J. N. Figgis and R.V. Laurance (London: Macmillan, 1907).

[7] Neil Ormerod, "Power and Authority—A Response to Bishop Cullinane," *The
Australasian Catholic Record* 82, no. 2 (April 2005): 155.

control are transformed into the power of reconciliation. In that school we discover the habits of power appropriate to followers of Jesus.

How might we conceptualize the kind of ecclesial reform that could bring about this redemption of power? A surprising resource lies in the work of the French poststructuralist, Michel Foucault. Foucault famously challenged the zero-sum conception of power, arguing that this framework depended too much on the exercise of sovereign power by the state and obscured more fundamental ways in which power is enacted. Power is not something that is acquired, seized, or shared, something that one holds onto or allows to slip away; power is exercised from innumerable points in the interplay of nonegalitarian and mobile relations.[8]

For Foucault, power is not a discrete and quantifiable entity or force but a reality that inheres within all relational networks. All social institutions are sustained by networks of power relations. This power is ubiquitous, moving in all directions. There is never really a question of the presence or absence of power, only how it is "disciplined" within particular "technologies" or mechanisms of power. Foucault offered a now-classic analysis of the history of the Western penal system as but one example of a "technology" of power, one governed by the logic of domination and control. He persuasively demonstrated that the penal system disciplined power in ways that affected both prisoners and guards alike.[9]

There is much that Catholic ecclesiology can glean from Foucault's analysis. Just as Foucault complained that contemporary accounts of power are too preoccupied with the sovereign power of the state, so too in the life of the church our analysis of power has been overly dependent on juridical power regulated by canon law. Catholic theology, without ignoring the role of juridical power, must recover that more comprehensive dimension of ecclesial power that comes from baptism and is animated by the Spirit.

Foucault's conviction that networks of power are often concerned with domination and control certainly finds confirmation in the harmful structures and habits of power enacted in the Catholic Church, past and present. The invisibility of these networks of control and domination,

---

[8] Michel Foucault, *The History of Sexuality* (New York: Vintage Books, 1990), 1:94. I am indebted to an unpublished seminar paper by Daniel Horan for encouraging me to explore the applicability of Foucault's analysis for ecclesiology.

[9] Michel Foucault, *Discipline and Punish: The Birth of the Prison* (New York: Vintage, 1977).

often obscured by high-minded spiritual rhetoric, makes these mechanisms particularly insidious. This is evident in the tragic and grievous abuse of children perpetrated by both clergy and professed religious under the veil of ecclesiastical respectability.

Particularly helpful is Foucault's conviction that power is not exercised unidirectionally. Those "in power" are affected as much by its exercise as are those who are the supposed objects of that power. As Hunter puts it, "power always generates its own resistances. . . . Even the weak possess the power to challenge, subvert, destabilize and oppose. It may not be easy and it may even be costly, but the power to act is always present within the relations of power itself."[10] This analysis reminds us that church reform cannot settle with a simple redistribution of power (e.g., giving more power to pastoral councils); it must seek a fundamental transformation of the very way that power is conceived and exercised.

One of the limitations of Foucault's analysis of power is that, in spite of his protests to the contrary, his analysis emphasizes the agonistic or contested nature of power and the "play of dominations" inherent in all social relationships.[11] If, however, power is always "disciplined" through certain "technologies of power," not all such disciplining need be negative or controlling. There is, if you will, a "discipline" of power proper to a school of "disciples." Power can be subverted, transformed, and redirected in alternative and unanticipated ways. From the perspective of Christian discipleship, we can imagine communal exercises for the disciplining of power; that is, there may be certain Christian technologies of power that are entirely appropriate to the church's mission.[12]

As a school of discipleship, the church is called to sustain distinctive technologies of power that transform power from the habits of domination and consumption to habits of power exercised in accord with the values of God's reign. This ecclesial disciplining of power can occur in many ways. The Eucharist, when it is ritually enacted in ways that fully display its transformative potential (that is, not simply as a display of clerical power and prerogative), offers such an alternative disciplining of ecclesial power, as do family practices of forgiveness and generosity

---

[10] Hunter, *To Change the World*, 179.

[11] Michel Foucault, "Nietzsche, Genealogy, History," in *Language, Counter-Memory, Practice*, ed. Donald F. Bouchard (Ithaca, NY: Cornell University Press, 1977), 150.

[12] James K. A. Smith, *Who's Afraid of Postmodernism? Taking Derrida, Lyotard, and Foucault to Church* (Grand Rapids, MI: Baker Academic, 2006), 102.

that constitute the household as a "domestic church."[13] Parishes discipline the exercise of power in their outreach to the poor, in their ministries, sacramental and nonsacramental, of reconciliation, and in their practices of solidarity with the marginalized.

The Rule of Benedict, one of the most authoritative sources for guidance in Western monasticism, offers a classic example of the Christian disciplining of power.[14] The life of the monastery is to be disciplined through the integration of prayer and labor. It is to be so structured as to accommodate hospitality to the stranger. The exercise of power by the abbot is similarly disciplined. Chapter 3 of the Rule attends to the obligation of the abbot to consult the monks before making any decision of note, including the youngest members of the monastery. In the opening weeks of his pontificate, Pope Francis provided a dramatic example of an alternative disciplining of ecclesial power when he celebrated an ancient Holy Thursday ritual, not by washing the feet of twelve males as liturgical law dictates, but by attending a juvenile prison and washing the feet of troubled youth, including women and Muslims.

The Empowerment of a Learning Church

This consideration of the church as a school of discipleship invites exploration of the Christian community of faith as both a learning and teaching church. We begin, however, with the primary posture of a disciple as listener and learner. To be sure, the church is also a teacher; but, at least since the French Revolution, consideration of the ecclesial dynamics of listening and learning have been eclipsed by ever more expansive considerations of the dynamics of ecclesial teaching. These dynamics presupposed what Lonergan referred to as a "classical cognitivist" framework in which God communicates a divine message through doctrines that are taught by the magisterium and passively received by the Christian faithful. In this account, a commitment to the epistemic objectivity of church doctrines overrode any concerns for subjective

[13] Richard R. Gaillardetz, "The Christian Household as School of Discipleship: Reflections on the Ecclesial Contributions of the Christian Household to the Larger Church," in *The Household of God and Local Households: Revisiting the Domestic Church*, ed. Thomas Knieps-Port Le Roi, Gerard Mannion, and Peter De Mey, Bibliotheca Ephemeridum Theologicarum Lovaniensium Series (Leuven: Peeters, 2013), 111–21.

[14] Terrence G. Kardong, *Benedict's Rule: A Translation and Commentary* (Collegeville, MN: Liturgical Press, 1996).

appropriation. The classical cognitivist perspective emphasized a sharp division between the teaching church (*ecclesia docens*), identified with the magisterium, and the learning church (*ecclesia discens*), identified with the lay faithful. This framework paid much greater attention to the distinctive assistance of the Holy Spirit given to the bishops than it did to the work of the Spirit in the life of the whole people of God.

In an address given to the Catholic Theological Society of America in 1996, Margaret O'Gara and Michael Vertin challenged the adequacy of this account and called for a shift toward a "historical cognitivist" framework in which the learning church takes priority over the teaching church and in which normative doctrine is "authentically discovered by the church."[15] This alternative account would locate the teaching ministry of the bishops within the community of the baptized. This priority is reflected in the opening lines of *Dei Verbum*:

> Hearing the word of God reverently and proclaiming it confidently, this holy synod makes its own the words of St. John: "We proclaim to you the eternal life which was with the Father and was made manifest to us—that which we have seen and heard we proclaim also to you, so that you may have fellowship with us; and our fellowship is with the Father and with his Son Jesus Christ." (DV 1)

The council further explored this insight, teaching that the Holy Spirit had empowered all the baptized with a supernatural instinct for the faith (*sensus fidei*) that allowed them to adhere to the faith they had received, penetrate its deepest meanings, and apply it more fully in their lives (LG 12). The Holy Spirit "moves the heart and converts it to God, and opens the eyes of the mind and 'makes it easy for all to accept and believe the truth'" (DV 5). That same Spirit allows ordinary believers to join with the bishops in the development of tradition (DV 8).

The *sensus fidei* represents a major theological category that, until Vatican II, had received far too little attention. The International Theological Commission (ITC) recently published an important study of the

---

[15] Margaret O'Gara and Michael Vertin, "The Holy Spirit's Assistance to the Magisterium in Teaching: Theological and Philosophical Issues," *Proceedings of the Catholic Theological Society of America* 51 (1996): 128. On the distinction between classical and historical consciousness, see Bernard Lonergan, "The Transition from a Classicist Worldview to Historical-Mindedness," in *Bernard Lonergan, A Second Collection: Papers,* ed. William F. Ryan and Bernard Tyrrell (Toronto: University of Toronto, 1974), 1–9.

topic.[16] Yet significant theological questions remain, many of which the ITC addressed but without always providing a theologically satisfying response. We can only briefly consider a few of them here.

What, for example, is the proper relationship between the wisdom of God's people (*sensus fidelium*) and church doctrine? The insight and wisdom of ordinary believers often eludes propositional form, embedded as it is in the concrete narratives and daily practices of Christian discipleship. There is a temptation to consider this nonpropositional form as inchoate doctrine, as if Christian wisdom cannot achieve its maturity until it has been received by the bishops and given normative expression as doctrine. But is this always the case? The church generally promulgates doctrine only in response to serious and enduring controversy regarding the substance of the Christian faith. It does not follow, however, that doctrine is the most profound expression of the faith. Few Christians are moved to heroic exercises of discipleship by a reading of the catechism or a profession of the Nicene Creed. Is it vital that the bishops consult the faithful prior to the formulation of church doctrine? Yes. Is it necessary that the comprehensive insight of all God's people find its final and definitive form in church doctrine? No.

A second question concerns the scope of our consideration of the *sensus fidei*. This supernatural instinct for the faith may be given at baptism but it surely is a gift that, like all gifts, must be properly cultivated. All things being equal (and in this matter they are often not), the exercise of the *sensus fidei* by a properly catechized, practicing Catholic ought to be more mature and discerning than its exercise by a baptized person whose shadow has seldom crossed the threshold of a church. But things quickly get more complicated. How do we evaluate the instinct for the faith of a person who is no longer a practicing Catholic, not because of indifference or poor catechesis, but because of a conscious decision to leave the church in response to difficulties with church doctrine or practice? How do we hear the voices of those who have remained in the church but are marginalized because of gender, sexual orientation, education, ethnicity, or economic status? To put it baldly, in the church in the United States, a wealthy, white lay male is more likely to have his faith witness taken seriously by those in leadership than a poor Latina whose immigration status may be in question. Finally, how are we to

---

[16] International Theological Commission, "*Sensus Fidei* in the Life of the Church," http://www.vatican.va/roman_curia/congregations/cfaith/cti_documents/rc_cti_20140610_sensus-fidei_en.html, accessed on November 8, 2014.

assess the faith contributions of Christians outside the Catholic communion? As the ITC rightly noted, Catholics share a common baptism with many other Christian communions. This simple fact compels Catholics to listen to the testimony of the baptized belonging to other Christian traditions.[17] But where does this actually happen?

A third question concerns processes of consultation, verification, and interpretation. The ITC is to be commended for its forthright admission that the Catholic Church is lacking sufficient ecclesial mechanisms for the adequate consultation of the faith of the baptized.[18] Yet the results of any consultation will still require careful verification and interpretation. There are many controversial matters in church doctrine and practice about which it would be impossible to say that there is a widespread agreement among the faithful. How does one verify whether the *sensus fidelium* actually represents a *consensus fidelium*? Is this more criteriological use of the category even possible?

The ITC insisted on "adherence to the magisterium" as a necessary disposition for the authentic exercise of the *sensus fidei*.[19] The crucial issue here concerns the meaning of "adherence." Recall the teaching of Vatican II in *Dignitatis Humanae* on the formation of conscience in which the council taught that one must "carefully attend to the sacred and certain doctrine of the Church" (DH 14). An amendment was proposed to the council's Theological Commission that this passage be revised so as to call for forming one's conscience "in accord with the doctrine of the church." The Theological Commission rejected the amendment as "unduly restrictive."[20] If adherence to the magisterium is understood in the sense of *Dignitatis Humanae*'s exhortation carefully to attend to magisterial teaching, there is no difficulty. If, on the other hand, adherence means simply conforming to the magisterial teaching, problems arise. The ITC hinted at the possibility that resistance of the faithful to current church teaching may signal the need for a reformulation of doctrine but it did not sufficiently spell out either the extent of the reformulation that may be required or the mechanisms through which this process would be undertaken.[21]

---

[17] Ibid., 56.

[18] Ibid., 74.

[19] Ibid., 97–98.

[20] Second Vatican Council, *Acta Synodalia* (Vatican City: Typis polyglottis Vaticanis, 1970–), IV/6, 769.

[21] ITC, "*Sensus Fidei*," 80.

There has been a wealth of theological reflection on the role of the sense of the faithful in the church, yet it has received precious little consideration in ecclesiastical documents, including the Code of Canon Law. Fortunately, in Pope Francis's apostolic exhortation, *Evangelii Gaudium*,[22] we come to the end of a de facto fifty-year moratorium on papal consideration of the council's teaching on the sense of the faithful. Francis specifically exhorts church leaders to attend to the graced wisdom of the whole people of God. He recalls the Second Vatican Council's teaching on the infallibility of the people of God in *credendo* (see LG 12). "The presence of the Spirit gives Christians a certain connaturality with divine realities, and a wisdom which enables them to grasp those realities intuitively, even when they lack the wherewithal to give them precise expression."[23] It is this firm conviction regarding the value of the *sensus fidei* in the life of the church that has motivated Pope Francis to call for the development of more robust ecclesiastical structures for consultation and dialogue.[24]

Up to this point we have been considering the need to listen to the Spirit-breathed insight of the entire community of faith. Yet the Spirit's empowerment of a listening and learning church must not be limited to a receptive posture toward the testimony of Scripture, tradition, theology, magisterial teaching, and the sense of the faithful. This posture of ecclesial listening and learning must also be directed outward toward the world. This is the thrust of *Gaudium et Spes*'s insistence on the church's dialogical stance toward the world. The council's claim that the church can learn from the world (GS 44), reinforced by Pope Francis's call for a "culture of encounter," presupposes a listening church open to discerning in human society those graced impulses that resonate with deep evangelical values.[25]

The empowerment of a listening and learning church finds a crucial biblical warrant in the Pentecost event. Although the story begins with

---

[22] Francis, *Evangelii Gaudium* (On the Joy of the Gospel), http://w2.vatican.va /content/francesco/en/apost_exhortations/documents/papa-francesco_esortazione -ap_20131124_evangelii-gaudium.html, accessed November 8, 2014.

[23] Ibid., 119.

[24] Ibid., 31.

[25] See Luke Bretherton, *Christianity and Contemporary Politics: The Conditions and Possibilities of Faithful Witness* (Malden, MA: Wiley-Blackwell, 2010); James Gerard McEvoy, *Leaving Christendom for Good: Church-World Dialogue in a Secular Age* (New York: Lexington Books, 2014).

the empowerment of the apostles in the proclamation of the Good News, the narrative clearly extends that empowerment to all who hear that proclamation in their own languages (Acts 2:8). The Spirit is as active in the listening and learning of the church as it is in the church's teaching.

The Empowerment of a Teaching Church

It is as a listening and learning community that the people of God may rightly assume its responsibility as a teaching church. Just as all Christians participate in the indispensable work of listening for God's Word, so too all Christians must participate in the church as teacher. We must resist the default Catholic tendency to contract our notion of the teaching church to include only the pope and bishops, necessary though their role is. The council gave us helpful direction in this regard as it expanded the prophetic office of the church to all the baptized. Consequently, as Ormond Rush argues, we can speak of the Spirit's empowerment of a threefold participation in the prophetic/teaching office of the church by the bishops, theologians, and the sense of the faithful.[26] Bishops teach by virtue of their ordination, by which they are charged to safeguard the integrity of the apostolic faith. Their doctrinal teaching carries a uniquely normative dimension not present in the other participations in the church's teaching office. Theologians offer the insight gained through their scholarship, and the baptized teach the wisdom gained by their experience in Christian living and the exercise of the *sensus fidei*. The teaching ministry of the church is best sustained by the fruitful interaction of these three exercises or modalities of the prophetic office of the church.

Regardless of who is exercising the teaching ministry of the church at any given moment, authentic church teaching ought to have as its principal goal a more profound understanding of God's Word. Nicholas Lash writes:

---

[26] Ormond Rush, *The Eyes of Faith: The Sense of the Faithful and the Church's Reception of Revelation* (Washington, DC: The Catholic University of America Press, 2009), esp. pt. 3. See also Ormond Rush, "The Prophetic Office in the Church: Pneumatological Perspectives on the Sensus Fidelium-Theology-Magisterium Relationship," in *When the Magisterium Intervenes: The Magisterium and Theologians in Today's Church*, ed. Richard R. Gaillardetz (Collegeville, MN: Liturgical Press, 2012), 89–112.

> The craft or process we call "teaching" is the art of helping people to understand. They have to do this for themselves, and it is a dangerous, exhilarating, fragile, never finished process . . . this achievement we call "understanding," which each of us has to do for ourself, is done in us by God. . . . If "teaching" were a mere matter of declaration or instruction, of telling people what is the case, or what they ought to do, then indeed spreading knowledge would be as easy as spreading butter. But this is not the traditional Christian understanding of what "teaching" involves.[27]

This brings us to what Lash argues is one of the most pervasive failings of the church's teaching ministry, the modern Catholic tendency to reduce authentic teaching to mere governance. When we consider the contemporary North American scene, evidence of teaching reduced to governance confronts us at every turn. Bishops weigh in on specific curricular matters in Catholic schools, often overruling experts in religious education. Assessing the competency of teachers is reduced to their willingness to take oaths and sign contracts assenting to all church teaching. The US bishops' conference now insists on directly evaluating and approving all catechetical materials prior to publication. Theologians are investigated not only in cases where there is an obvious rejection of the apostolic faith but also in many instances where the matter in dispute is more theological than doctrinal.[28]

When we conceive of the teaching ministry of the church as governance we will naturally look to our teachers to "police" the faith, and we will imagine the appropriate response to such teaching less as understanding and more as obedience. Whereas early Christian thought presented revelation as a divine pedagogy aimed at the transformation of humankind, the reduction of teaching to governance has reduced the richness of the Christian faith to a "digital genre," as Juan Luis Segundo put it. This "digital" presentation of the Christian story purges dogma of its imaginative character within an eschatological horizon and renders

---

[27] Nicholas Lash, "Authors, Authority, and Authorization," in *Authority in the Roman Catholic Church: Theory and Practice*, ed. Bernard Hoose (Burlington, VT: Ashgate Publishers, 2002), 65.

[28] The investigation of Elizabeth Johnson by the USCCB Committee on Doctrine offers a good example of this. The entire dossier of the Elizabeth Johnson case can be found in Richard R. Gaillardetz, ed., *When the Magisterium Intervenes: The Magisterium and Theologians in Today's Church* (Collegeville, MN: Liturgical Press, 2012), 177–294.

it strictly informational—a collection of truths subject to mere intellectual assent.[29]

Catholicism's longstanding preoccupation with teaching over learning led to an inadequate theology of the assistance of the Holy Spirit given to the magisterium. These theological treatments often ignored the historical conditioning of the church and its ministers. If the church is pilgrim, then its official teachers must share in that pilgrim status. The Holy Spirit, to be sure, assists the bishops in the exercise of their ministry, but always under the conditions and limitations of human history, finitude, and sin. Heribert Mühlen's evocation of the kenosis of the Holy Spirit may be helpful here.[30] Mühlen reminds us of the Pauline teaching that the Word embraced human limitation in Jesus of Nazareth as an act of kenosis, a divine self-emptying in which God in Christ embraced the full limitations of human history. According to Mühlen, we must consider an analogous "self-emptying" of the Spirit in history as it consents to work through a church subject to all those constraints that are part of the human condition.

The failure to take seriously the historical conditioning of the church has been compounded, according to Thomas O'Meara, by a reliance on a baroque theology preoccupied with actual grace. Episcopal action is reduced to a weak instrumental causality within a crass "mechanics of grace."[31] The church needs to pay greater attention, he insists, to the human processes necessary for authentic learning and teaching. O'Meara reminds us, "Teaching always involves study, learning, and reflection. It seems unlikely that when those three are absent a divine power replaces them."[32] Karl Rahner warns of

> a tendency tacitly to proceed from the assumption that there is a kind of "synergism" at work here, to point to forces that are extrinsic to human debate, and so to regard God's intervention as commencing only at that point at which human efforts are suspended. In reality, however, God works precisely in and through these human

---

[29] Juan Luis Segundo, *The Liberation of Dogma: Faith, Revelation and Dogmatic Teaching Authority* (Maryknoll, NY: Orbis Books, 1992), 108.

[30] Heribert Mühlen, *Una Persona Mystica: Die Kirche als das Mysterium der heilsgeschichtlichen Identität des Heiligen Geistes in Christus und den Christen: Eine Person in vielen Personen* (Munich: Schöningh, 1968), 255ff.

[31] Thomas F. O'Meara, "Divine Grace and Human Nature as Sources for the Universal Magisterium of Bishops," *Theological Studies* 64, no. 4 (2003): 688–89.

[32] Ibid., 694.

efforts and his activity does not constitute a distinct factor apart from this. Precisely for this reason we should bring these human factors into the open. Instead of concealing them we should throw light upon them and make it possible to assess them at their true worth. For in themselves they constitute something more than merely a supplement to the divine activity, a prior condition for it, or an obscure residue, otherwise unaccounted for, in the exercise of the teaching office. Rather these human factors constitute an intrinsic element in the exercise of the teaching office itself.[33]

Avoiding this reductive "mechanics of grace" requires much more emphasis on the active cooperation of the bishops with the action of the Spirit. Bishops must give due diligence to the demands of their teaching ministry. The term "due diligence" comes from the legal profession and refers to the obligation to proper investigation before entering into a binding contract of some kind. In our context it can help illuminate the obligation of the bishops to engage in requisite prayer, consultation, dialogue, and study before exercising their teaching responsibilities. Again, this manifold engagement does not just establish the conditions for the assistance of the Spirit—they are not mere natural processes necessary before the work of the Spirit can "kick in." Rather, the Spirit acts through these human processes.

In this regard, Pope Francis made a remarkable assertion in his interview published under the title, "A Big Heart Open to God": "When the dialogue among the people and the bishops and the pope goes down this road and is genuine," he contended, "then it is assisted by the Holy Spirit."[34] Admittedly, this was a comment offered extemporaneously and we should be careful not to give it too much theological weight. Nevertheless, we cannot ignore the audacity of his claim. Francis appears to suggest that we can be confident of an assistance of the Holy Spirit to the bishops on the condition that they are open to listening to others. The pope offers a striking alternative to the still dominant "mechanics of grace" so frequently encountered in ecclesiastical attitudes today. He

---

[33] Karl Rahner, "The Teaching Office of the Church," in *Theological Investigations*, vol. 12, *Confrontations* (New York: Seabury Press, 1974), 12.

[34] Antonio Spadaro, "A Big Heart Open to God: The Exclusive Interview with Pope Francis," trans. Massimo Faggioli, Sarah Christopher Faggioli, Dominic Robinson, Patrick Howell, and Griffin Oleynick, *America* 209, no. 8 (September 30, 2013): 22.

calls for the bishops to acquire new habits of teaching power structured around listening, dialogue, and a ministry of accompaniment.[35]

Finally, the dominance of the teaching as governance paradigm has also handicapped the church's stance as teacher before the world. The council did not shy away from asserting what the church as teacher can offer the world through the Gospel of Jesus Christ (GS 22, 33, 40). Yet the council placed this teaching function within a dialogical framework that took seriously the pluralistic context of humanity today and insisted that the teaching modalities the church assumes in its relation with the world must be characterized by a genuine openness to the other, a receptivity to the contributions of its interlocutors, and a respect for the integrity of all who seek the truth (DH 1–3).[36]

The Ecclesial Exercise of Authority in the Church

We turn now to consider the variety of authoritative relationships within which authentic ecclesial power is exercised. One of the unfortunate by-products of the Enlightenment is a pervasive suspicion of authority as inherently dominating, coercive, and opposed to the exercise of human freedom. Freud would later assert that all claims to authority were infantile while Marx would associate authority with false consciousness and Nietzsche with the will to power.[37] Even Weber considered power and authority as constraining more than enabling features within a society. As John Courtney Murray observed almost fifty years ago, while some posit a crisis of authority today, and others warn of a crisis of freedom, the real challenge may be a crisis of community, since it is only by way of an authentic account of human community that freedom and authority can be brought into their proper relationship.[38]

---

[35] The call for episcopal "accompaniment" with the people was a central theme in Francis's July 2013 address to the coordinating committee of CELAM during his visit to Brazil. The citation for this address is Francis, "Address to the Leadership of the Episcopal Conferences of Latin America during the General Coordination Meeting," http://www.vatican.va/holy_father/francesco/speeches/2013/july/documents/papa-francesco_20130728_gmg-celam-rio_en.html, accessed November 8, 2014.

[36] See McEvoy, *Leaving Christendom*, 163–75.

[37] Ormerod, "Power and Authority," 160.

[38] John Courtney Murray, "Freedom, Authority, Community," *America* 115 (December 3, 1966): 734–41.

Authority in Service of Human Flourishing
and the Common Good

Critics of Weber's work have challenged his focus on persons and institutions and his neglect of the fundamentally relational and performative character of authority. David Stagaman, for example, has criticized our modern tendency to speak of authority as if it were the property of persons or things. Although we may speak of the Bible as an authority, that authority actually resides in the relation established between the Bible and those who look to it as a source of revelation.[39] This is just as true when speaking of the authority of a theologian or the authority of a pope. Healthy authoritative relationships do not exist as an abstraction; they are performed cooperatively in the life of a community.[40]

According to Victor Lee Austin, "authority is built into what it means to be human, and we never will escape from needing it for our flourishing."[41] Austin distinguishes between substitutionary and nonsubstitutionary forms of authority. The former is evident in parental exercises of authority inasmuch as the parent's authority is filling in for some lack of maturity or experience in the child. Understood as such, substitutionary authority compensates for a fundamental lack in the person subject to that authority.[42] It also functions as a corrective against some defect in the other. The authority exercised by law enforcement is substitutionary to the extent that it is a response to the social defects of criminals. Here one assumes that, as a person matures and develops, the exercise of substitutionary authority would diminish correspondingly.

The more mature exercise of authority, Austin contends, is nonsubstitutionary and functions so as to coordinate individual human activity for the sake of corporate action. Nonsubstitutionary authority creates the conditions for individuals and groups to make the most of their gifts and abilities. This form of authority is most reflective of its etymological roots inasmuch as the person exercising nonsubstitutionary authority "authorizes" the actions of others. Austin uses the example of the authority

[39] David Stagaman, *Authority in the Church* (Collegeville, MN: Liturgical Press, 1999), 24–28.

[40] Joseph Komonchak also considers authority as a particular kind of social relationship in his "Authority and Magisterium," in *Vatican Authority and American Catholic Dissent*, ed. William May (New York: Crossroad, 1987), 103–4.

[41] Victor Lee Austin, *Up with Authority: Why We Need Authority to Flourish as Human Beings* (New York: Continuum, 2010), 2.

[42] Ibid., 15–16.

of the symphony conductor who exercises her authority to maximize the individual gifts of the musicians in order to produce a coordinated human activity.[43]

Austin is drawing on the work of the late French Thomist and political theorist Yves Simon, who argued that since communal action is more than the coincidence of individual purposes, it requires some instrument of unity that allows a community to engage in common action.[44] The more complex the coordinated action, the more there is a need for an authority to help unify that action. This framework brings authority and freedom into their proper relation by introducing, as Murray insisted, a third term—community. Authority enables the exercise of freedom to serve the life of communion: "self-fulfillment is the achievement of freedom for communion with others."[45]

In service of his argument, Simon distinguishes between materially and formally willing the common good.[46] Every member of a community is obligated to formally will the common good of the community. For example, as a member of a Catholic Jesuit university, I am formally committed to serving the university's mission. At the same time, it is each member's responsibility materially to will particular goods in keeping with their own ability and expertise. Thus while formally I am committed to serving the common good of the university and its mission, materially I accomplish this by dedicating myself to the practice of theology and the initiation and formation of our students into that practice. It is for those directly responsible for the leadership of the university not only formally but also materially to will the achievement of the university's mission. We want to be careful not to assume too much from this distinction. I can both materially will the particular good of developing an excellent theology program and participate in the material willing of the realization of the university's mission by, for example, participation in a faculty senate or by being part of a consultation conducted by the university president.

The point that Simon is making is that those in authority are charged with acting in such a way as to best bring about, materially, the common good through the empowerment and coordination of those in the com-

---

[43] Ibid., 18–19.

[44] Yves R. Simon, *A General Theory of Authority* (Notre Dame, IN: University of Notre Dame Press, 1962), 30–31.

[45] Murray, "Freedom, Authority, Community," 735.

[46] Simon, *A General Theory of Authority*, 50–67.

munity who are working to achieve a vast array of particular goods. This argument offers insight into the authentic exercise of governing authority in the church.

One of the principal contributions of the council was its recovery of the pneumatological conditioning of the church and its appropriation of the biblical understanding of charism. The council taught that the Spirit "guides the church in the way of all truth (see John 16:13) and, uniting it in fellowship and ministry, bestows on it different hierarchic and charismatic gifts, and in this way directs it and adorns it with his fruits" (LG 4). In this passage, the phrase "hierarchic gifts" refers to stable church office while "charismatic gifts" refers to those many charisms that the Spirit distributes among all the faithful. In council teaching, charism and office are not opposed to one another since both have the Spirit as their origin. Ordained pastoral leadership need not compete with the exercise of the many gifts of the faithful. Each requires the other. According to conciliar teaching, those ordained to pastoral leadership are not to absorb into their own ministry all the tasks proper to building up the church. Rather, the distinctive authority exercised by the church's pastors must be directed toward recognizing, empowering, and ordering the gifts of all God's people. Those who have charge over the church should judge the genuineness and orderly use of these gifts, and it is especially their office not to extinguish the Spirit but to test all things and hold fast to what is good (LG 12, see also AA 3, PO 9).

The council situated ordained pastoral ministry within the Christian community. The ordained minister is responsible, among other things, for the discernment and coordination of the charisms and ministries of all the baptized. To transpose the council's teaching into Simon's account, we might say that the ordinary believers' exercise of their particular charisms is directed toward the material pursuit of particular goods that will contribute to the common good of the church. The authority of the pastor lies with materially pursuing the common good of the church by identifying, empowering, and ordering the exercise of individual charisms toward the church's larger mission. It follows that the reform of the processes by which the church calls forth its leaders should attend carefully to discovering candidates for office who manifest a distinctive aptitude for recognizing, empowering, and ordering the gifts of others. This positive discernment of a charism for pastoral leadership is in too little evidence in our current structures.

Consider the situation in the church's process of calling forth and forming candidates for ordination to the diocesan priesthood. Our current process is frequently dominated by a dubious theology of vocation as the private possession of an individual.[47] When a man presents himself to a vocation director with the claim that he might have a vocation to the priesthood, there will almost certainly be an initial investigation into whether there are canonical impediments to his ordination. There will be, one hopes, some assessment of the candidate's sanctity and basic mental health. If no obstacles present themselves, the candidate will likely be accepted into the seminary. Now let us presume that over the course of his period of formation he passes all of his courses, dutifully attends daily Mass, sees his spiritual director regularly, and does not manifest heretical or "dangerous" views in his academic work, preaching, pastoral counseling, or field education. Even if this candidate manifests no aptitude for genuine pastoral leadership, is there any doubt he will be ordained? This system is constructed more to discern impediments to ordination than to discern the existence of a charism or aptitude for the exercise of genuine pastoral authority.

Authority, Trust, and Accountability

Gerard Mannion contends that the church today is facing a fundamental crisis regarding the legitimation of authority, a crisis fueled by "the continued assumption by many bishops, clergy, and other church leaders that respect is theirs by right and that they are entitled to expect and even demand obedience and deference to their decisions."[48] Mannion calls our attention to the crucial question of authority's legitimation. Weber held that authority could be legitimated in three distinct ways.[49] (1) Traditional authority was legitimated by way of past precedents for determining present action. This authority finds warrants in customs, founding myths, and so on. In the life of the church, the exercise of this kind of authority usually takes the form of "as the Bible says . . ." or "according to the teaching of the Council of Trent . . ." According to Weber, such exercises of authority are largely resistant to change. (2) Legal-rational authority depends on accepted rules and con-

---

[47] Edward Hahnenberg offers an informative consideration of the history of theologies of vocation in *Awakening Vocation: A Theology of Christian Call* (Collegeville, MN: Liturgical Press, 2010).

[48] Gerard Mannion, " 'A Haze of Fiction': Legitimation, Accountability, and Truthfulness," in *Governance, Accountability, and the Future of the Catholic Church*, ed. Francis Oakley and Bruce Russett (New York: Continuum, 2004), 162.

[49] Weber, *Economy and Society*, 1:215–45.

ventions that are associated with a bureaucratic entity of one kind or another. Here too we can see an ecclesial example in the highly bureaucratized activity of the Roman Curia and the application of canon law at all levels of ecclesial life. (3) Charismatic authority is legitimated by the distinctive gifts of an individual or group of individuals that makes them heroic or exemplary in some way and thereby elicits allegiance or adherence. In the life of the church we might think of the authority of a figure like St. Francis of Assisi.

One difficulty with Weber's account, Neil Ormerod reminds us, is that Weber does not recognize any normative component in the legitimation of authority.[50] For Weber, authority is legitimate only to the extent that people consent to it. In our contemporary ecclesial context, however, the nature of this consent requires more attention. The authentic legitimation of authority requires more emphasis on the trustworthiness of those who exercise authority. Thus Joseph Komonchak characterizes authority not just as legitimate power but as "trustworthy power."[51]

This trustworthiness can be established in multiple ways. First, we must recognize the good will of those who exercise authority. Those who consent to the authority relationship must be able to trust that the subject of a particular authoritative relationship is acting out of good intentions and a commitment to act in support of the common good. Second, the trustworthiness of one in authority requires competency. When I visit my doctor to complain of shortness of breath, I do so presupposing her competence as a physician and the consequent trustworthiness of her diagnosis. That trust in her competence allows me to accept her quite reasonable diagnosis that I need to lose some weight. The presumption of competence that I grant her, however, is not absolute. Should she suggest to me that my shortness of breath is the direct consequence of my failure to trim my toenails, I might call her competence and therefore her authority into question! Authority cannot function in any meaningful way when competency is lacking.

Standard accounts of the exercise of authority generally distinguish between those who are *in authority* (exercising authority by virtue of office) and those who are *an authority* by virtue of some specialized knowledge, wisdom, competence, or aptitude.[52] Yet this distinction,

---

[50] Ormerod, "Power and Authority," 157.

[51] Komonchak, "Authority and Magisterium," 107.

[52] Richard E. Flathman gives detailed consideration to this distinction in his *The Practice of Political Authority: Authority and the Authoritative* (Chicago: University of Chicago Press, 1980).

particularly as it is realized in the life of the church, can be overdrawn.[53] The authority of office, after all, generally presupposes that the office-holder is in some sense *an authority*, that is, a person who has a specialized knowledge, wisdom, competence, or aptitude for a set of tasks. It is possible, of course, and in fact rather common, that one would assent to the exercise of authority by an officeholder who lacks the requisite knowledge, experience, competence, or aptitude in the short run. This does not mean, however, that such an exercise of authority is likely to be effective in the long run. Over time, the exercise of authority by those who, in spite of their office, do not possess the requisite competence is bound to damage the life of the community. It is true that a loyal Catholic might acknowledge a particular exercise of a bishop's authority such as his decision to close a parish, for example. Absent the recognition that the bishop is also, however, an authority possessing some specialized knowledge, wisdom, competence, or aptitude for this kind of pastoral decision, his actions will have more the features of dominating power than of legitimate authority. Any society will suffer in the long run, and no less the church, when those who are in authority fail to demonstrate that they are in some meaningful way also an authority on matters related to their exercise of leadership.

Finally, we must speak of the relationship between trustworthiness and accountability. Paul Lakeland insists that where the exercise of authority is concerned, "credibility is directly proportional to the level of practice of accountability."[54] Unfortunately, discussion of accountability in the church has been handicapped because of the term's association with the political and business sectors. As bishop of Pittsburgh, Donald Wuerl (now the cardinal archbishop of Washington) made a helpful contribution to a volume on governance and accountability in the church. Wuerl was frank in his admission that Catholic Church leadership needed to be more transparent in its exercise of authority, but he also cautioned that "when we address accountability in the church, we must be careful not to use a political model for a reality that transcends human

---

[53] See Gerard Mannion's helpful treatment of this in his "What Do We Mean by 'Authority'?" in *Authority in the Roman Catholic Church: Theory and Practice*, ed. Bernard Hoose (London: Ashgate, 2002), 19–36.

[54] Paul Lakeland, "Accountability, Credibility, and Authority," *New Theology Review* 19, no. 1 (2006): 8.

political institutions."[55] Ecclesial accountability, he insisted, differs from its political analogue because the authority of the apostolic tradition and the divine origins of the apostolic office bind the church in distinctive ways.[56] Wuerl defined ecclesial accountability as requiring an openness and transparency sufficient to allow one to assess whether church leaders are acting in fidelity to their divine mandate.

Wuerl's views reflect something close to a consensus position among ecclesiastical leadership. Many bishops are willing to admit that "mistakes have been made" by those in authority, and they will often affirm the need for a more transparent and collaborative style of leadership. There seems, however, to be a default assumption that the divine origins of the church and its apostolic office preclude the bishops from being accountable to the baptized. Church leaders are accountable to their hierarchical superiors and ultimately to God. Accountability to the church itself is limited to the faithful's verification of the bishops' fidelity to Christ—to the truth of Christ found in church teaching and to the institutions and structures founded by Christ. As John Beal has pointed out, this attitude toward ecclesial accountability is enshrined in canon law.

> Since all lines of accountability point upward in canon law, only hierarchical superiors are competent to judge whether their subordinates have adequately fulfilled the obligations of their offices or abused their powers. Bishops, pastors, and other officeholders are accountable for their stewardship to those who appointed them, not to those they serve. The faithful may express disgruntlement about the shoddy performance, nonfeasance, and malfeasance of their pastors and even bishops to their hierarchical superiors, but superiors are free to give these complaints as much or as little weight as their discretion dictates when deciding whether to retain, remove, or discipline their subordinates.[57]

---

[55] Donald W. Wuerl, "Reflections on Governance and Accountability in the Church," in *Governance, Accountability, and the Future of the Catholic Church*, ed. Francis Oakley and Bruce Russett (New York: Continuum, 2004), 18.

[56] Ibid., 13.

[57] John P. Beal, "Something There Is That Doesn't Love a Law: Canon Law and Its Discontents," in *The Crisis of Authority in Catholic Modernity*, ed. Michael J. Lacey and Francis Oakley (New York: Oxford University Press, 2011), 150.

According to this logic, any other form of ecclesial accountability would reflect at best an unacceptable Protestantizing and at worst a capitulation to the secular culture.

This view suffers from an inadequate appreciation for the trinitarian foundations of the church. Accountability to Christ must not be separated from accountability to the Spirit alive in the church today. As Yves Congar reminded us, "[T]he Spirit did not come simply in order to animate an institution that was already fully determined in all its structures." In fact, the Spirit "is really the co-instituting principle" of the church.[58] Accountability to Christ and his Spirit require both a fidelity to the apostolic tradition and openness to the witness of the Spirit in the church today, including the Spirit-breathed witness of all God's people reflected in the exercise of the *sensus fidei.* Faithful obedience to Christ will be manifested in practices of communal discernment that listen for the voice of the Spirit speaking through a faith-filled people. When all in the church come to discover the dignity and demands of their baptism and the concrete shape of discipleship in service of the Spirit's promptings, accountability becomes simply another word for *koinonia,* our "shared communion" in Christ.

The Enlightenment first instigated what has been a longstanding suspicion regarding the role of authority in modern society. Since the eighteenth century, the Catholic Church has relied on a naïve sacralization of power and authority that has enabled significant abuse. Catholicism must not abandon this sacral framework entirely. The church is a sacrament of salvation in the world. Yet the Holy Spirit animates the church, working through a network of authority relationships that order and enhance the freedom of believers and empower the church for its mission. This divine power is mediated through human subjects and its efficacy depends, at least in part, on its being appropriately "disciplined" within a "school" for Christian discipleship. As a school of discipleship the church must cultivate the habits of power exercised within a network of authority relationships in imitation of the One who came not to be served but to serve.

---

[58] Yves Congar, "The Church Is Made by the Spirit," in *I Believe in the Holy Spirit* (New York: Crossroad, 1997), 2:9.

For Further Reading

Austin, Victor Lee. *Up with Authority: Why We Need Authority to Flourish as Human Beings*. New York: Continuum, 2010.

De George, Richard T. *The Nature and Limits of Authority*. Lawrence: University Press of Kansas, 1985.

Gaillardetz, Richard R. *By What Authority? A Primer on Scripture, the Magisterium, and the Sense of the Faithful*. Collegeville, MN: Liturgical Press, 2003.

———, ed. *When the Magisterium Intervenes: The Magisterium and Theologians in Today's Church*. Collegeville, MN: Liturgical Press, 2012.

Hoose, Bernard, ed. *Authority in the Roman Catholic Church: Theory and Practice*. Burlington, VT: Ashgate Publishers, 2002.

Komonchak, Joseph. "Authority and Conversion or: The Limits of Authority." *Cristanesimo nella storia* 21 (2000): 207–29.

Loomer, Bernard. "Two Conceptions of Power." *Process Studies* 6, no. 1 (Spring 1976): 5–32.

Oakley, Francis, and Bruce Russett, eds. *Governance, Accountability, and the Future of the Catholic Church*. New York: Continuum, 2004.

Oakley, Francis, and Michael J. Lacey, eds. *The Crisis of Authority in Catholic Modernity*. New York: Oxford University Press, 2011.

Rahner, Karl. "The Teaching Office of the Church." In *Confrontations*, vol. 12, *Theological Investigations*, 3–30. New York: Seabury Press, 1974.

Stagaman, David. *Authority in the Church*. Collegeville, MN: Liturgical Press, 1999.

Sullivan, Francis A. "Magisterium." In *Dictionary of Fundamental Theology*, edited by René Latourelle and Rino Fisichella, 614–20. New York: Crossroad, 1995.

CHAPTER 6

A Feminist Reflection on Postconciliar Catholic Ecclesiology

Mary Ann Hinsdale, IHM

If anyone has this task of advancing the dignity of women in the Church and society, it is women themselves who must recognize their responsibility as leading characters.

—Pope John Paul II

If one were to ask what the Second Vatican Council had to say about women, the answer would be "not much." Nevertheless, given the past misogynist words of many church fathers and the general invisibility of women in the history of the Catholic Church (aside from Mary and the saints), what Vatican II *did* say struck many women as revolutionary. The council's document *Gaudium et Spes* (The Pastoral Constitution on the Church in the Modern World) asserted women's equality with men as *imago Dei* and acknowledged that "women claim parity with men in fact as well as of right" (GS 9). During the council, the bishops voiced a strong plea for the eradication of sex discrimination, noting that since women are fully human, they too, deserve fundamental human rights.

> But any kind of social or cultural discrimination in basic personal rights on the grounds of sex, race, color, social conditions, language, or religion must be curbed and eradicated as incompatible with God's design. It is deeply to be deplored that these basic personal rights are not yet being respected everywhere, as is the case with

women who are denied the chance freely to choose a husband, or a state of life, or to have access to the same educational and cultural benefits as are available to men. (GS 29)

Under the heading of "reverence for the human person," the council singled out a whole host of injustices that should be eliminated, including slavery and the trafficking of women and children (GS 27).

Since these words were written, the church has seen five popes and three generations of feminist theologians. This chapter aims to sketch some of the opportunities and challenges that have emerged for women and for Catholic ecclesiology since the Second Vatican Council. Such an assessment is timely, not only in light of the council's fiftieth anniversary but also because the current pope has expressed new interest in increasing the number of women in church leadership positions and in forging "a profound theology of the woman."[1] To this end, the first part of this chapter reviews the involvement of women at Vatican II—before, during, and immediately after the council. Next, I trace the development of what for many feminists has become "the issue under the issue" in Catholic ecclesiology, namely, a theological anthropology of "gender complementarity" and the way in which it presents an impasse for the full inclusion of women in the church. Finally, I offer some examples influenced by feminist thought that seek to provide the necessary "disciplining" of power relations in the church in order that women followers of Jesus might truly be recognized for who they are in the "discipleship of equals" that is the church.[2]

---

[1] See Antonio Spadaro, "A Big Heart Open to God: The Exclusive Interview with Pope Francis," trans. Massimo Faggioli, Sarah Christopher Faggioli, Dominic Robinson, Patrick Howell, and Griffin Oleynick, *America* 209, no. 8 (September 30, 2013): 28.

[2] This phrase, of course, comes from the title of Elisabeth Schüssler Fiorenza's *Discipleship of Equals: A Critical Feminist Ekklesia-logy of Liberation* (New York: Crossroad, 1993). Richard Gaillardetz, in his chapter in this volume, uses Michel Foucault's concept of the "technologies of power" in explaining how power relations in the church might be "disciplined" (i.e., transformed) in accord with Jesus's vision of the reign of God. In the third section of this chapter, I suggest some ways in which feminist theologians and other groups of women are involved in the disciplining of power imbalances in the church.

Women and Vatican II

Women's Preconciliar Involvement

The Second Vatican Council coincided with what commentators have called the "second wave" of feminism.[3] Given the advances for women in society taking place during the 1960s, it was inevitable that women would become excited about the possibilities that Vatican II might afford women in the Catholic Church. During the council's preparatory phase, several international Catholic women's organizations submitted suggestions (*vota*) for the bishops' consideration. A particularly direct petition came from the Swiss lawyer Gertrud Heinzelmann (d. 1999). Heinzelmann sent a detailed request to the conciliar Preparatory Commission in May 1962 calling for dialogue regarding "the intolerable situation dictated by tradition" and demanding equality for women "at every level of ecclesial life."[4]

Heinzelmann's petition found its way to four other Catholic women: Iris Müller and Ida Raming, who were studying philosophy and theology in Germany, and Americans Rosemary Lauer, a philosopher from St. John's University in New York, and Mary Daly, a doctoral student at the University of Fribourg. Together with Josefa Theresia Münch, who in 1959 had petitioned the Vatican about a revision of canon 968 in the 1917 Code of Canon Law, they published *Wir schweigen nicht länger!* (*We Won't Keep Silent Any Longer! Women Speak Out to the Vatican Council II*). This book included the resolutions of the Saint Joan's International Alliance, a group of Catholic women who held gatherings in 1963 and 1964 arguing for women's admission to the diaconate and the priesthood, as well as for the inclusion of women in the commissions of the council.[5]

Pope John XXIII's announcement of the council and his encyclical *Pacem in Terris* (1963), which declared that the dignity and rights of women were among the chief "signs of the times," also served to heighten the expectations of Catholic women. It was Cardinal Leo Jozef Suenens of Belgium (1904–1996), however, who during the council's second

---

[3] This "second wave" followed the "first wave" that marked the struggle for women's suffrage. For a critique of the metaphor of waves, see Nancy Hewitt, ed., *No Permanent Waves: Recasting Histories of U.S. Feminism* (Piscataway, NJ: Rutgers University Press, 2010).

[4] See Gertrud Heinzelmann, *Wir schweigen nicht länger! Frauen äussern sich zum II Vatikanischen Konzil* (Zurich: Interfeminas-Verlag, 1965).

[5] For an account of this whole process, see Ida Raming, *A History of Women and Ordination*, vol. 2, *The Priestly Office of Women: God's Gift to a Renewed Church*, 2nd ed., trans. and ed. Bernard Cooke and Gary Macy (Lanham, MD: Scarecrow Press, 2004).

session, electrified the assembled bishops with this intervention: "Why are we even discussing the reality of the church when half of the church is not even represented here?"[6]

Women's Involvement During the Council

Thanks in part to Suenens's intervention, twenty-three women were eventually invited to become auditors at Vatican II (fourteen arrived in 1964, nine more joined them in 1965). While some commentators dismiss the influence of these women (since they could neither address the assembly nor vote), two scholars of the council, Carmel McEnroy and Catherine Clifford, present a different assessment.[7] According to Clifford, the fact that Vatican II did not contain a specific reflection on the role of women as "a uniquely identifiable group within the structure of the church" does not mean that women's voices were ignored.[8] In fact, as McEnroy points out, the women auditors were quite deliberate in refusing to be put on a pedestal, and they rejected the idea that they had "a special nature" that differentiated them as human beings. A case in point is the influence they exerted in the debate on the 1963 "Schema on the Lay Apostolate." The original plan was to have two separate articles, one on men (*De Viris*) and one on women (*De Mulieribus*). As Clifford notes,

> The women at the council preferred to be considered under the inclusive heading of the generic "men" (*hominum*) over being exalted in flowery discourse, or defined according to rigid categories. Pilar Bellosillo cautioned those well-intentioned bishops who in their exuberance, were looking for ways to elaborate a poetic tribute to women. "That kind of language is detached from life and puts women on a pedestal instead of on the same level as man."[9]

---

[6] Second Vatican Council, *Acta Synodalia* (Vatican City: Typis polyglottis Vaticanis, 1970–), II/3 177, 356. See also, Mary Luke Tobin, "Women in the Church Since Vatican II," *America* 155, no. 12 (November 1, 1986): 242–46. Tobin herself was in the first group of women Paul VI subsequently invited to the council as "auditors."

[7] Carmel McEnroy, *Guests in Their Own House: The Women of Vatican II* (New York: Crossroad, 1996; repr. Eugene, OR: Wipf and Stock, 2011); citations are to the Wipf and Stock reprint. Catherine Clifford, *Decoding Vatican II: Interpretation and Ongoing Reception* (New York: Paulist Press, 2014).

[8] Clifford, *Decoding Vatican II*, 73.

[9] Ibid., 73; cf. McEnroy, *Guests in Their Own House*, 155. As the first woman to be named a permanent member of a curial congregation (The Pontifical Council on the Laity), Bellosillo was very influential in several subcommissions.

The American auditor Sr. Mary Luke Tobin later recalled that it was the Redemptorist *peritus*, Bernard Häring, who was instrumental in having some of the women participate in the commissions formulating the documents. She tells how she and the Australian auditor, Rosemary Goldie, were invited to speak "as freely as we wished in whatever language we chose; and each of us did speak."[10] Goldie likewise insisted on women being "recognized as the full human persons they are, and treated accordingly."[11]

Thus Vatican II's "teaching on women" includes not only the handful of specific references to women but also the many places in the council documents that treat the *whole* church. In recovering the biblical notion of "the people of God" as a fundamental image of church, the council called on both hierarchy and laity to recognize the implications of their common baptism. This recognition provided a new understanding of the laity that regarded both men and women equally as disciples. The council further acknowledged that "there is one single vocation of all the baptized,"[12] underlining an equality that is "prior to any distinctions that derive from particular roles in the church."[13] The features of this vocation include: (1) the universal call to holiness; (2) the common priesthood of all the baptized; (3) the call to mission; and (4) a renewed appreciation of the Holy Spirit's animation of the church through the distribution of charisms (LG, 4, 10, 12, 31, 37).

Clifford points out that this renewed emphasis on the laity as equal sharers in the priestly, prophetic, and royal office of Christ, as well as the co-responsibility in mission that flows from it, makes an implicit statement about women. After all, women constitute more than half of the Catholic laity. In *Lumen Gentium, Apostolicam Actuositatem,* and *Ad Gentes,* women are treated equally with men in being encouraged to assume roles of service to their brothers and sisters in Christ—in catechetics, in

---

[10] Mary Luke Tobin, "Women in the Church: Vatican II and After," *Ecumenical Review* 37, no. 3 (July 1, 1985): 296.

[11] Rosemary Goldie, quoted in Clifford, *Decoding Vatican II*, 126n16. Much of Goldie's contributions are hidden away in some of the early commentaries on the council documents. For example, see her "Un point de vue 'féminin'?" in *L'église dans le monde de ce temps*, vol. 3 (Paris: Cerf, 1967), 93–106.

[12] Paul Lakeland, *A Council That Will Never End:* Lumen Gentium *and the Church Today* (Collegeville, MN: Liturgical Press, 2013), 74.

[13] Richard Lennan, "Roman Catholic Ecclesiology," in *The Routledge Companion to the Christian Church*, ed. Gerard Mannion and Lewis S. Mudge (New York: Routledge, 2008), 239.

the care of souls, and in administration of the church's goods (AA 9–10). For such roles they ought to be provided with "adequate formation," including "access to theological education," as well as given a "just wage" and "a decent standard of living" (AG 17). Their participation in various apostolic fields was encouraged in the same measure that they were moving into new fields in society that were hitherto closed to women. As Clifford reminds us, "The substance of these teachings is almost taken for granted today. At the time of the Second Vatican Council, they signified substantial progress in understanding the role of women in the life of the church and society. These few lines of teaching opened the way for women to devote themselves to new forms of pastoral ministry and to the study and teaching of theology."[14]

Postconciliar Involvement of Women

The council unleashed an overwhelming response on the part of women to a renewed understanding of their baptismal vocation. This response can be seen nowhere more dramatically than in the reception of the council among women religious in the United States. Catholic sisters in North America were the vanguard of conciliar renewal. They implemented an *aggiornamento* of their lifestyles and apostolates by taking to heart the council's *Perfectae Caritatis* (Decree on the Appropriate Renewal of Religious Life)—often more fully than did male religious orders. Their endeavors received "pushback" from the hierarchy who were not used to women taking their own initiative (though actually, one could say the sisters were "just being obedient" in implementing conciliar directives). Nor had they reckoned with the effects of the "Sister Formation" movement in spawning a cadre of well-educated female leaders.[15]

Following the council, women religious embraced new ecclesial ministries and pursued degrees in biblical studies, theology, and canon law

---

[14] Clifford, *Decoding Vatican II*, 72.

[15] To appreciate the challenges that the response of women religious to Vatican II presented to the institutional church in the decades after Vatican II, see Lora Ann Quinonez and Mary Daniel Turner, *The Transformation of American Catholic Sisters* (Philadelphia, PA: Temple University Press, 1992); Anita M. Caspary, *Witness to Integrity: The Crisis of the Immaculate Heart Community of California* (Collegeville, MN: Liturgical Press, 2003); and Margaret R. Brennan, *What Was There for Me Once* (Toronto: Novalis Press, 2009).

in order to prepare for them. For the first time, women were not only allowed but actually encouraged to become theologians. Thus, several North American religious congregations made it a priority to educate a number of their own sisters as theologians.[16]

In heeding Vatican II's call to mission, women religious in apostolic congregations began to move beyond the traditional apostolates of nursing and teaching to embrace peace and social justice ministries. The 1971 Synod of Bishops document "Justice in the World," the civil rights and antiwar movements in the United States, and the emergence of liberationist theologies imbued many sisters and lay women with a zeal for the structural transformation not only of society but also of the church itself. The rapid growth of "lay ecclesial ministries" during the fifty years since Vatican II has also created great expectations on the part of many women.[17] It is beyond the scope of this chapter to give a complete account of these movements, but a snapshot of the impetus toward justice that stirred many women is captured in two excerpts from "Justice in the World": (1) that "action on behalf of justice and participation in the transformation of the world fully appear to us as a constitutive dimension of the preaching of the Gospel"; and (2) "While the Church is bound to give witness to justice, she recognizes that anyone who ventures to speak to people about justice must first be just in their eyes. Hence we must undertake an examination of the modes of acting and of the possessions and life style found within the Church herself."[18]

Gender Complementarity:
The "Issue Under the Issues" in Ecclesiology

In this section I want to argue, to borrow a phrase from John O'Malley, that gender—especially gender complementarity—is *the* "issue under the issues" in ecclesiology today.[19] For the most part, the council documents do not treat women as a separate group in the church but include

---

[16] See my *Women Shaping Theology* (New York: Paulist Press, 2006).

[17] Some of these issues are discussed in Zeni Fox, ed., *Lay Ecclesial Ministry: Pathways for the Future* (Lanham, MD: Rowman and Littlefield, 2010).

[18] 1971 Synod of Bishops, "Justice in the World," 6, 40, http://www.shc.edu /theolibrary/resources/synodjw.htm, accessed December 31, 2014.

[19] See John W. O'Malley, *What Happened at Vatican II* (Cambridge, MA: Harvard University Press, 2008), 8–9.

them in the church's new understanding of itself.[20] As baptized laity and vowed religious, women belong to the "people of God" as do men; they share in the priestly, prophetic, and kingly mission of Christ and are therefore to be respected as *imago Dei*. Yet during the pontificates of John Paul II and Benedict XVI, we see an ever-increasing endorsement of gender essentialism in the form of gender complementarity, to the point that it now appears to have achieved the status of an official theological anthropology.

A reflection on this development seems especially important in the face of the recent statements by Pope Francis expressing a desire to "investigate further the role of the woman in the church."[21] The very idea that the role of woman (note the singular, collective usage of the term) in the church is singled out by the pope is troubling. Are not women church just as much as men are church?[22] In his interview with Antonio Spadaro, the editor of *La Civiltà Cattolica*, Pope Francis said, "We have to work harder to develop a profound theology of the woman. Only by making this step will it be possible to better reflect on their function within the church. The feminine genius is needed wherever we make important decisions. The challenge today is this: to think about the specific place of women also in those places where the authority of the church is exercised for various areas of the church."[23] Since Spadaro's interview, Pope Francis has continued to make statements about women and "femininity." In June 2014, in an interview with Franca Giansoldati of *Il Messaggero*, he again indicated that a study of "the feminine question" was underway: "Women are the most beautiful thing God has made. The

---

[20] Paul VI's "Address to Women" at the closing ceremony of the council might be viewed as an exception here. His address in fact does give a special status and mission to women that might be regarded as espousing gender complementarity. See Walter M. Abbott, ed., *The Documents of Vatican II* (New York: Guild Press, 1966), 732–34.

[21] Spadaro, "A Big Heart Open to God," 28.

[22] See, for example, Mary Hunt, "The Trouble with Francis: Three Things that Worry Me," *Religion Dispatches*, January 6, 2014, http://religiondispatches.org/the-trouble -with-francis-three-things-that-worry-me/, accessed November 20, 2014; and Mary T. Malone, "Some Definitive 'No's,'" in *The Francis Factor: A New Departure*, ed. John Littleton and Eamon Maher (Dublin: Columba Press, 2014), 17–24. A more hopeful but still critical assessment is that of Tina Beattie, "The Revolution of Tenderness: The Theology of Pope Francis," in *The Francis Factor: A New Departure*, ed. John Littleton and Eamon Maher (Dublin: Columba Press, 2014), 141–49.

[23] Spadaro, "A Big Heart Open to God," 28.

Church is a woman. Church is a feminine word. We cannot do theology without this femininity. You are right, we don't talk about this enough. I agree that we have to work more on the theology of woman. I said it and we are working on it . . . have to study the feminine question more deeply, otherwise we cannot understand the Church herself."[24]

While willing to give Pope Francis the time "to study the question more deeply," I want to offer some suggestions as well as some cautions for how such a study might be undertaken. But first, it is important to review the trajectory of papal and curial statements that have addressed gender issues in the church since the council. It will be interesting to see to what extent, ultimately, Francis's goal can be achieved given the positions expressed in these statements and to what extent he is open to further dialogue.

"Gender" and "Sex" as Unstable Categories

The term "gender" never appears in the documents of Vatican II. This is understandable given the time period during which the council took place. Women's studies, feminist theory, feminist ethics, and feminist theologies were just beginning to reflect on the meaning of sex and gender in the context of a theological anthropology that took embodiment seriously. Elisabeth Schüssler Fiorenza reminds us that only in the 1970s did the field of women's studies start to distinguish socially constructed gender roles from biological sex, so that "by the mid-1980s gender studies emerged as a distinct field of inquiry" that not only called into question seemingly universal beliefs about women and men but also attempted "to unmask the cultural, societal, and political roots of gender."[25] Catholic ethicist Margaret Farley also points out that feminist theorists have held various, sometimes competing, positions on the "sex/gender" issue. These arguments include: (1) stressing the equality of

---

[24] Interview with Pope Francis by Franca Giansoldati, *Aleteia*, June 30, 2014, http://www.aleteia.org/en/religion/article/pope-francis-women-are-the-most-beautiful-thing-god-has-made-5860471114563584, accessed July 4, 2014.

[25] Elisabeth Schüssler Fiorenza, "Between Movement and Academy: Feminist Biblical Studies in the Twentieth Century," in *Feminist Biblical Studies in the Twentieth Century: Scholarship and Movement*, ed. Elisabeth Schüssler Fiorenza (Atlanta: Society of Biblical Literature, 2014), 6. For a classic, historical treatment of this subject, see Joan Wallach Scott, "Gender: A Useful Category of Historical Analysis," in *Feminism & History: Oxford Readings in Feminism*, ed. Joan Wallach Scott (New York: Oxford University Press, 1996), 152–80.

persons, with gender simply a secondary human attribute; (2) a reevaluation of women's embodiment that gives gender an even greater importance; (3) the "denaturalization" of notions of gender; and (4) a social constructivism that radically destabilizes not only gender but also sex.[26] Theories that emphasized the "social construction" of sex and gender began to be used to challenge a number of official church teachings, such as the prohibition of women's ordination and "the intrinsic disorder" of homosexual activity.

Gender Complementarity in Papal and Curial Pronouncements

The possibility of women's admission to the ministerial priesthood (which, as we have seen, was raised even before Vatican II) reached a tipping point in the mid-1970s with the "irregular" ordination of eleven women to the priesthood in the US Episcopal Church and the first Catholic Women's Ordination Conference, held in Detroit, which petitioned the Vatican to "Ordain women now!" The Congregation for the Doctrine of the Faith, with the approval of Pope Paul VI, responded by publishing "The Declaration on the Question of the Admission of Women to the Ministerial Priesthood" (*Inter Insigniores*) on October 15, 1976.[27]

The primary argument advanced in *Inter Insigniores* is that fidelity to the intention of Christ and the constancy of tradition do not allow the church today to overturn the longstanding prohibition against ordaining women to the ministerial priesthood. In addition, the document includes several arguments "from fittingness" in support of this position. Among them is the claim that the maleness of Jesus determines that the priest, who sacramentally acts *in persona Christi*, must be a man, in order that there be a "natural resemblance" to Christ, who was male.[28] Although the CDF document also acknowledged that priests equally represent the church as the Body of Christ in the sacraments (*in personae ecclesiae*), it appealed to Vatican II which regarded the priest as "representing Christ the head and the shepherd of the church" (LG 28 and PO 2). Underlying

[26] Margaret Farley, *Just Love: A Framework for Christian Sexual Ethics* (New York: Continuum, 2008), 135.

[27] Congregation for the Doctrine of the Faith, "The Declaration on the Question of the Admission of Women to the Ministerial Priesthood" (*Inter Insigniores*), in *Women Priests: A Catholic Commentary on the Vatican Declaration*, ed. Leonard Swidler and Arlene Swidler (New York: Paulist Press, 1977), 319–37.

[28] The argument "from fittingness" is presented in ibid., 25–27.

these arguments are gendered understandings of the patriarchal "head" of the family. But this document does not have a strong emphasis on gender *complementarity* with respect to women in relation to men. In fact, the equality of women with men is frequently invoked throughout the document, notwithstanding its admonition that "equality is in no way identity."[29]

In 1994, on the feast of Pentecost, Pope John Paul II issued the apostolic letter "On Reserving Priestly Ordination to Men Alone" (*Ordinatio Sacerdotalis*). Addressed to the bishops of the Catholic Church, this document reaffirmed much of the same reasoning expressed in *Inter Insigniores*, though it did not repeat the argument that women could not image Christ. John Paul II concluded the document in very forceful terms: "In order that all doubt may be removed regarding a matter of great importance, a matter which pertains to the Church's divine constitution itself, in virtue of my ministry of confirming the brethren (cf. Lk 22:32) I declare that the Church has no authority whatsoever to confer priestly ordination on women and that this judgment is to be definitively held by all the Church's faithful."[30] The pope does say that women have an important role to play "in the divine plan." Although Jesus did not choose women to serve in the role of priest, this is not a matter of discrimination. The pope praises women as "true disciples, witnesses to Christ in the family and in society, as well as in total consecration to the service of God and of the Gospel."[31]

Ordinatio Sacerdotalis was followed by a *Responsum ad Dubium* from the Congregation for the Doctrine of the Faith, which declared that the teaching of *Ordinatio Sacerdotalis* was to be understood as "definitive," and hence, infallibly taught and irrevocable, precluding any further discussion of women's ordination. Serious doubts were expressed by individual theologians and major Catholic theological societies regarding

---

[29] "It therefore remains for us to meditate more deeply on the nature of the real equality of the baptized which is one of the great affirmations of Christianity; equality is in no way identity, for the Church is a differentiated body, in which *each individual has his or her role*. The roles are distinct, and must not be confused; they do not favor the superiority of some vis-á-vis the others, nor do they provide an excuse for jealousy; the only better gift, which can and must be desired, is love" (CDF, *Inter Insigniores* 39, emphasis mine).

[30] John Paul II, *Ordinatio Sacerdotalis*, 4, http://w2.vatican.va/content/john-paul-ii/en/apost_letters/1994/documents/hf_jp-ii_apl_19940522_ordinatio-sacerdotalis.html, accessed August 15, 2014.

[31] Ibid., 3.

the legitimacy of the *Dubium*'s claim.[32] The important thing to note here is that—with the exception of the argument for an "iconic resemblance" necessary in order to act *in persona Christi*—none of the statements prohibiting ordination specifically discuss gender complementarity. Rather, the focus is on an unchanging understanding of revelation and the authority of the church.

The first specific papal endorsement of gender complementarity occurs in John Paul II's 1988 apostolic letter, *Mulieris Dignitatem* (On the Dignity and Vocation of Women).[33] For the purpose of this chapter it is important to remember that the timing of this letter effectively derailed the US bishops' attempt to write a third pastoral letter on "Women in Society and the Church." The bishops were forced to abandon their practice of "listening sessions" in which lay women and women religious of all ages, ethnicities, and geographical locations were invited to voice concerns based on their lived experience as women in church and society. In addition, certain topics were now "off the table," especially since *Mulieris Dignitatem* continued to reaffirm the impossibility of the ordination of women.

Mulieris Dignitatem begins by noting that the dignity and vocation of women is a "sign of the times." Its main reference, however, is to Paul VI's 1965 "Address to Woman," given at the end of the Second Vatican Council.[34] Even then, Paul VI's words struck many women as quaint. This appeal to past papal statements in discerning the "signs of the times" was a far cry from the consultative and pastorally sensitive process behind the drafting of the US bishops' letter on women. Not only did *Mulieris Dignitatem* reaffirm the impossibility of women's ordination, it also outlined an anthropology of complementarity whose essentialist arguments would lay the groundwork for what many feminist theologians regard as women's *inequality* in the church.

---

[32] For examples, see Nicholas Lash, "On Not Inventing Doctrine," *The Tablet* (December 2, 1995): 1544; Francis A. Sullivan, "Guideposts from Catholic Tradition: Infallibility Doctrine Invoked in Statement against Ordination by Congregation for the Doctrine of the Faith," *The Tablet* (December 23–30, 1995): 1646; and Ad Hoc Committee on Tradition and Ordination, Catholic Theological Society of America, "Tradition and the Ordination of Woman: A Question of Criteria," *Proceedings of the Catholic Theological Society of America* 51 (1996): 333–42.

[33] John Paul II, On the Dignity and Vocation of Women (*Mulieris Dignitatem*), http://www.vatican.va/holy_father/john_paul_ii/apost_letters/documents/hf_jp-ii_apl_15081988_mulieris-dignitatem_en.htm, accessed August 15, 2014.

[34] See above, n. 20.

The document ostensibly was meant to take up the issue of the vocation and dignity of women that had been requested by the members of the recent Extraordinary Synod on the Laity held in the same year. Thus in his postsynodal apostolic exhortation, *Christifideles Laici*, John Paul II explicitly stated, "The condition that will assure the rightful presence of woman [*sic*] in the Church and in society is a more penetrating and accurate consideration of the *anthropological foundation for masculinity and femininity* with the intent of clarifying woman's personal identity in relation to man, that is, a diversity yet mutual complementarity, not only as it concerns roles to be held and functions to be performed, but also, and more deeply, as it concerns her make-up and meaning as a person."[35] John Paul went on to encourage all, especially those "who devote their lives to the human sciences and theological disciplines," to read *Mulieris Dignitatem* as a biblical meditation and to undertake "critical study" that will "enlighten and guide the Christian response to the most frequently asked questions, oftentimes so crucial, on the *'place' that women can have and ought to have in the Church and in society.*"[36]

It is clear, however, that the encouragement to study critically the issue of women is predetermined by "a plan that 'from the beginning' has been indelibly imprinted in the very being of the human person— men and women—and, therefore, in the make-up, meaning and deepest workings of the individual."[37] With the help of an "informed discernment," scholars, while not forgetting the help that can come from different human sciences and cultures, "will be able to help gather and clarify the values and requirements that belong to the enduring essential aspects of women and those bound to evolve in history."[38]

---

[35] John Paul II, *Christifideles Laici*, 50 (italics in original), http://www.vatican.va /holy_father/john_paul_ii/apost_exhortations/documents/hf_jp-ii_exh_30121988 _christifideles-laici_en.html, accessed November 20, 2014.

[36] Ibid.; italics in original.

[37] Ibid. Here John Paul II makes explicit appeal to his catechetical orations on Genesis as well as his first encyclical: "The Apostolic Letter on the Dignity and Vocation of Woman gives much attention to the anthropological and theological foundation of woman's dignity as a person. The document seeks to again treat and develop the catechetical reflections of the Wednesday General Audiences devoted over a long period of time to the theology of the body, while at the same time fulfilling a promise made in the Encyclical *Redemptoris Mater* and serving as a response to the request of the Synod Fathers."

[38] John Paul II, *Christifidelis Laici*, 50.

As did *Gaudium et Spes*, *Mulieris Dignitatem* argues that both men and women are created as *imago dei* and thus are equally human.[39] As Susan Ross points out, however, the anthropology in this document was derived not from Christology but from Mariology.[40] Michele Gonzalez echoes Ross and notes that what professes to be an "egalitarian anthropology" in *Mulieris Dignitatem* "is quickly amended with a gender complementarity that defines the ethical vocation of women as one in which she 'can only find herself by giving love to others' (no. 30). Woman is characterized as giving by her nature, almost to the point that she appears naturally self-effacing. Women have a special capacity to care and love based on a Marian anthropology of motherhood."[41]

This Marian-centered anthropology characterizes femaleness by receptivity and maternal nurturing, while maleness consists of initiation and agency. Thus, at the heart of John Paul's anthropology is a nuptial symbolism based on his reading of the creation narratives in Genesis. His "Theology of the Body," which began as catechetical orations on the book of Genesis, stressed this symbolism and leads to an essential difference between "man" and "woman." Such symbolism implies

> a conception of men and women as (a) essentially different and (b) "complete" only in relation to each other. According to this understanding, maleness and femaleness constitute the original dimorphic condition of humanity as intended by God and as evidenced in the two creation accounts. In John Paul II's understanding however, gender complementarity has also come to include a definition of what is "essential" to being male and female. A certain form of "essentialism" has long been a part of official Vatican teaching on womanhood, but it has taken on enhanced importance in the writings of John Paul II.[42]

---

[39] John Paul II, *Mulieris Dignitatem*, 6.

[40] Susan Ross, "The Bridegroom and the Bride: The Theological Anthropology of John Paul II and Its Relation to the Bible and Homosexuality," in *Sexual Diversity and Catholicism: Toward the Development of Moral Theology*, ed. Patricia Beattie Jung with Joseph Andrew Coray (Collegeville, MN: Liturgical Press, 2001), 43.

[41] Michelle Gonzalez, *Created in God's Image: An Introduction to Feminist Theological Anthropology* (Maryknoll, NY: Orbis Books, 2007), 142.

[42] Ross, "The Bridegroom and the Bride," 40. See also Ross's *Anthropology: Seeking Light and Beauty* (Collegeville, MN: Liturgical Press, 2012), esp. 86–104.

The use of nuptial symbolism has a long and noble history in the Christian mystical tradition and it has often been used to illustrate the love and intimacy between married partners and between the soul and God. But "it has not," Ross writes, "for the most part, served as a prescriptive model for gender roles."[43]

Ross, along with Tina Beattie, Michelle Gonzalez, Susan Rakoczy, and others, attribute John Paul II's theory of sex complementarity to an understanding of the church highly influenced by Hans Urs von Balthasar.[44] Balthasar, who prefers a highly symbolic, rather than historical-critical reading of New Testament texts, often interpreted Scripture through the imaginative personal piety of the visionary and mystic Adrienne von Speyr. This interpretation connects to a rather distinctive ecclesiology that sees ministerial roles and the church itself as instantiated in certain archetypes drawn from principal figures in the New Testament (i.e., Mary, Peter, John, Mary and Martha, Mary Magdalene). Fundamentally, von Balthasar understood the church as being comprised of a "Marian" and a "Petrine" principle.[45] Mary is at the center of the church,

> because her faith represents "the all-inclusive, protective and directive form of all ecclesial life" (p. 208), "the model of all being and acting" in the church (p. 206). . . . The Church, after all, begins in the chamber at Nazareth, in the faith of the Virgin "through which the Son of God becomes man," and by which "he also forms the truly universal Church" (p. 207). . . . In her is seen "the nuptial encounter between God and the creature." "The entire Church is Marian," von Balthasar says . . . because "Mary disappears into the heart of the Church to remain there as a real presence which, however, always gives place to her Son" (pp. 158–59). For von Balthasar, the radiant heart of the Church is *lay, faithful, and holy*, characterized by contemplative receptivity in relation to God, and symbolized by the femininity and virginal maternity of Mary: as she is, so is the church.[46]

---

[43] Ross, "The Bridegroom and the Bride," 41.

[44] See Susan Rakoczy, "Mixed Messages: John Paul II's Writings on Women," in *The Vision of John Paul II: Assessing His Thought and Influence*, ed. Gerard Mannion (Collegeville, MN: Liturgical Press, 2008), 159–83.

[45] Hans Urs von Balthasar, *The Office of Peter and the Structure of the Church* (San Francisco: Ignatius Press, 1986).

[46] John McDade, "Von Balthasar and the Office of Peter in the Church," *The Way* 44, no. 4 (2005): 101. McDade is quoting from Hans Urs von Balthasar, *The Office of Peter and the Structure of the Church*, trans. Andrée Emery (San Francisco: Ignatius, 1986).

The essentialist view of women and its corresponding gender complementarity expressed in *Mulieris Dignitatem* appears again in John Paul II's 1995 "Letter to Women," written on the eve of the Fourth United Nations World Conference on Women. "Womanhood and manhood are complementary not only from the physical and psychological points of view, but also from *the ontological*. It is only through the duality of the 'masculine' and the 'feminine' that the 'human' finds full realization."[47] In this letter the pope also gives thanks for "the feminine genius" of women—a phrase that henceforth will characterize the "semiofficial" understanding of the role of women in the church. The "Letter to Women" concludes, "It is thus my hope, dear sisters, that you will reflect carefully on what it means to speak of the 'genius of women,' not only in order to be able to see in this phrase a specific part of God's plan which needs to be accepted and appreciated, but also in order to let this genius be more fully expressed in the life of society as a whole, as well as in the life of the Church."[48]

Earlier in 1995, in his encyclical *Evangelium Vitae* (On the Value and Inviolability of Human Life), the pope described contemporary society as "a culture of death" and asked women to create a "new feminism"— clearly indicating his disdain for "secular feminism," which in his estimation was opposed to life and espoused a reverse form of sex domination: "In transforming culture so that it supports life, women occupy a place, in thought and action, which is unique and decisive. It depends on them to promote a 'new feminism' which rejects the temptation of imitating models of 'male domination,' in order to acknowledge and affirm *the true genius* of women in every aspect of the life of society, and overcome all discrimination, violence and exploitation" (EV 99; emphasis mine). Specifically urging women "to transform culture so that it supports life" is not in itself an objectionable summons; however, to single out women as bearing a special responsibility in this regard continues to canonize a construal of gender that concentrates on "women's special nature and gifts as mothers."

As prefect of the Congregation for the Doctrine of the Faith, then-Cardinal Joseph Ratzinger continued to champion the "new feminism" (or, as it is often called, "John Paul II feminism" or simply, "the feminine

---

[47] "Letter of Pope John Paul II to Women," http://w2.vatican.va/content/john -paul-ii/en/letters/1995/documents/hf_jp-ii_let_29061995_women.html, accessed November 20, 2014 (emphasis mine).

[48] "Letter of Pope John Paul II to Women," 10.

genius"). The "Letter to Bishops of the Catholic Church on the Collaboration of Men and Women in the Church and the World," issued by the CDF with the pope's approval in 2004, castigated what it termed "radical feminism," and reiterated the "definitive" teaching concerning the inadmissibility of women to priestly ordination, while insisting at the same time that such an exclusion "does not hamper in any way women's access to the heart of Christian life." This document continued to stress sexual difference as "a fundamental component of personality" and taught that it is "women's vocation" to love and nurture life and to take primary responsibility for human relationships, based on "her capacity for the other."[49] Such a theological anthropology certainly would have rankled the women auditors at Vatican II and continues to disturb many women today.

Why Is This a Problem?

What is problematic for many feminists about John Paul II's anthropology in the statements just reviewed is the elevation of gender complementarity to a metaphysical and theological category "that corresponds to the entire 'order of creation.' "[50] Furthermore, John Paul II's understanding of spousal relationships is "completely dyadic," and does not give enough attention to the multiplicity of roles that exist in human relationships.[51] This is not to say that there are not differences among theologians, including Catholic feminist theologians, with regard to "sexual difference" or the gender roles of women and men. Tina Beattie, Nancy Dallavalle, Lisa Cahill, Michelle Gonzalez, Christine Gudorf, and Margaret Farley, each in different ways, acknowledge the complexity of the meaning and importance of gender and sexual arrangements among human beings. Perhaps Margaret Farley puts it most clearly:

> Considerations of sex and gender do not begin as neutral examinations of "interesting" aspects of what it means to be human, embodied and inspirited. They begin as efforts to correct or reinforce previous understandings and to challenge or deny imbalances of

---

[49] See Mary Ann Hinsdale, "Women Theologians as Gift of an Inculturated US American Church," in *Inculturation and the Church in North America*, ed. T. Frank Kennedy (New York: Crossroad Publishing, 2006): 44–60.

[50] Ross, "The Bridegroom and the Bride," 47.

[51] Ibid., 53.

power based on gender. They continue as investigations into "the political stakes in designating as an *origin* and a *cause* those identity categories that are in fact the *effects* of institutions, practices and discourses with multiple and diffuse points of origin."[52]

Importantly, discussions about sex, gender, and women's roles in the church have not involved a sufficiently wide representation of theologians—particularly women theologians—and social scientists, as was called for during the synod on the laity in 1987. Instead, there have been concerted efforts on the part of the hierarchy to undertake a campaign against what in many countries is called "gender-theory" or "gender-ideology." In the *Instrumentum Laboris* for the 2014 extraordinary synod on the family, four different paragraphs mention concerns about "gender ideology."[53] Gerhard Marschütz, an ethicist on the Catholic Theological Faculty at the University of Vienna, described the ecclesial campaign being waged against "gender theory" and "gender mainstreaming" in Europe in an article in *Herder Korrespondenz*. He noted that a charitable agency sponsored by the Vatican has distributed tens of thousands of booklets denouncing "gender ideology" and that three conferences of bishops (Portugal, Slovakia, and Poland), acting independently of one another, have issued pastoral letters warning against the danger of "gender ideology."[54]

Getting Beyond Impasse

Most Catholics know that Pope Paul VI wrote *Humanae Vitae*, but few have heard of his first encyclical, *Ecclesiam Suam*. Written during the council, this encyclical offered a bold call for dialogue as the fundamental way of proceeding in the life of the church. According to John O'Malley, there was hardly a word that was more celebrated during Vatican II than *dialogue*: "No single word, with the possible exception of *aggiornamento*, would be more often invoked to indicate what the council was all

---

[52] Farley, *Just Love*, 136.

[53] See nos. 23, 114, 117 and 127 of the *Instrumentum Laboris*, http://www.vatican.va /roman_curia/synod/documents/rc_synod_doc_20140626_instrumentum-laboris -familia_en.html, accessed October 14, 2014.

[54] See Gerhard Marschütz, "Wachstumspotenzial für die eigene Lehre: Zur Kritik an der vermeintlichen Gender-Ideologie," *Herder Korrespondenz* 68, no. 9 (2014): 457–62.

about."[55] Since the council, however, it appears that dialogue (especially with women) is a word more to be feared rather than celebrated.

For many women, particularly those imbued with a feminist consciousness, the raising of gender complementarity to an ontological status presents a tragic situation of ecclesial impasse that is an affront to women's baptismal equality in the church. Thus, in this concluding section, I want to lift up four proposals for dialogical practice that might be undertaken in response to this situation.

A particularly egregious illustration of ecclesial impasse is the recent investigations concerning US women religious—both the apostolic visitation of women's religious communities, which took place between 2009 and 2011, and the "doctrinal assessment" of the Leadership Conference of Women Religious (LCWR) mandated by the Congregation for the Doctrine of the Faith.[56] While on the surface these investigations do not seem to bear directly on "gender complementarity," at the root of the conflict is the exercise of women's agential power.

Thus the first example of dialogical practice is the way in which the LCWR responded to the CDF's investigation. One outcome of the doctrinal assessment, which at the time of this writing is still ongoing, was the imposition of an overseer, Archbishop Peter Sartain of Seattle. Sartain and two bishop assistants were given a mandate to "implement a process of review and conformity to the discipline of the Church" which involves (1) revising the LCWR's statutes; (2) reviewing its programs, including its general assemblies, speakers, and occasional publications; (3) reforming its programs for future superiors and formators; (4) offering guidance with respect to liturgical norms and texts; and (5) reviewing LCWR links with its affiliated organizations such as the social justice lobby NETWORK and the Resource Center for Religious Life.

The responses of the officers of the LCWR to the CDF's doctrinal assessment offer an excellent example of the exercise of "disciplinary power" proper to Christian discipleship that Richard Gaillardetz proposes in his chapter in this volume. In implementing its "Call 2010–2015"

---

[55] O'Malley, *What Happened at Vatican II*, 80.

[56] See Congregation for the Doctrine of the Faith, "The Doctrinal Assessment of the Leadership Conference of Women Religious," http://www.usccb.org/upload /Doctrinal_Assessment_Leadership_Conference_Women_Religious.pdf, accessed October 10, 2014.

the LCWR asked its members to engage in a contemplative process during its regional meetings in order to create a national conversation among all women religious about the critical questions facing religious life. The hope is that such a national conversation would enable greater contemplative engagement with the emerging questions being faced by the world and church, strengthen and shape the mission of US women religious, and strengthen the solidarity among all women religious.[57]

Drawing on the passage from Isaiah 43:19, "Behold, I am doing something new. . . . Can you not perceive it?" the contemplative process begins with a leader inviting participants to breathe deeply, relaxing their bodies in order to settle into a space of reflective quiet. Next, the passage from scripture is repeated and a song is played. This period of reflection is followed by a structured, ninety-minute meeting, punctuated by times of contemplative silence and reflection on significant questions (provided in a handout from the meeting planners). Before beginning their reflection, participants are asked to "imagine themselves looking upon the world with no judgments, no questions, but with just a contemplative gaze: what significant events capture your attention?" They then are invited to keep these realities in their hearts as they discuss the input and discussion that will take place in the meeting.

Small- and large-group interaction takes place with emphasis on "contemplative listening" to one another, including self-reflection on what might be impeding one's own perception and understanding of what is being shared. The sharing in small groups leads to the discerning of one insight to be shared with the rest of the region. Then, after a large-group discussion, consideration moves to discerning one insight that the region wishes to share with the rest of the LCWR membership. The process concludes with the group creating a brief statement that captures at least one of the key insights emerging from their contemplative inquiry into "'the new' to which God is leading us," which is then posted on the LCWR website.

Many leaders in the LCWR have participated in a series of contemplative workshops designed by a team led by former LCWR president, Nancy Sylvester. Called "Engaging Impasse: Circles of Communal Contemplation and Dialogue," these retreat-like gatherings began in 2002

---

[57] For the entire process, see The Leadership Conference of Women Religious, "The 'Behold I Am Doing Something New' Process," https://lcwr.org/resources /leadership-pathways/behold, accessed November 20, 2014.

and comprised a series of three, three-day sessions.[58] The first gathering focused on accessing more deeply participants' personal stories of impasse; the second gathering focused on understanding the causes of impasse, including one's own complicity; and the third gathering focused on contemplating one's stance in impasse—which did not mean resolution necessarily, but how to engage and embrace impasse.[59] During its first ten years the Institute for Communal Contemplation and Dialogue (ICCD) focused on the Engaging Impasse Circles. ICCD's focus during its second decade has been on "Exercising Contemplative Power." Blogs are used to reflect on a series of issues, including: human trafficking, globalization, immigration, church, global climate change, political climate, the Middle East, inequality and our political reality. For each topic the question posed is, "What does it mean to 'exercise contemplative power' with respect to these issues?"[60]

Clearly, *an invitation to dialogue and discernment* is at the heart of exercising contemplative power. This element has been largely absent, not only in interactions between the magisterium and women religious but also in the magisterium's interventions with theologians. The practice of contemplative prayer opens up our capacity to enter a space in which we hear in a new way what the other is saying. Where the process breaks down is when one encounters fear, particularly fear of women's power.

A second dialogical practice that would serve the church is the recent movement of ecclesiologists who employ ethnography in their work. Focusing on the concrete reality of women's lives would provide a primary locus for an ecclesiology "from below" and qualitative research could provide ways to get beyond the "romantic abstraction" of the anthropology of complementarity. Nicholas M. Healy, for example, has argued that Christianity

---

[58] Sylvester's approach to engaging impasse is derived from Constance FitzGerald, "Impasse and Dark Night," in *Living With Apocalypse*, ed. Tilden Edwards (San Francisco: Harper and Row, 1984), 93–116. See also FitzGerald's "From Impasse to Prophetic Hope: Crisis of Memory," *Proceedings of the Catholic Theological Society of America* 64 (2009): 21–42.

[59] For a description and commentary on the first "Circles of Communal Contemplation and Dialogue," see Nancy Sylvester and Mary Jo Klick, eds., *Crucible for Change: Engaging Impasse through Communal Contemplation and Dialogue* (San Antonio, TX: Sor Juana Press, 2004).

[60] The ICCD process of exercising contemplative power is described at "Exercising Contemplative Power," http://www.iccdinstitute.org/home/exercising-contemplative-power/, accessed October 14, 2014.

is not properly understood as a set of beliefs, a system of doctrine or a religious theory about the way things are. It is, rather, a way of life experienced concretely in and through one's beliefs, practices and attitudes as these are formed by one's church, one's social, cultural and political situation, and personal history. Experience is always contextual, and the context particular, so Christianity can be adequately understood only if one gives an account of its local, concrete forms to complement broader, more generalizing description.[61]

Along with Joseph Komonchak, Healy has decried "blueprint ecclesiologies" which are based on "models" and which, while appealing in their conception and design, fail to address the realities of church life in the concrete. Often, they are "divorced from the confusions and sinfulness of ordinary Christian life."[62] This "turn to the concrete" has been the subject of several ecclesiological conferences in the United States, Great Britain, and Norway that have focused on the use of ethnography as a way of developing a "practical ecclesiology."[63] With regard to gender complementarity, I believe that the use of ethnographic methods would provide access to "the full complexity of women's concrete experience on this issue."[64] Feminist Natalie Watson has long challenged ecclesiologists to provide "a narrative, embodied ecclesiology." One of the best

---

[61] Nicholas M. Healy, "Ecclesiology and Practical Theology," in *Keeping Faith in Practice: Aspects of Catholic Pastoral Theology*, ed. James Sweeney, Gemma Simmonds, and David Lonsdale (London: SCM Press, 2010), 117.

[62] Ibid., 121.

[63] Conferences on Ecclesiology and Ethnography were held at Yale in 2007, in Oxford in 2008, and, since 2012, under the sponsorship of the Ecclesiology and Ethnography Network, in Norway, Durham, St. Paul, and Boston. The leaders of this movement are Pete Ward, Christian Scharen, Paul Fiddes, John Swinton, and James Nieman. Their journal is *Ecclesial Practices*, published by Brill. See https://ecclesiology andethnography.wordpress.com/2014/11/, accessed November 20, 2014.

[64] Healy, "Ecclesiology and Practical Theology," 125. It is important to note that Healy does not eschew doctrine; rather, his caution is based on the belief that the church too easily forgets the basic doctrine of its "giftedness," its inability to function as it should without grace. Forgetting its pneumatological origin, "the Church too often turns to some created thing it can possess: apostolic succession; a revelatory tradition; a centralized, bureaucratic and authoritarian hierarchy; a supernatural liturgy; its status as a *societas perfecta*; an infallible pope" (124).

ways to do so is to gather by means of qualitative research the myriad experiences of women regarding gender and roles in the church.[65]

Third, the issue of the social construction of gender, especially gender complementarity, has often been assumed to be the crusade of first world, dominant culture, North Atlantic feminists. As Brazilian theologian Ivone Gebara has pointed out, however, not acknowledging the social construction of gender fails to acknowledge how evil and suffering are seen differently by women, especially poor women.[66] Basing her understanding of gender theory on the work of the sociologist Pierre Bourdieu, Gebara maintains that

> distinct identities are established as habits through an immense and continuous work of socialization. A game of opposition, verified in every culture, occurs between what is attributed symbolically to men and what is attributed symbolically to women. It leads us to perceive the world according to the principles of the dominant social structure, that is, that this structure seems to be something natural, something that has always operated that way. Based on a social construction of sex, or more precisely on a social definition of sexual identity, this structure is equally responsible for the way the behaviors for each sex are rigidly fixed.[67]

In relationship to the experience of evil, Gebara sees gender analysis as enabling women "to do away with the universalism of male discourse about evil and allows us to enter into the relativity of difference."[68] In using the term "relativity of difference," Gebara intends not to deny biological differences but to disclose something more profound: namely, the fact that the victims are not only the weak, the marginalized of society, but also belong to "the other sex," where maleness is presumed to be the norm. For her, "gender" is a hierarchical and dualistic framework

---

[65] Natalie Watson, *Introducing Feminist Ecclesiology* (Cleveland, OH: The Pilgrim Press, 2002). Mary McClintock Fulkerson's *Places of Redemption: Theology for a Worldly Church* (New York: Oxford University Press, 2007) also provides an excellent example of ecclesiology that utilizes qualitative research and incorporates a feminist perspective.

[66] Ivone Gebara, *Out of the Depths: Women's Experience of Evil and Salvation* (Minneapolis, MN: Fortress Press, 2002), 66–68.

[67] Ibid., 68.

[68] Ibid., 66.

that is culturally produced and is "one of the special locations in which evil demonstrates its work."[69] Thus, she concludes,

> Gender (analysis) calls us to go beyond those fixed models that, for example, oppose Eve to Mary and present them as two contradictory exemplars. The concept of gender exposes the complexity of these symbolic models and leads us to decipher them in the light of social power games between men and women. In this way we can see how culture and politics fabricate gender and how gender builds culture and politics.[70]

Finally, in academic considerations of women's leadership in the church there has been a call to amend the terms of the discussion and move beyond "gender issues" to the analytic of "intersectionality." Such a move, it is argued, would prove to be more inclusive and would provide a needed response to the critiques that gender analysis is primarily a Western preoccupation. As Elisabeth Schüssler Fiorenza has observed,

> gender studies have tended to focus on male/masculine power over wo/men but not on race, class, heteronormativity, disability, colonialism and other structures of domination, a new mode of analysis has become necessary. . . . Conceptualizing gender as a practice that produces sex differences that are infected by race, class, sexual preference, culture, religion, age, and nationality allows one to see that individual wo/men are much more than simply gendered."[71]

Proposing the analysis of "intersectionality" recognizes that identity "is not only constituted by gender, but also by immigrant status, class, education, nationality, sexuality, ability, race, religion, and more. . . . Identity must be seen as multiplex and shaped by intersecting structures of domination."[72] Coined by the African-American legal scholar Kimberlé Crenshaw,[73] this term has been critiqued in terms of its workability "in

---

[69] Ibid., 67.

[70] Ibid.

[71] Schüssler Fiorenza, "Between Movement and Academy," 9–10.

[72] Ibid., 11.

[73] Kimberlé Crenshaw, "Demarginalizing the Intersection of Race and Sex: A Black Feminist Critique of Anti-discrimination Doctrine, Feminist Theory, and Anti-racist Politics," *The University of Chicago Legal Forum 1989: Feminism in the Law; Theory, Practice and Criticism* (1989): 139.

the concrete."[74] Its importance, however, for the discussion of gender complementarity as "the issue under the issues" is to underline that we are dealing with a very complex question when it comes to "a theology of woman." Here again, the use of ethnography in ecclesiology may provide the most fruitful approach to ensuring that the diversity of women's "daily lives" receives a hearing in the formulations of ecclesiology and theological anthropology that intend to include the experience of women in the church.[75]

It has been twenty years since the US Catholic bishops wrote "Strengthening the Bonds of Peace: Pastoral Reflections on Women in the Church and in Society,"[76] their replacement statement for the ill-fated pastoral letter on women in church and society. Writing ten years after that document, Lisa Cahill lamented that "few if any of the bishops' recommendations have been put into practice or even seriously explored by the church hierarchy."[77] We are now ten years more removed from that document, and fifty years removed from the Second Vatican Council. Given the ongoing impasse, it is difficult for many women not to become cynical about the possibility of addressing "the issue under the issues" regarding women's full inclusion in the community of disciples. Cahill cites Elizabeth Johnson, another theologian who continues in her writing to "discipline power" by reminding us of the *productive* power of women who continue to listen attentively to the stirrings of the Spirit: "Brokenness and sin are everywhere. . . . Spirit-Sophia is the source of transforming energy among all creatures. She initiates novelty, instigates change, transforms what is dead into new stretches of life."[78]

---

[74] See, for example, Jennifer C. Nash, "Re-thinking Intersectionality," *Feminist Review* 89 (2008): 1–15. Nash points out the difficulties involved in assessing the "demarcation points" of intersectionality, such as how many are there and how does one pay attention to them?

[75] Ivone Gebara discusses the importance of "daily life" as important sites in recounting the historiography of women in *Out of the Depths*, 77–78.

[76] USCCB, "Strengthening the Bonds of Peace: Pastoral Reflections on Women in the Church and in Society," http://www.usccb.org/about/laity-marriage-family -life-and-youth/womens-issues/strengthening-the-bonds-of-peace.cfm, accessed November 22, 2014.

[77] Lisa Sowle Cahill, "Feminist Theology and a Participatory Church," in *Common Calling: The Laity & Governance in the Catholic Church*, ed. Stephen J. Pope (Washington, DC: Georgetown University Press, 2004), 145.

[78] Elizabeth A. Johnson, *She Who Is: The Mystery of God in Feminist Theological Discourse* (New York: Crossroad, 1992), 135.

For Further Reading

Abraham, Susan, and Elena Procario-Foley, eds. *Frontiers in Catholic Feminist Theology*. Minneapolis, MN: Fortress Press, 2009.

Cahill, Lisa Sowle. "Feminist Theology and a Participatory Church." In *Common Calling: The Laity & Governance in the Catholic Church*, edited by Stephen J. Pope, 127–49. Washington, DC: Georgetown University Press, 2004.

Gebara, Ivone. *Out of the Depths: Women's Experience of Evil and Salvation*. Minneapolis, MN: Fortress Press, 2002.

Griffith, Colleen M., ed. *Prophetic Witness: Catholic Women's Strategies for Reform*. New York: Herder and Herder, 2009.

Gudorf, Christine. "Encountering the Other: The Modern Papacy on Women." In *Change in Official Catholic Moral Teachings, Readings in Moral Theology*, vol. 13, edited by Charles E. Curran, 269–84. New York: Paulist Press, 2003.

Hines, Mary E. "Community for Liberation: Church." In *Freeing Theology: The Essentials of Theology in Feminist Perspective*, ed. Catherine Mowry LaCugna, 161–84. San Francisco: HarperSanFrancisco, 1993.

Hinsdale, Mary Ann. *Women Shaping Theology*. New York: Paulist Press, 2006.

Johnson, Elizabeth A., ed. *The Church Women Want: Catholic Women in Dialogue*. New York: Herder and Herder, 2002.

McEnroy, M. Carmel. *Guests in Their Own House: The Women at Vatican II*. New York: Crossroad, 1996. Reprint. Eugene, OR: Wipf and Stock, 2011.

Patrick, Anne E. *Conscience and Calling: Ethical Reflections on Catholic Women's Church Vocations*. New York: Bloomsbury, 2013.

Schüssler Fiorenza, Elisabeth. *Discipleship of Equals: A Critical Feminist Ekklesia-logy of Liberation*. New York: Crossroad, 1993.

Watson, Natalie K. *Introducing Feminist Ecclesiology*. Cleveland, OH: The Pilgrim Press, 2008.

CHAPTER 7

Liturgical Ecclesiology

Susan K. Wood, SCL

The liturgy provides a rich resource for developing an ecclesiology based on the principle that that which is celebrated symbolically in liturgical time reflects what is lived out ecclesially in historical time. The chief manifestation of the church is liturgical according to *Sacrosanctum Concilium* (The Constitution on the Sacred Liturgy): "the principal manifestation of the church consists in the full, active participation of all God's holy people in the same liturgical celebrations, especially in the same Eucharist, in one prayer, at one altar, at which the bishop presides, surrounded by his college of priests and by his ministers" (SC 41). The liturgical assembly reflects the diversity of the people of God as an ordered communion according to the various charisms and offices of that people. Thus it is not surprising that there have been various attempts to construct a sacramental or liturgical ecclesiology.

This chapter begins with an ecumenical consideration of sacramental ecclesiologies rooted in either baptism or in Eucharist. It then examines some possibilities for how an analysis of liturgical relationships, such as the role of the assembly in the liturgy, may elucidate ecclesiology. As we will see, one advantage of mining liturgical and sacramental theology for an ecclesiology is that the liturgy provides an alternative to secular political models, such as democracy or monarchy, as the basis for articulating ecclesial relationships.

Eucharistic Ecclesiologies

Although a eucharistic ecclesiology is a development of the twentieth century, particularly in the work of Orthodox theologians such as Nicholas Afanasiev (1893–1966) and John D. Zizioulas (b. 1931), its roots go back to St. Ignatius of Antioch (c. 35–107), who wrote, "Take care to observe one Eucharist: for there is one flesh of our Lord Jesus Christ, and one cup for union in his blood, one altar, just as there is one bishop, together with the presbytery and the deacons my fellow-servants."[1] The church is one because it is assembled around one altar under the presidency of one bishop, and receives communion in the one Body and Blood of Christ. In his *Letter to the Smyrneans*, Ignatius also emphasizes the role and person of the bishop, especially with respect to the Eucharist: "Let the Eucharist be considered valid which is held under the bishop or under someone whom he appoints. Wherever the bishop appears, there let the people be, just as wherever Jesus Christ is, there is the Catholic Church. . . . He who does anything without the bishop's knowledge is serving the devil."[2] A eucharistic ecclesiology is particularly suited for considering church structures and ordained ministries since a theology of the episcopacy derives from a theology of the Eucharist, and the celebration of the Eucharist is conditioned by its authoritative minister.

Nicolas Afanasiev's eucharistic ecclesiology, drawn from the letters of St. Ignatius of Antioch, the *Didache*, and certain other early Christian texts, is in opposition to what he called a "universal ecclesiology," which he attributes to St. Cyprian.[3] Afanasiev stresses the local over the universal:

> As the body of Christ, the Church manifests herself in all her fullness
> in the eucharistic assembly of the local church, because Christ is

---

[1] "Ignatius of Antioch to the Philadelphians," in *The Apostolic Fathers*, ed. and trans. J. B. Lightfoot and J. R. Harmer (London: Macmillan, 1893), 124.

[2] "Ignatius of Antioch to the Smyrnaeans," in *The Apostolic Fathers*, ed. and trans. J. B. Lightfoot and J. R. Harmer (London: Macmillan, 1893), 129–30.

[3] See Nicolas Afanasiev, "Una sancta," in *Tradition Alive: On the Church and the Christian Life in Our Time; Readings from the Eastern Church*, ed. Michael Plekon (New York: Rowman & Littlefield, 2003), 3–30; Afanasiev, "Le sacrement de l'assemblie," *Internationale Kirchliche Zeitschrifte* 4 (1956); Afanasiev, "The Church which Presides in Love," in *The Primacy of Peter*, ed. John Meyendorff (London: The Faith Press, 1963), 57–110; and Afanasiev, *The Church of the Holy Spirit* (Notre Dame, IN: University of Notre Dame Press, 2007).

present in the Eucharist in the fullness of his body. This is why the local church possesses all the fullness of the Church. Put differently, she is the Church of God in Christ. The fullness of the nature of the Church determines her unity, which finds its expression in the eucharistic assembly of each local church.[4]

The eucharistic assembly is the empirical sign of the church. Those who participate in the assembly belong to the church and the limits of the church are determined by the limits of the eucharistic assembly. Afanasiev's eucharistic ecclesiology does not exclude the bishop since the eucharistic assembly cannot exist without its president, that is, the bishop, who by definition is the one who presides at the eucharistic assembly.

The eucharistic model for the church's life is evident when all the clergy and faithful in their diversity are gathered together under the presidency of the one bishop. Since the Eucharist is only celebrated locally, at a specific assembly of the faithful gathered in the same place, and since Christ is wholly present at each Eucharist, it follows that the local church celebrating the Eucharist in a particular place is wholly church, the church catholic in this particular place. Each local church, no matter where it is located, possesses the same unity and the same fullness. Afanasiev's fundamental principle of eucharistic ecclesiology claims, "Where the eucharist is, there is the fullness of the Church."[5] This unity of the local churches means that their bishops possess the same unity and equality, although some local churches may "preside in love." This unity does not negate the diversity inherent to unique locales of the churches. Afanasiev uses a eucharistic ecclesiology to justify intercommunion between Orthodox and Roman Catholics.

John A. Zizioulas (Metropolitan John of Pergamon) is a contemporary Orthodox theologian who has modified Afanasiev's eucharistic theology. He points to the need for churches to share the same teaching and communion among bishops in order to share eucharistic communion.[6] Zizioulas cautions that the theory of eucharistic ecclesiology, taken to its

---

[4] Afanasiev, "Una sancta," 14.

[5] Afanasiev, "The Church which Presides in Love," 76.

[6] John Zizioulas, *Being as Communion: Studies in Personhood and the Church* (Crestwood, NY: St. Vladimir's Seminary Press, 1985); John Zizioulas, *Eucharist, Bishop, Church: The Unity of the Church in the Divine Eucharist and the Bishop in the First Three Centuries*, trans. Elizabeth Theokritoff (Brookline, MA: Holy Cross Orthodox Press, 2001); John Zizioulas, *Communion and Otherness* (New York: T & T Clark, 2006).

ultimate conclusion, can lead to unacceptable and dangerous positions since other essential elements such as right faith are required.[7] Zizioulas challenges Afanasiev's eucharistic theology beginning with his analysis of the contrast between the eucharistic ecclesiology of Ignatius and the universal ecclesiology of Cyprian, criticizing him for giving priority to the local over the universal aspects of the church. He says, "while the view of the Eucharist as the element incarnating and expressing the Church *par excellence* is correct, the view that this is the *sole sine qua non* condition for the notion of the Church and her unity could not be accepted so unreservedly."[8] Zizioulas has spent much of his career developing a theology of the relationship between the local churches and the universal church based on a relationship of unity and difference in analogy to trinitarian relations of persons-in-communion.

In doing so, Zizioulas broadened eucharistic ecclesiology into an ecclesiology of communion.[9] Where Afanasiev emphasized the qualitative and intensive aspect of catholicity in the Eucharist, Zizioulas identifies the communion existing among the churches as essential to catholicity. Where Afanasiev's eucharistic theology, with its historical basis in the second-century patristic model of the bishop presiding at the Eucharist, tended to identify the local church with the parish (a model no longer viable because most parishes are led by presbyters rather than bishops), Zizioulas identifies the fullness of the local church with the diocese as the community that incorporates all the ecclesial orders inclusive of the deacon, bishop, and even the laity.[10] Zizioulas laments what he considers to be a rupture in Orthodox eucharistic ecclesiology, hoping that "one day the bishop will find his proper place which is the Eucharist, and the rupture in eucharistic ecclesiology caused by the problem 'parish-diocese' will be healed."[11] For eucharistic ecclesiology to become viable, he sees the necessity of small episcopal dioceses.

Zizioulas has been criticized for being too strongly episcopo-centric, implying that the bishop is the sole channel of grace and authority within the church, which leads him to omit things like the inner appropriation

---

[7] Zizioulas, *Eucharist, Bishop, Church*, 257.

[8] Ibid.

[9] See John H. Erickson, "The Church in Modern Orthodox Thought: Towards a Baptismal Ecclesiology," *International Journal for the Study of the Christian Church* 11, nos. 2–3 (2011): 143.

[10] Zizioulas, *Being as Communion*, 251.

[11] Ibid.

of the grace of the Eucharist by each believer personally, the succession of "elders," that is, of spiritual mothers and fathers in the church, and a robust discussion of other sacraments.[12] Despite these shortcomings, Kallistos Ware judges that in the period from 1965 onward, no new ecclesial model has emerged within Orthodoxy to replace or to rival the eucharistic approach upheld by Afanasiev and Zizioulas.[13]

John Erickson, an Orthodox theologian, aptly questions whether Zizioulas and other proponents of eucharistic ecclesiology have adequately reflected on how the present context of the church has affected the meaning of "place" and "local" where one's "place" is no longer a small city and "local" does not necessarily imply geographic territoriality.[14] He identifies some of the problems associated with a eucharistic ecclesiology such as an idealized second-century church order considered as normative in every detail for all ages and situations; the tendency for a local church to become self-satisfied, introverted, with little tolerance for diversity and little concern for mission; the danger of triumphalism if a theology of the Eucharist as banquet of the kingdom loses sight of its proleptic nature; and the danger of "ecclesiological and soteriological exclusivism" when the limits of the church are identified too rigidly with the limits of the Orthodox Church's eucharistic fellowship.[15]

Baptismal Ecclesiologies

Eucharistic ecclesiologies do not necessarily neglect a theology of baptism. In fact, the great attention given to Orthodox eucharistic ecclesiology may obscure the importance of Orthodox insights into baptism. Paul Meyendoff, while recognizing the positive contributions of a eucharistic ecclesiology, calls for a baptismal ecclesiology to help his own Orthodox tradition improve relations with other Christians, counteract increased clericalism, recover a robust theology of the priesthood of the baptized, make more explicit the role of the Holy Spirit, and find a middle

---

[12] Kallistos Ware, "Sobornost and Eucharistic Ecclesiology: Aleksei Khomiakov and His Successors," *International Journal for the Study of the Christian Church* 11, nos. 2–3 (2011): 231–33.

[13] Ibid., 231.

[14] Erickson, "The Church in Modern Orthodox Thought," 144–45. See also Radu Bordeianu, "Orthodox-Catholic Dialogue: Retrieving Eucharistic Ecclesiology," *Journal of Ecumenical Studies* 44, no. 2 (Spring 2009): 239–65.

[15] Erickson, "The Church in Modern Orthodox Thought," 147–49.

ground between full ecclesial communion and no communion.[16] Both Afanasiev and Zizioulas speak of baptism and chrismation as an ordination of the royal priesthood to participate in the eucharistic assembly.[17] This is not an ordination of lay people but of "laics," understood as all the members of God's people.[18] Afanasiev interprets this ordination saying, "The newly baptized, spiritually born in the sacrament of baptism, is ordained for service in the Church, for carrying out his calling as a member of God's people, a nation of kings and priests."[19] Thus the church consists of those who are ordained. A lay person cannot be viewed in opposition to the consecrated but only in opposition to the nonconsecrated, that is, to those who are not in the church or members of God's people.[20] Theologically, "there can be no 'lay people' in the church."[21] This Orthodox insight bears enormous implications for a theology of the laity in general, lay ministry in particular, and for a theology of the liturgical assembly.

The attention to baptism found in these Orthodox theologians is even more prominent within recent Anglican reflections. A baptismal ecclesiology gains prominence within the Anglican Communion, especially in the American context, beginning in the latter part of the twentieth century. Colin Podmore traces the foundations of a baptismal ecclesiology within the Episcopal Church to the 1979 *Book of Common Prayer*,[22] as well as to the significant changes in baptismal practice and theology—away from a rite focused primarily on the individual to a sacrament constituting the church understood as the community of the baptized.[23]

---

[16] Paul Meyendorff, "Towards a Baptismal Ecclesiology," in *Liturgies in East and West: Ecumenical Relevance of Early Liturgical Development; Acts of the International Symposium Vindobonense I, Vienna, November 17–20, 2007*, ed. Hans-Jürgen Feulner (Berlin: Lit Verlag, 2013), 285–94.

[17] Afanasiev, *The Church of the Holy Spirit*, 24; Zizioulas, *Being as Communion*, 216.

[18] Afanasiev, *The Church of the Holy Spirit*, 25.

[19] Ibid., 30.

[20] Ibid., 31.

[21] Ibid.

[22] Episcopal Church, *The Book of Common Prayer and Administration of the Sacraments and Other Rites and Ceremonies of the Church: Together with the Psalter or Psalms of David According to the Use of the Episcopal Church* (New York: Seabury Press, 1979).

[23] Colin Podmore, "The Baptismal Revolution in the American Episcopal Church: Baptismal Ecclesiology and the Baptismal Covenant," *Ecclesiology* 6 (2010): 14. Podmore reports that Ruth Meyers, who succeeded Louis Weil as liturgics professor at the Church Divinity School of the Pacific in 2009, traces the Episcopal Church's adoption of a baptismal ecclesiology in a developed sense to a 2003 booklet by

As Podmore observes, the American Episcopalian understanding of baptismal ecclesiology goes beyond seeing baptism as constitutive of the church to seeing it "as the fount of all ministry within it, lay and ordained."[24] He attributes the warm reception of baptismal ecclesiology on the part of the American Episcopal Church to its democratic, egalitarian, and antihierarchical nature.[25]

A group known as the Associated Parishes for Liturgy and Mission (AP) published two booklets in 1978, the year before the appearance of the revised *Book of Common Prayer*. The first booklet, titled *Ministry I: Holy Baptism*, developed the understanding of baptism as ordination to ministry. It included the statement, "in the anointing, the person has been ordained to the lay ministry of the church completely."[26] This was most likely in response to an intra-Anglican discussion of whether or not confirmation constituted an ordination to lay ministry. The second booklet, titled *Ministry II: Laity, Bishops, Priests, and Deacons*, continued this baptismal emphasis, stating, "The full ministry of the Church is given in Holy Baptism. . . . In this sense, everyone baptized into the Body of Christ is ordained into the ministry. Every Christian functions as a minister of the Gospel and participates in the functioning of the episcopate, the priesthood, and the diaconate."[27] The second text comments, "The Spirit was given in baptism and it is clear that there can be nothing more to give to the Christian person. Rather, ordination 'activates' the gift of the Spirit for a particular function within the Body of Christ."[28] The booklet concludes, "It would be difficult to distinguish completely among the four ministries of the Church. Each ministry seems to flow into the others and partake of their richness."[29] These statements suggest that nothing further is given to an individual in ordination other

---

C. Kilmer Myers, *Baptized into the One Church* (New York: Seabury, 1963), 19, published by the Episcopal Church's Department of Initiation. For an Episcopal baptismal ecclesiology, see also Ruth Meyers, *Continuing the Reformation: Re-Visioning Baptism in the Episcopal Church* (New York: Church Publishing, 1997).

[24] Podmore, "The Baptismal Revolution," 14–15.

[25] Ibid., 15.

[26] Associated Parishes for Liturgy and Mission, *Ministry I: Holy Baptism* (Alexandria, VA: Associated Parishes, 1978), 4, 8.

[27] Associated Parishes for Liturgy and Mission, *Ministry II: Laity, Bishops, Priests, and Deacons* (Alexandria, VA: Associated Parishes, 1978), 1.

[28] Ibid., 4.

[29] Associated Parishes, *Ministry II*, 6.

than perhaps an authorization to exercise what has already been received in baptism, reflecting a fundamentally egalitarian approach to ministry.

The Catechism of the Episcopal Church in the back of the *Book of Common Prayer* reflects this baptismal ecclesiology when it identifies the ministers of the church as lay persons, bishops, priests, and deacons, and then describes the ministry of the laity as "to represent Christ and his Church; to bear witness to him wherever they may be; and, according to the gifts given them, to carry on Christ's work of reconciliation in the world; and to take their place in the life, worship, and governance of the Church."[30]

In 2001, the Sixth International Anglican Liturgical Consultation issued the statement *To Equip the Saints*, which promoted a baptismal ecclesiology as the appropriate foundation for understanding Anglican orders. "Understanding baptism as the life and ministry of the church (that is, having a baptismal ecclesiology) leads us to see ordained ministers as integral members of the body of Christ"[31] and baptism as foundational for any understanding of ministry.

This baptismal theology is developed in opposition to a view of ministry as conferring a status elevating ordained ministers above the laity and as a correction to a clericalism implying a separation between clergy and the laity.[32] While the intention of the 2001 report was not to be minimalist or reductionist, to exclude other dimensions of ecclesiology, or to imply that there is no differentiation of ministerial roles, it raises questions about whether such egalitarianism is possible and whether baptism is sufficient to support a theology of ministry. Paul Gibson, for example, questions whether "the equality established by baptism can carry the full freight of a theology of ministry and order."[33] In his opinion, a theology of ministry and order should be built on a eucharistic ecclesiology since Jesus' table fellowship appears to be more central to his ministry

---

[30] Episcopal Church, *Book of Common Prayer*, 855–56.

[31] "Baptism and Ministry," in *To Equip the Saints*, ed. Paul Gibson (Cambridge, UK: Grove Books Limited, 2002), http://www.anglicancommunion.org/resources/liturgy/docs/berkeley.pdf, accessed August 7, 2014.

[32] Louis Weil, "Baptismal Ecclesiology: Uncovering a Paradigm," in *Equipping the Saints*, ed. Paul Gibson (Dublin: Columba Press, 2006), 22, cites the remarks of Professor William Crockett, the IALC consultant, to the Inter-Anglican Standing Commission on Ecumenical Relations.

[33] Paul Gibson, "A Baptismal Ecclesiology—Some Questions," in *Equipping the Saints*, ed. Paul Gibson (Dublin: Columba Press, 2006), 35.

than baptism, especially as practiced by John.[34] Commenting that he does not believe baptism is about the structure of the church, he says, "Baptism is the door; the table is where structure and order are defined."[35]

While Roman Catholics can affirm many of the principles of this baptismal ecclesiology, it raises questions about the relationship between the ordained ministry and the priesthood of the baptized. Catholics would certainly affirm that ordained ministers are integral members of the Body of Christ and that ordained ministry is situated within the church, not above it. Thus baptism is the ground for all discussion of ministry. Catholics would also agree that the ordained priesthood enables the priesthood of the faithful to exercise their priesthood in the liturgy.[36]

The framework provided by *Lumen Gentium* (The Dogmatic Constitution on the Church), which situates the chapter on the church as the people of God prior to the chapter on the hierarchy, reflects this relationship between the priesthood of the baptized and the ordained. All Christians belong to the people of God before there are any distinctions between lay and ordained. Once ordained, a deacon, priest, or bishop does not lose his baptismal character but always remains a member of the baptized people of God. His ordination is a repositioning within that people and within the liturgical assembly such that he is able to function *in persona Christi capitis* and *in persona ecclesiae*.[37] Thus ordained ministry is always within the community of the baptized, not apart from it or above it. All the baptized put on Christ and become, in some sense, an *alter Christus*, as the Episcopalians would hold, but differences in how the baptized represent Christ and how the ordained represent Christ become particularly evident in church governance and in liturgical ministry. Catholics hold that the priesthood of the baptized and the ministerial priesthood are interrelated, but that they "differ essentially and not only in degree," a difference that exceeds a difference in authorization to perform certain functions (LG 10).

What is unclear for a Catholic listening in on the Anglican discussions of baptismal ecclesiology is whether there is any differentiation in how

---

[34] Ibid., 41.

[35] Ibid., 44.

[36] *Catechism of the Catholic Church* (Collegeville, MN: Liturgical Press, 1994), 1547.

[37] See Richard R. Gaillardetz, "Ecclesiological Foundations of Ministry in an Ordered Communion," in *Ordering the Baptismal Priesthood*, ed. Susan K. Wood (Collegeville, MN: Liturgical Press, 2003), 36.

the laity, bishop, priest, and deacon represent Christ. The tendency in this theology seems to be that ordination does not confer a distinct grace of office but that it is an authorization to exercise publicly a priesthood already given to every Christian in baptism. The weight of argument bears on the meaning of the assertion that all ministry is "derived" from baptism. There is a difference, however, between deriving ordained ministry from baptism and holding that baptism is foundational for all ministry. To affirm the latter does not necessitate the former insofar as baptism is prior to any subsequent differentiation of vocation, state in life, or ministry.

If the egalitarianism in the Episcopalian baptismal theology accurately represents the Episcopalian position, this stands in some tension with the 1973 statement of the Anglican-Roman Catholic International Commission, "Ministry and Ordination": "Their [Christian ministers] ministry is not an extension of the common Christian priesthood but belongs to another realm of the gifts of the Spirit. It exists to help the church to be 'a royal priesthood, a holy nation, God's own people.'"[38] One senses here a distinct difference between the baptismal theology of the Church of England and that of the Episcopal Church (ECUSA). Paul Avis, a prominent theologian of the Church of England, for example, differs from the Episcopal Church on the notion of completeness being achieved in baptism.[39] A conclusion of the report of the Church of England's Faith and Order Advisory Group, *The Mission and Ministry of the Whole Church*, contrasts with the view of the Episcopal Church that all the baptized have a ministry when it states, "Discipleship is intrinsic to being a baptized follower of Jesus Christ. Ministry is something that is subsequently discerned and for which we need to be called and equipped. All ministers should be disciples, but not all disciples are necessarily ministers."[40] A final difference noted by Podmore is the change in the

---

[38] Anglican-Roman Catholic International Commission, *The Final Report* (London: CTS /SPCK, 1982), 13; also in *Ecumenical Documents*, vol. 2, *Growth in Agreement*, ed. Harding Meyer and Lukas Vischer (New York: Paulist Press, 1984), 82.

[39] See Paul Avis, "Is Baptism 'Complete Sacramental Initiation'?" in *The Journey of Christian Initiation: Theological and Pastoral Perspectives* (Church House Publishing: Faith and Order Commission of the General Synod of the Church of England, 2011), 6–21. There are also differences in the theology and practice of confirmation, but these will not be discussed here.

[40] Faith and Order Advisory Group, Church of England, *The Mission and Ministry of the Whole Church: Biblical, Theological, Historical and Contemporary Perspectives* (London: General Synod, 2007), 25.

fifth question of the Baptismal Covenant. The Episcopalian question asks: "Will you strive for justice and peace among all people and respect the dignity of every human being?" The question in the Church of England's 1998 Common Worship Baptism and Confirmation services locates this question within a more comprehensive context, "Will you acknowledge Christ's authority over human society, by prayer for the world and its leaders, by defending the weak and by seeking peace and justice?" The latter question asks the baptized to seek peace and justice as members of an ordered society, not merely as individuals.[41] Furthermore, the question in the rite for the Church of England occurs after baptism and does not appear to be a condition for baptism by occurring before baptism as in the Episcopal rite.

This very brief overview of eucharistic and baptismal ecclesiologies points to each having an ecclesiological agenda supported by a particular sacramental ecclesiology. Afansiev supported a theology of the local church over the universal church. Zizioulas's ecclesiology of communion seeks to reconcile a local and universal ecclesiology at the same time it serves an ecumenical agenda by developing a model of church unity. John Erickson expresses the desire to transcend the issue of local and universal in order to promote mission and counteract the dangers of triumphalism and exclusivism through the adoption of a baptismal ecclesiology. The Episcopalian adoption of a baptismal ecclesiology provides a theological justification of a democratic and egalitarian approach to ministry as well as the ordination of women and homosexual persons.[42] Obviously a balanced ecclesiology needs to appeal to both its eucharistic and its baptismal foundations. A more comprehensive liturgical ecclesiology emerges from the dynamics embedded within the liturgy itself as well as in principles of liturgical renewal and implementation.

---

[41] Podmore, "The Baptismal Revolution," 34.

[42] See Podmore's discussion of the significance of a baptismal ecclesiology for the ordination of women (ibid., 23–26) and the relationship between the baptismal covenant and the ordination of women and homosexual persons (ibid., 31). In 1974 and 1975, fifteen women were irregularly ordained in the Episcopal Church, but ecclesiastical authorities did not recognize their ordinations. The Rev. Jacqueline Means was ordained January 1, 1977 under a new canon that had been approved at the General Convention in September 1976. See Episcopal News Service, "First Woman Regularly Ordained to Episcopal Priesthood" (January 6, 1977), http://www.episcopalarchives .org/cgi-bin/ENS/ENSpress_release.pl?pr_number=77002, accessed August 9, 2014.

A Liturgical Theology of the Assembly

As the above paragraphs imply, a number of ecclesiological themes can be developed through the lens of the liturgy. Chapter 2 of *Lumen Gentium* states that the sacred character and the organic structure of the priestly community are brought into effect by means of the sacraments and the virtues (LG 11). Thus one can expect to find an ecclesiology embedded in the liturgy.

For example, a theology of authority can be enhanced by attention to the liturgical foundations of authority within the worshipping assembly. In particular, a theology of episcopal authority can be extracted both from the rite of episcopal ordination and from the eucharistic liturgy at which the bishop presides.[43] In the liturgy, authority is envisioned not as power over another but as empowerment to fulfill one's responsibilities among the differentiated members that make up the Body of Christ. The words in *Lumen Gentium* that describe episcopal authority as "proper, ordinary and immediate" (LG 27) give us a theology of the bishop who is not simply a delegate of the Vatican but who exercises his own authority within a theology of communion with the other bishops in union with the bishop of Rome. Similarly, liturgical rituals "speak" of various kinds of authority. A married couple exercises authority within the family based on the covenant they forge in marriage. The whole people of God exercises an authority based on their reception of the gift of the Holy Spirit in baptism and confirmation, which confer on all disciples a supernatural sense of the faith to recognize and receive the truth of the Gospel (*sensus fidei*) (LG 12).

The remainder of this chapter demonstrates how ecclesiology is embedded within the dynamics of liturgical action by examining a theology of the liturgical assembly.[44] As Alexander Schmemann reminds us, "[T]he purpose of worship is to constitute the church."[45] To this Gordon Lathrop adds, "[T]o interpret the assembly is to interpret the meaning of 'church' and the church's faith."[46]

---

[43] See Susan K. Wood, "A Liturgical Theology of the Episcopacy," in *Unfailing Patience and Sound Teaching: Reflections on Episcopal Ministry in Honor of Rembert G. Weakland, O.S.B.*, ed. David A. Stosur (Collegeville, MN: Liturgical Press, 2003), 31–44.

[44] Gordon W. Lathrop, a Lutheran, does this from a different perspective in his *Holy People: A Liturgical Ecclesiology* (Minneapolis, MN: Fortress Press, 1993).

[45] Alexander Schmemann, *Introduction to Liturgical Theology* (New York: St. Vladimir's Press, 1975), 19.

[46] Lathrop, *Holy Things*, 9.

A theology of the liturgical assembly provides a theology for how the various orders in the church interrelate with one another. A theology of the assembly is not simply a theology of the laity since the liturgical assembly includes all those present at liturgy—bishop, presbyters, deacons, and lay faithful. In other words, the liturgical assembly is not simply those folks who sit in the nave of the church. It is not the people vis-à-vis the priest celebrant, but rather the entire people of God gathered by word and sacrament in liturgical prayer, inclusive of the ordained presider. Nevertheless, the assembly provides insight into the interrelationship between the laity and the ordained clergy. Since this liturgical assembly is the subject or agent of the liturgical action, the lay members of the assembly are not simply passive observers of liturgical actions performed by the ordained but active participants along with the presider.

The historical origins of the liturgical assembly lie in Jewish self-consciousness and in the continuity between the Jewish synagogue in the Second Temple period and the early church.[47] The Jews officially described themselves as an assembly. In the postexilic literature, terms such as *qahal* and *ekklesia*, both meaning "to call" or "to convene," were used to designate the Jewish people as the Israelites came to a self-understanding as a people convened or assembled by God. Paul used *ekklesia* to refer to Christians gathered in a house (Phlm 2), for Christians assembled for worship (1 Cor 11:18), or to designate a number of house churches in a city (1 Thess 2:14).[48]

The sacred character of this assembly, its sacred origins, and its liturgical identity is expressed in *Lumen Gentium* 26:

> This church of Christ is really present in all legitimately organized local groups of the faithful which, united with their pastors, are also called churches in the New Testament. For these are in fact, in their own localities, the new people called by God, in the holy Spirit and with full conviction (see 1 Thess 1:5). In them the faithful are gathered together by the preaching of the Gospel of Christ, and the mystery of the Lord's Supper is celebrated "so that, by means of the flesh and blood of the Lord the whole brotherhood and sisterhood of the

[47] See R. Kevin Seasoltz, "The Liturgical Assembly: Light from Some Recent Scholarship," in *Rule of Prayer, Rule of Faith: Essays in Honor of Aidan Kavanagh, O.S.B.* (Collegeville, MN: Liturgical Press, 1996), 307.

[48] Margaret Mary Kelleher, "Assembly," in *The New Dictionary of Theology*, ed. Joseph A. Komonchak, Mary Collins, and Dermot A. Lane (Wilmington, DE: Michael Glazier, 1987), 68. See also Judith M. Kubicki, *The Presence of Christ in the Gathered Assembly* (New York: Continuum, 2006), 33–59.

body may be welded together." In any community of the altar, under the sacred ministry of the bishop, a manifest symbol is to be seen of that charity and "unity of the mystical body, without which there can be no salvation." In these communities, though they may often be small and poor, or dispersed, Christ is present through whose power and influence the one, holy, catholic and apostolic church is constituted.

Thus, even though a eucharistic community is not a local church in and of itself, Catholicism defines a particular church eucharistically in terms of word, sacrament, and ministry. As Joseph Komonchak notes, a first dimension of the local churches is liturgical.[49]

In the liturgy, this theological understanding of assembly is essential, for God is the one who convokes the assembly. The assembly is not just any human gathering or an arbitrary congregation but the assembly *of God*. Moreover, within a Christian understanding, this people of God is also the Body of Christ and therefore not a profane gathering but a sacred gathering for a sacred people with a sacred identity. As Hans Küng aptly puts it, "the *congregation fidelium* only exists as *con-vocatio Dei*, the *communio sanctorum* only exists as *institutio Dei*."[50] Aspects of the liturgy that focus on the assembly cannot therefore be accused of a "horizontalism" that detracts from the liturgy's sacred character but instead should be considered as elements respectful of the incarnational economy of Christianity.

According to *Sacrosanctum Concilium*, the liturgy is an ecclesial event. The document clearly states, "Liturgical services are not private functions but are celebrations of the church which is 'the sacrament of unity,' namely, the holy people united and organized under their bishops" (SC 26). This inclusive character of the liturgy is evident in several principles.

First, the primary principle of liturgical renewal is that "all of the faithful should be led to take that full, conscious, and active part in liturgical celebrations which is demanded by the very nature of the liturgy, and to which the Christian people, 'a chosen race, a royal priesthood, a holy nation, a redeemed people' (1 Pet 2:9; 4-5) have a right and to which they are bound by reason of their Baptism" (SC 14). This active participation goes beyond laws governing valid and lawful celebration (SC 11).

---

[49] Joseph A. Komonchak, "The Significance of Vatican Council II for Ecclesiology," in *The Gift of the Church*, ed. Peter Phan (Collegeville, MN: Liturgical Press, 2000), 80.
[50] Hans Küng, *The Church* (New York: Sheed and Ward, 1967), 86.

Second, Christ is present most of all in the eucharistic species, but also in the person of the minister, in the word, and in the assembly (SC 7). Even though *Sacrosanctum Concilium* says that Christ is present "most of all" in the eucharistic species, his presence in the assembly is not just a pious platitude or afterthought. It is actually essential to the dynamism of the eucharistic anaphora insofar as the doxological and trinitarian movement of the liturgy is oriented to the transformation of the people of God into the Body of Christ that they may return with him in his self-offering to the Father. The assembly gives thanks and praise to the Father, remembers the Son, and invokes the Holy Spirit to transform the gifts into the Body and Blood of Christ and to transform the assembly into a community of unity. The liturgy commemorates the great *exitus-reditus* wherein the people of God recognizes the Father as the Creator who gives the gifts that are transformed in the power of the Holy Spirit into the Body of Christ and returned in offering to the Father. The ultimate purpose of the eucharistic liturgy is not the confection of the *res et sacramentum*—the consecration of bread and wine into the real Body and Blood of Christ. Instead, the real presence of Christ in the Eucharist, the *res et sacramentum*, is itself oriented to the *res*, the unity of the assembly in Christ, both personally, in an individual's reception of communion, and communally, as all are united in Christ by partaking of one bread (1 Cor 10:16-17). The Body of Christ does not exist sacramentally for its own sake, but, in the words of St. Augustine, is given to us that we may become what we eat—the Body of Christ. Sacramental unity effects ecclesial unity in and through union with Christ.

The eucharistic prayer offers a theologically rich indication of the ordained minister's engagement of the priesthood of the faithful. While it is true that the priest recites the words of institution in the first person and recites the anaphora by himself, aside from the words of institution, the anaphora is in the first person plural. Thus the priest is speaking it in the name of the rest of the assembly. Hervé Legrand's analysis of the liturgical vocabulary of the first millennium shows in the Roman sacramentaries the subject of the verb "celebrate" is always the "we" of the assembly, never the "I" of the priest.[51] The liturgical "we" made Lombard say that a priest cut off from the Church could not validly

---

[51] Hervé-Marie Legrand, "The Presidency of Eucharist According to the Ancient Tradition," *Worship* 53 (1979): 432; also published in *Living Bread, Saving Cup: Readings on the Eucharist*, ed. R. Kevin Seasoltz (Collegeville, MN: Liturgical Press, 1987), 196–221; Benedicta Droste, *"Celebrare,"* in *Der römischen Liturgiesprache* (Munich: Max Hueber, 1963), 3–80. Droste notes on page 80 of her study an exception in the rubrics

celebrate Mass since he could not say *offerimus quasi ex persona Ecclesiae* in the anamnesis.[52]

This liturgical "we" is further emphasized in the dialogue between priest and people in the liturgy. For example, in the exchange, "The Lord be with you," and the response, "And with your spirit," there is a reciprocal recognition of the Lord's presence in both the assembly and in the minister.[53] St. John Chrysostom commented that the eucharistic prayer is a common prayer because the priest does not give thanks (which is to say that he does not celebrate the Eucharist, the "thanksgiving") alone but only with the people. He does not begin the eucharistic prayer without first gathering the faithful and assuring their agreement to enter into this action through the dialogue: "Lift up your hearts." "We lift them up to the Lord." "Let us give thanks to the Lord our God." "It is right to give him thanks and praise."[54] In our own time, the *General Instruction of the Roman Missal* states that the dialogue between the celebrant and the faithful gathered together and the acclamations "are not simply outward signs of the community's celebration, but . . . encourage and achieve a greater communion between priest and people."[55]

---

of the *Gelasian Sacramentary* but comments that even there it is clear that the priest does not celebrate alone but with the community.

[52] P. Lombard, *Sent.* 4.13. See B. D. Marliangeas, *Clés pour une théologie du ministère: 'In persona Christi, in persona Ecclesiae'* (Paris: Beauchesne, 1978), 55–60.

[53] Yves Congar, "L'Ecclesia ou communauté chrétienne, sujet intégrale de l'action ligurgique," in *La Liturgie après Vatican II*, ed. J.-P. Jossua and Yves Congar, *Unum sanctam* 66 (Paris: Cerf, 1967), 277.

[54] "The eucharistic prayer is common; the priest does not give thanks alone, but the people with him, for he begins it only having received the accord of the faithful. . . . If I say that, it is so that we learn that we are all a single body. Therefore let us not rely on the priests for everything, but let us, too, care for the Church." John Chrysostom, *Com. in 1 Cor.* Hom. 8, 3, in *Patrologia Graeca*, ed. Jacques Paul Migne (Paris: Impremerie Catholique, 1857–1866), 61, 527. This is a frequently cited text, attesting to its importance; Congar, " 'L'ecclesia' ou commmunauté chrétienne," 277–78; Legrand, "The Presidency of Eucharist according to the Ancient Tradition," 435.

[55] *General Instruction of the Roman Missal* (*Institutio Generalis Missalis Romano*), including Adaptations for Dioceses of the United States, 34, http://www.vatican.va /roman_curia/congregations/ccdds/documents/rc_con_ccdds_doc_20030317 _ordinamento-messale_en.html, accessed November 11, 2014. The Latin edition, *Institutio Generalis Missalis Romani* (GIRM) was published in 2000. The English translation of the *General Instruction of the Roman Missal* was canonically approved for use by the United States Conference of Catholic Bishops on November 12, 2002, and was subsequently confirmed by the Holy See by decree of the Congregation for Divine Worship and the Discipline of the Sacraments on March 17, 2003.

Following the Second Vatican Council, this relationship was made clear by the decree *Prece Eucharistica* (May 23, 1968), which promulgated three new eucharistic prayers and gave guidelines to assist catechesis on the anaphoras of the Mass. These guidelines explained that the faithful are directly involved in four places in the prayer: the Introductory Dialogue, the Sanctus, the Memorial Acclamation, and the Great Amen. In the revised Communion Rite, the communion preparation of the priest and the people occur together in the one recitation of the "Lord, I am not worthy." These elements of the eucharistic prayer, along with the use of the vernacular and the series of acclamations throughout, facilitate the active participation of the common priesthood. This is not only a desirable characteristic of liturgical celebration but also a right and duty which the Christian people have by reason of their baptism.[56] The conclusion of the prayer, the "Great Amen," represents an affirmation, endorsement, and commitment on the part of the assembly to what has just been accomplished together.

The *General Instruction of the Roman Missal* explicitly affirms that the entire assembly is the primary agent of the liturgical action, for the celebration of the Eucharist is the action of Christ and the Church (par. 19). The new *Catechism of the Catholic Church* reiterates this affirmation: "it is the whole *community*, the Body of Christ united with its Head, that celebrates" (no. 1140). These passages confirm the teaching of *Sacrosanctum Concilium* that the gathered people should learn to offer their own lives, just as they offer Christ in the sacrifice of the Eucharist, "not only through the hands of the priest but also together with him" (SC 48).

Ecclesiological Conclusions

A number of ecclesiological conclusions can be drawn from this theology of the liturgical assembly. First, the liturgical assembly is an ordered community reflecting an ordered church. The various orders within the church reveal the nature of the church. Within the Eucharist the primary identity of the church is that it is constituted as the Body of Christ by partaking in the eucharistic Body of Christ (1 Cor 10:16-17). The assembly is ordered to Christ as head of the body, and we are ordered to each other as members of the body. The ordained office of priest, inclusive of both bishop and presbyter, is ordered to the headship of Christ in relation to the body. The service of the deacon reveals *diakonia* to be

---

[56] *General Instruction of the Roman Missal*, 18.

essential to the nature of the church. The service of reader reveals that the church is always and everywhere a servant of the Word. The diversity among the members of the assembly reveals the diversity of charisms within the Body of Christ. As a whole, the assembly is a sign of the church at prayer.

Second, the people of God are engaged in a process of transformation into Christ and are oriented toward a goal of final fulfillment. This reality reflects the relationship between chapter 2 and chapter 7 of *Lumen Gentium*. Chapter 2 identifies the origin of the new people of God in baptism (LG 9). This people comprise the church, which is identified as the Body of Christ (LG 7), evidence that a eucharistic ecclesiology cannot be in opposition to a baptismal one. In chapter 2 the kingdom is inaugurated "to be further extended until, at the end of time, it will be brought to its completion" (LG 9). Chapter 7 describes the eschatological character of the pilgrim church and its union and completion with the heavenly church. The sacraments and institutions of the church belong to this interim time and will eventually pass away (LG 48).

Third, the relationship between the laity and ordained ministers as evidenced in the liturgy is profoundly dialogical and interactive. If the laity are to be full, active participants in the liturgy, such participation must also be their role in the church. This does not negate role differentiation, but it does mean that structures for lay participation and lay voice such as synods and councils need to be utilized much more than they have been in recent memory of the church.[57]

Fourth, the problem of the relationship between the local and universal church is a question of how various eucharistic assemblies relate to one another within a theology of communion. Even as an individual *ekklesia* fully represents the church, it is not the whole church, nor is it either a subdivision or a section of it. The local churches and universal church exist in a relationship of mutual interiority, for it is in and from these particular churches, formed in the likeness of the universal church, that there exists the one unique catholic church (LG 23). Clearly, the liturgy of a single eucharistic celebration cannot be addressed in isolation from its other manifestations.

---

[57] The Anglican-Roman Catholic International Commission (ARCIC) statement, *The Gift of Authority (Authority in the Church III)* (1999) challenges Catholics on this very point. See http://www.vatican.va/roman_curia/pontifical_councils/chrstuni/documents/rc_pc_chrstuni_doc_12051999_gift-of-autority_en.html, accessed August 10, 2014.

Fifth, the laity are called to full, active, conscious participation in the church. This is not a democratic principle but a liturgical one and, when applied to ecclesial life, it suggests a theology of conciliarity and synodality inclusive of the laity. The theological foundation for consultation of the laity lies not only in this liturgical principle but also in the fact that the Christian faithful, anointed by the Holy Spirit, are in possession of the sense of the faith (*sensus fidei*) and are responsible for actively promoting that sense of the faithful (*sensus fidelium*) in word and deed.[58] As the baptized, they participate in the prophetic, priestly, and kingly offices of Christ and bear responsibility for witnessing to their faith, participating in the worship of the church as well as in appropriate forms of church service and leadership.

Sixth, the people of God are a people sent on mission. In this interim time, the messianic people are sent as a mission to the whole world "as the light of the world and the salt of the earth (see Mt 5:13-16)" (LG 9). Both baptism and the Eucharist embody a theology of mission. In the dismissal of the Eucharist the presider addresses the assembly and may say, "Go and announce the Gospel of the Lord." The dominical command to baptize in Matthew 28:28 tells the disciples to "go," to "make disciples," to "baptize," and to "teach." In the Rite of Christian Initiation of Adults, the celebrant addresses the newly baptized before the laying on of hands for the sacrament of confirmation, saying that the promised strength of the Holy Spirit will help the baptized to be witnesses to Christ's suffering, death, and resurrection and will strengthen them to be active members of the church, building up the Body of Christ in faith and love.[59]

While questions of ministry—both lay and ordained—tended to dominate ecclesiological discussions in the twentieth century, if the young pontificate of Pope Francis is any indication, mission and missionary discipleship will be the dominant ecclesiological category of the twenty-first century.[60] All the baptized clearly share in the mission of the church.

---

[58] *Sensus fidelium*: GS 52; *sensus fidei*: LG 12, 35; PO 9. See also John Paul II, *Christifideles Laici*, 14 and John Paul II, *Ut Unum Sint*, 80.

[59] *The Rites of the Catholic Church as Revised by the Second Vatican Ecumenical Council*, vol. 1 (Collegeville, MN: Liturgical Press, 1990), 162.

[60] See Pope Francis, *Evangelii Gaudium* (On the Joy of the Gospel), 119–21, http://w2.vatican.va/content/francesco/en/apost_exhortations/documents/papa-francesco_esortazione-ap_20131124_evangelii-gaudium.html, accessed November 10, 2014.

Mission is prior to ministry, for ministry is differentiated according to how mission is carried out by a particular individual. This means that the church's primary purpose is not self-maintenance or self-service but rather to transform the world in service of the reign of God. The whole church must "be a leaven and, as it were, the soul of human society in its renewal by Christ and transformation into the family of God" (GS 40). A few, both lay and ordained, are called to ecclesial ministry, but this is a subset of a much larger mission that belongs to the whole church. Baptism inaugurates this mission; Eucharist nourishes it and sends out the people of God to enact this mission in the world.

The liturgy offers a rich resource for developing an ecclesiology, with the caution that it needs to be approached holistically, allowing the various aspects of the liturgy to balance and complement one another. If the church believes as it prays according to the principle of *lex orandi, lex credendi*, it also enacts what it prays in its own life.

For Further Reading

Afanasiev, Nicholas. *The Church of the Holy Spirit*. Translated by Vitaly Permiakov. Notre Dame, IN: University of Notre Dame Press, 2007.

Congar, Yves. *At the Heart of Christian Worship: Liturgical Essays of Yves Congar.* Translated and edited by Paul Philibert. Collegeville, MN: Liturgical Press, 2010.

Faggioli, Massimo. *True Reform: Liturgy and Ecclesiology in* Sacrosanctum Concilium. Collegeville, MN: Liturgical Press, 2012.

Irvine, Christopher, ed. *Anglican Liturgical Identity: Papers from the Prague Meeting of the International Anglican Liturgical Consultation*. Norwich, UK: SCM-Canterbury Press, 2008.

Kubicki, Judith M. *The Presence of Christ in the Gathered Assembly*. New York: Continuum, 2006.

Lathrop, Gordon. *Holy People: A Liturgical Ecclesiology*. Minneapolis, MN: Fortress Press, 1999.

Ploeger, Mattijs. *Celebrating Church: Ecumenical Contributions to a Liturgical Ecclesiology.* Gronigen: Instituut voor Liturgiewetenschap Rijksuniversiteit Gronigen, 2008.

Wood, Susan K. "A Liturgical Theology of the Episcopate." In *Unfailing Patience and Sound Teaching: Reflections on Episcopal Ministry*, edited by David A. Stosur, 31–44. Collegeville, MN: Liturgical Press, 2003.

Zizioulas, John D. *Eucharist, Bishop, Church: The Unity of the Church in the Divine Eucharist and the Bishop During the First Three Centuries*. Translated by Elizabeth Theokritiff. Brookline, MA: Holy Cross Orthodox Press, 2001.

CHAPTER 8

Learning from Experience: Attention to Anomalies in a Theology of Ministry

Edward P. Hahnenberg

For anyone who writes on ministry, experience as well as research should be a mentor.

—Thomas F. O'Meara, OP

In the years following the Second Vatican Council, new and various experiences of ministry began to emerge and rapidly expand. Priests and religious reimagined their roles while tens of thousands of lay women and men entered into direct ministries within their parishes and dioceses. This transformation of the church's ministerial life was not the result of a Vatican mandate or a national pastoral plan. Instead, ministerial forms grew from the ground up, as expanding needs in the community were met by a new sense of active participation among the people of God.

How quickly a new paradigm took hold. Within a few years, preconciliar models of lay engagement—and even Vatican II's own language of *lay apostolate*—gave way to a new vocabulary. Catholics in the United States began to speak of *coordinators, directors of religious education, ministerial teams, the parish staff, pastoral associates*, and, above all, *lay ministers*. By the end of the 1970s, the sociologist John Coleman would point out that the term *ministry* had already become a pervasive catch phrase among Catholic religious professionals—so taken for granted that it was rarely defined. He noted that it is precisely those things that are taken for granted that constitute a culture in possession: "What we do not need to define itself defines our world and charts our view of reality."[1] The term *ministry* finessed the centuries-old distinction between clergy and laity and signaled a dramatic shift in emphasis—from ordination to baptism, office to charism, status to competency, and hierarchy to collegiality—hidden, as it were, behind "our pervasive, often unreflected and undefined use of the new language."[2]

This is the context in which postconciliar theologies of ministry emerged and to which they contributed. The following chapter is less a survey of books on ministry or a grappling with the many neuralgic issues of recent decades than it is an attempt to understand the changed landscape that Coleman saw by exploring the tectonic plates moving below the surface. I will argue that the most important shift for Catholic theologies of ministry over the past fifty years has been a shift in method—a move away from an approach that was deductive, doctrinal, and universalist to one that is inductive, empirical, and particularist. This methodological shift can be seen especially in two pervasive features of contemporary theologies of ministry: an awareness of history and an appeal to experience. I will further suggest that the best hope for advancing theologies of ministry over the next fifty years lies in greater attention to the ministerial anomalies that shaped our past, mark our present, and point toward the future.

Past Tradition

Vatican II spoke a language both attentive to contemporary concerns and deeply rooted in scripture, liturgy, and early Christian thought. In doing so, the council confirmed a theological revival in Europe, launched major theological movements in Latin America and the Global South, and inspired a generation of Catholic thinkers in the United States. In the years following, new theologies of ministry appeared. While each new volume had its own distinctive contribution to make, several com-

---

[1] John A. Coleman, "The Future of Ministry," *America* 144 (March 28, 1981): 243. The definition of ministry (*diakonia*) lies at the heart of John N. Collins's trenchant critique of contemporary ministerial language. See his most recent collection, *Diakonia Studies: Critical Issues in Ministry* (Oxford: Oxford University Press, 2014). The most successful attempt at a definition of the reality Coleman describes remains that of Thomas O'Meara, *Theology of Ministry*, rev. ed. (New York: Paulist Press, 1999), 150.

[2] Coleman, "The Future of Ministry," 245.

mon themes characterize the most influential texts—the first of which is attention to the history of ministry.

Return to the Sources

The turn to history in theologies of ministry had its proximate source in the *ressourcement* that marked mid-twentieth-century Catholic theology. The liturgical movement, developments in biblical studies, and historical research began to impact how Catholics understood ministry. Scholars discovered gradually-evolving church offices and learned that the baroque model of the priest was not an eternal ecclesial form but merely one chapter in an unfolding narrative. Drawing on this scholarship, the documents of Vatican II prefer the images of Scripture and the theologies of the patristic period to the definitions of the Counter-Reformation and the antimodern polemic of neoscholastic theology. It was only after the council that the historical *ressourcement* Vatican II embraced began to be felt within dogmatic theology, transforming, among many things, the theology of ministry.

Bernard Lonergan famously described this broader transformation as a shift from a classicist worldview (privileging the eternal and the universal) to a historical worldview (preferring change and particularity).[3] With the end of neoscholasticism, theology moved irreversibly from a deductive to an empirical science[4]—and no treatment of ministry after the council could afford to ignore the concrete reality of history. Thus one of the first major postconciliar systematic works on ministry by a theologian in the United States, Bernard Cooke's *Ministry to Word and Sacraments*, adopted a thoroughly historical approach—with theological reflection coming after, and dependent on, the historical data.[5] Following the example of Yves Congar, Hans Küng, and Edward Schillebeeckx,

---

[3] See, for example, Bernard Lonergan, "The Transition from a Classicist World-View to Historical-Mindedness," in *A Second Collection*, ed. William Ryan and Bernard Tyrrell (Philadelphia: Westminster Press, 1974), 1–9; Lonergan, *Method in Theology* (London: Darton, Longman & Todd, 1971), 175–234.

[4] Bernard Lonergan, "Theology in Its New Context," in *A Second Collection*, ed. William Ryan and Bernard Tyrrell (Philadelphia: Westminster Press, 1974), 59.

[5] "The theological portions are presented as relatively freestanding. Yet, I feel that they are inextricably bound up with the historical study that precedes them; it was the study of the historical process of Christian ministry that led me to the theological positions I present." Bernard Cooke, *Ministry to Word and Sacraments: History and Theology* (Philadelphia: Fortress Press, 1976), ix. The introduction and footnotes reveal

widely read volumes by Thomas O'Meara, David Power, Kenan Osborne and others followed a historical-theological methodology—surveying how earlier eras understood ministry in order to offer fresh ideas for the contemporary church. The most recent, and one of the most ambitious, attempts at employing such a methodology is the three-volume project of Roger Haight.[6] *Christian Community in History* locates ministry within the context of a transdenominational "ecclesiology from below" whose first characteristic is a historical consciousness shaped by the radical pluralism of postmodernity.

This historically critical reevaluation of ministry recovered a number of common themes: baptism as the primary sacrament of ministry, St. Paul's notion of charisms as ordinary and widely available, ordained priesthood as grounded in the priesthood of all believers, leadership as service, authority as collegial, and the church as *koinonia* or *communio*. Perhaps the greatest insight of all was the simple recognition that the great Christian tradition of ministry is in fact many traditions. History gives witness to an ever-changing plurality of ministerial forms, activities, and understandings.

Widening the Lens

The historical work of recent decades has been groundbreaking for Catholic theology, but it has not unearthed everything. The postcolonial critique and the rise of various liberation, feminist, and contextual theologies have challenged the limited historical vision of "mainstream" Eurocentric accounts. Even within that mainstream, twentieth-century theologies of ministry have been further constrained by a widely shared set of historiographical assumptions. In a too-often overlooked article written over twenty-five years ago, John O'Malley identified several unexamined biases shaping Catholic treatments of ministry, including: the tendency to deal almost exclusively with the biblical and patristic periods to the neglect of ministerial developments of the Middle Ages through the modern period; a focus on *ideas* about ministry found in past theologians or *ideals* of ministry found in official documents rather than attending to what was actually happening "on the ground" through

---

Cooke's dependence on—and impressive familiarity with—the historical and theological studies coming out of France and Germany around the time of the council.

   [6] Roger Haight, *Christian Community in History*, 3 vols. (New York: Continuum, 2004–2008).

evidence gathered from unofficial sources such as letters, diaries, and reports from the field; and an implicit assumption that the Second Vatican Council stands as the final criterion for assessing the life of the church and the culmination of the historical evolution of ministry, paradoxically forestalling the possibility of future, unforeseen developments.[7]

The impact of this way of reading history can be seen no more clearly than in recent appropriations of the patristic model of *communio* as the fundamental framework for ecclesiology in general and for a theology of ministry in particular.[8] The most enthusiastic proponents of communion ecclesiology lift up the fourth and fifth centuries as the golden age of ministry, when presbyters, deacons, a host of other ministers, and the whole community gathered around their bishop at the eucharistic liturgy—an earthly communion symbolizing the heavenly communion of the triune God. Everything since reads as a story of decline in ministry, an ossification and juridicalization of earlier, more pristine forms of ecclesial life. Such a reading follows on the historical biases that O'Malley described. When we set aside these historiographical blinders and look at what was actually happening during these neglected centuries, what we see is not so much a deviation from an early church ideal but a diversity of ministerial forms more intense and variegated than at first realized.

The thirteenth century is a case in point. At that time, the pervasive, grassroots enthusiasm for the "apostolic life" that pervaded late medieval Christendom burst forth into a new and lasting ministerial form: the friars. With the friars—the most well-known are the Dominicans and the Franciscans, but this movement also included the Carmelites, Augustinians, Servites, and many others—we find a new form of service emerging out of pastoral need and personal experience. For example, good teaching and good preaching were in short supply, so the Dominicans (the Order of Preachers) stressed education for their members. The opulence of the clergy was condemned by the Albigensians, so the vow of poverty was

---

[7] John W. O'Malley, "Priesthood, Ministry, and Religious Life: Some Historical and Historiographical Considerations," *Theological Studies* 49, no. 2 (1988): 225–29.

[8] "For the Church, there is only one way into the future: the way pointed by the Council, the full implementation of the Council and its communion ecclesiology." Walter Kasper, *Theology and Church*, trans. Margaret Kohl (New York: Crossroad, 1989), 150. See also Extraordinary Synod of Bishops, "The Final Report," *Origins* 15 (December 10, 1985): 448; and Edward P. Hahnenberg, "The Mystical Body of Christ and Communion Ecclesiology: Historical Parallels," *Irish Theological Quarterly* 70, no. 1 (2005): 3–30.

embraced, in part, in order that the Dominicans might get a hearing. Mobility was required to respond to a rapidly spreading movement, so the friars abandoned the monastery and successfully campaigned for freedom from the jurisdiction of local bishops.

This last point—exemption from episcopal oversight—O'Malley calls "astounding."[9] We forget how radical this departure must have been at the time. Almost nothing that the mendicants did fit into the patristic model of pastoral ministry. Did that make their ministry inappropriate? Something quite different came into existence, something that was not just a slight variation on the monastic life or a new set of tasks for the ordained priest. What we see in the friars is an experimentation not only with new ministries but also with new ministerial forms.

The sixteenth and seventeenth centuries mark another moment in ministry's metamorphoses—suggesting the danger, not only of overlooking this era but also of relying too heavily on texts of the official magisterium. During this period, Catholic ministry went through one of its most innovative and exciting transformations in history. But reading the decrees of the Council of Trent, you would never know it. The mendicant orders saw tremendous growth in both size and influence; and new apostolic orders, like the Jesuits, burst onto the scene, experimenting with everything from directing retreats, spiritual counseling, and social ministries to using schools, artists, and the press as instruments of ministry. The catechesis, evangelization, and missionary outreach was intense, immense, and unprecedented—a thrust seen nowhere more dramatically than in the massive efforts directed toward evangelizing the newly "discovered" worlds of the Americas and Asia. But, as O'Malley ironically observes, just as this global missionary movement was at its peak in the mid-sixteenth century, the bishops gathered at Trent bypass it "without a word."[10]

The proliferation of active communities of women religious since the sixteenth century—founded precisely for ministry—represents another innovation, something official church documents consistently fail to recognize. By expanding our sources and widening our historical vision, we go deeper into our past. We see that a lot has happened since the sixth century. The tendency among twentieth-century theologians to

---

[9] O'Malley, "Priesthood, Ministry, and Religious Life," 236.

[10] John W. O'Malley, "One Priesthood: Two Traditions," in *A Concert of Charisms: Ordained Ministry in Religious Life*, ed. Paul K. Hennessy (New York: Paulist Press, 1997), 17.

favor official documents and to privilege the early church is understand-able, given their desire to offer an alternative to a vision of priestly ministry shaped by medieval hierarchies, seventeenth-century French spirituality, and neoscholastic sacramental theology. The point here is not to deny the enduring value of the biblical witness, the success of Vatican II, or the ecumenical fruit bore by a rediscovery of patristic sources.[11] It is simply to suggest that there is greater diversity marking ministry in the past than even the best postconciliar accounts show, and that it may very well be those moments and ministerial forms that do *not* fit within the dominant ecclesiological narratives that offer the most potential for future theological development.

Contemporary Experience

If history reveals diversity in ministry and development in ministerial structures, ought not we open ourselves to the same today? The *ressource-ment* of the years leading up to Vatican II met the *aggiornamento* of the postconciliar period. In the midst of the social upheavals of the 1960s and the energies released by the council, ministries began to change. These changes became a point of departure for theology.

The Explosion of Ministry

The explosion of ministry after the council was largely unexpected, and it came quickly. The change is particularly evident in the worldwide expansion of lay ministries. Early on, the German bishops moved to establish formal ministerial roles for laity, with specific educational re-quirements and clearly delineated responsibilities. The more informal structure of base ecclesial communities, led by laity, spread from Brazil across Latin America into Africa and Asia.[12]

---

[11] See World Council of Churches, *Baptism, Eucharist and Ministry*, Faith and Order Paper no. 111 (Toronto: Anglican Book Centre, 1982); Thomas F. Best and Günther Gassmann, eds. *On the Way to Fuller Koinonia*, Faith and Order Paper no. 166 (Geneva: WCC Publications, 1994); and World Council of Churches, *The Nature and Mission of the Church: A Stage on the Way to a Common Statement*, Faith and Order (Geneva: WCC Publications, 2005), 198.

[12] See Edward P. Hahnenberg, "Think Globally, Act Locally: Responding to Lay Ecclesial Ministry," *New Theology Review* 17, no. 4 (2004): 52–65; and Edward L. Cleary, *The Challenge of Priestless Parishes: Learning from Latin America* (New York: Paulist Press, 2014).

In the United States, lay ministry flourished on multiple fronts. At the national level, Hispanic leaders organized the first of several Encuentro gatherings in 1972, in order to draw attention to the gifts and needs of Latino/a Catholics. In the late 1970s, the US bishops sponsored the broadly consultative "Call to Action" meeting in Detroit and established a Committee on the Laity at its national headquarters in Washington, DC. Meanwhile, at the local level, lay women and men entered the sanctuary to proclaim the Scriptures at Mass and distribute communion. Pastors began to hire their best volunteers to coordinate emerging religious education programs—giving rise to a new ministerial role, the "coordinator" or director of religious education, which became a model for other positions on the parish staff. General assistants, called pastoral ministers or pastoral associates, appeared, as did youth ministers, liturgical coordinators, and directors of social concerns. The work of organists and other liturgical musicians was recognized as ministry. At the same time, colleges and universities began to offer graduate courses and programs in theology for laypeople. Women religious and lay students filled summer sessions and received degrees in religious education and theology. Pastoral centers opened. National organizations for lay ministers emerged and expanded, promoting professionalization, competency standards, and networking beyond the parish.

This was the period that produced the first great wave of postconciliar studies on ministry. One of the most influential of these studies, Thomas O'Meara's *Theology of Ministry*, is paradigmatic. O'Meara wrote his book as a response to the ministerial transformations he observed happening around him. He later described *Theology of Ministry* not as "a prescription for what should be done in the church nor an insistent prediction of the future but a reflection on diocese and parish as they were changing after 1968." His work had one goal: "to reflect on the expansion and reconfiguration of ministry in the church."[13]

Attention to the revelatory power of contemporary experience stands as one of the hallmarks of postconciliar Catholic theology. The seminal work of Gustavo Gutierrez—emerging out of his pastoral work among the poor of Lima, Peru—lifted up praxis, solidarity, and experience as the beginning and end of theological method. His example inspired diverse liberation theologies and opened out into feminist, black, Latino/a, and a host of contextual theologies—all committed to an analysis of experience as key to theological reflection.

---

[13] O'Meara, *Theology of Ministry*, 1, 5.

Roger Haight makes explicit what is often implicit in many theologians now writing on ministry: "an ecclesiology from below does not hesitate to find the sources of ministry in the actuality of the community at any given time."[14] This openness to the ongoing evolution of church ministry is a marked contrast to neoscholastic treatises, whose ahistorical reading of the New Testament and appeal to past doctrinal authorities implied an eternal ecclesiastical order. New experiences can reveal new insight into the Gospel—a claim grounded in a theology of grace permeating nature, a notion of charisms as broadly available, and an eschatological vision of the church as a pilgrim people of God.

Incorporating Ethnography

But how do we determine "the actuality of the community at any given time"? In this question lies one of the greatest weaknesses of mainstream systematic theologies of ministry. We (and I include my own work here) have failed to apply a consistent and credible methodology in our appeal to the lived experience of ministry. Pete Ward speaks for many ecclesiologists when he says: "It has become acceptable to make assertions where there is no evidence. We assume a common perception of contemporary church life between author and reader. We base whole arguments on anecdote and the selective treatment of experience. We are prone to a sleight of hand that makes social theory appear to be a description of social reality—which of course it is not."[15] Ward is speaking not so much about the theoretical justification for incorporating experience (by appealing, for example, to a theology of grace or the Holy Spirit); instead, he is describing a general lack of interest among ecclesiologists in laying out a method for determining what "the experience" actually is. This "methodological laziness" becomes clear when we compare the way ecclesiologists talk about experience with the way we talk about history. When we appeal to the history of ministry in the construction of our theologies, we abide by the disciplinary conventions, academic rigor, and hermeneutical sensitivity demanded by the historian. But when we talk about the contemporary experience of ministry, "completely different rules seem to apply."[16]

---

[14] Haight, *Christian Community in History*, 1:63.
[15] Pete Ward, "Introduction," *Perspectives on Ecclesiology and Ethnography* (Grand Rapids, MI: Eerdmans, 2012), 4.
[16] Ibid.

There have been extensive and excellent sociological studies of ministry conducted over the past thirty years. In the United States, one only has to turn to the work of Andrew Greeley, Dean Hoge, Katarina Schuth, Philip Murnion, and David DeLambo—or visit the data-rich website of the Center for Applied Research in the Apostolate—to see the ministerial shifts of recent decades. It is unclear, however, to what extent all this data has been incorporated into the theologies of the postconciliar period—beyond the general assertion that changes in the church call for changes in theology. Moreover, the quantitative data derived from sociological surveys has a tendency to level out the diverse and multifaceted reality of ministry, resulting in a portrait of generic ministers serving generic parishes.[17] Survey data can only tell us so much. As Steven Tipton put it in another context, "Opinions are like noses, in short or at length, if you will: everyone has one and everybody's is a little different. All you can do is count them up in polls and check for the sociological equivalent of family resemblances."[18]

These family resemblances are not without value. And quantitative sociological research has been essential for charting changes in ministerial roles, attitudes toward ministry, and the self-perception of ministers. The limitations inherent in the enterprise, however, suggest that this research be complemented by more qualitative methodologies intent on "thick descriptions" of what is actually happening in our church communities. Just as theology has long drawn on philosophy and philology, and more recently on history, sociology, and critical theory, perhaps it is time for theology—particularly the theology of ministry—to draw on ethnography.[19]

---

[17] In their 1999 study, Philip Murnion and David DeLambo paint a portrait of the average lay ecclesial minister: She is "a fifty-year-old white woman of European ancestry, who has been a Catholic since birth and has a master's degree." *Parishes and Parish Ministers: A Study of Parish Lay Ministry* (New York: National Pastoral Life Center, 1999), 26. Compare this generic summary to the rich personal testimony of Mary M. Foley, "Exceptional Pastoring: Women in Parish Leadership," *America* 200 (March 9, 2009): 11–13.

[18] Steven Tipton, "A Response: Moral Languages and the Good Society," *Soundings* 69, nos. 1–2 (1986): 165, cited in Christian Scharen, " 'Judicious Narratives,' or Ethnography as Ecclesiology," *Scottish Journal of Theology* 58, no. 2 (2005): 130.

[19] Joseph Komonchak has been at the forefront in calling for ecclesiologists to pay greater attention to the social sciences. See his *Foundations in Ecclesiology*, supplementary issue of the *Lonergan Workshop*, vol. 11 (Boston: Boston College, 1995). An early call for an "ethnographic ecclesiology" was Nicholas M. Healy, *Church, World and the*

Although ethnography developed as a particular type of qualitative research within the field of anthropology (usually involving sustained immersion within a "foreign" cultural system[20]), ecclesiologists tend to define the method more inclusively as referring to any social research that involves "direct, qualitative observation of situations or settings using the techniques of participant observation, intensive interviewing, or both."[21] This type of qualitative research has long been the preserve of Protestant congregational studies and the evolving field of practical theology. For Catholic systematic theologians, the incorporation of ethnographical methods may feel as strange today as the inclusion of historically critical methods must have felt to the neoscholastics of the early twentieth century. It is a demanding call, for such research requires a form of fieldwork that is painfully time consuming and labor intensive—an investment of hard work that may or may not have any theological payoff. Nor is this call entirely unproblematic, insofar as it draws ecclesiology into the ongoing debate within the social sciences over the proper place of qualitative research in general.[22]

Nevertheless, by aspiring for a thick description of social spaces, ethnography opens up the contemporary experience of ministry. It allows some slice of this complex reality to stand forth—with its rough edges and clashing colors—as a source for theological reflection. One only has to read the work of Latino/a theologians such as Ada María Isasi-Díaz to realize the theologically productive force of close attention to experience.[23]

Christian Life: Practical-Prophetic Ecclesiology (Cambridge, UK: Cambridge University Press, 2000), 168–85. See, more recently, Neil Ormerod, *Re-Visioning the Church: An Experiment in Systematic-Historical Ecclesiology* (Minneapolis, MN: Fortress Press, 2014); Pete Ward, ed., *Perspectives on Ecclesiology and Ethnography* (Grand Rapids, MI: Eerdmans, 2012); and Christian B. Scharen, ed., *Explorations in Ecclesiology and Ethnography* (Grand Rapids, MI: Eerdmans, 2012). Gutierrez's *A Theology of Liberation*, trans. Caridad Inda and John Eagleson (Maryknoll, NY: Orbis Books, 1973) stands as a now-classic example of early theological engagement with the modern social sciences, revealing implications for ecclesiology.

[20] The postcolonial critique of ethnography as study of "the other" applies here. See Martyn Hammersley and Paul Atkinson, *Ethnography: Principles in Practice*, 3rd ed. (London: Routledge, 2007), 1–19.

[21] Scharen, "Judicious Narratives," 125. See Ward, "Introduction," 6–9.

[22] Neil Ormerod draws attention to the impact of these difficulties on theology in *Re-Visioning the Church*, 31–59.

[23] See the methodological comments in Ada María Isasi-Díaz, *En la Lucha, In the Struggle: Elaborating a Mujerista Theology*, 10th anniversary ed. (Minneapolis, MN: Fortress Press, 2004), 80–103.

Ethnography seeks not a representative voice but an authentic one.[24] It pushes below ideas to the actual practices of ministry, inviting a way of thinking marked by engagement and participation. As Mary McClintock Fulkerson rightly notes, qualitative methods do not lead to causal or explanatory claims such as are sought by quantitative research.[25] Nor are the observations about particular cases generalizable in the way survey data is. This fact implies a different mode of arriving at insight. Ethnographic description is *suggestive*—it encourages not a logical inference from exhaustive data but rather an imaginative leap from particular experience to broader truths. If the survey is generic, careful observation is genetic.[26] It sparks theological insight. It gives birth to new ideas or different ways of looking at old ideas. The concrete becomes creative, usually through the unexpected, the anomalous, the distinctive voice in all its messy particularity. What does not fit within our present theologies is what inspires future theological development.

Future Directions

The expansion and diversification of ministry that marked the second half of the twentieth century was deeply intertwined with a basic methodological shift in theologies of ministry. I have described this methodological shift as a move from a deductive to an inductive approach—a conversion among theologians away from repeating eternal church forms to discovering changing historical realities, from stating church doctrine to listening to experience. I have also argued that this inductive approach can go even deeper by unearthing the complexity of ministerial diversity in our past and attending more carefully to the lived experience of ministry in our present. What this attention to the concrete reveals is a constantly adapting, remarkably flexible procession of ministerial forms—some long lasting, some short-lived—taking on flesh to serve the mission of Christ. John O'Malley challenges theologians and church leaders to look back and to look ahead: "Do we not need, therefore,

---

[24] Ward, "Introduction," 8.

[25] Mary McClintock Fulkerson, "Interpreting a Situation: When Is 'Empirical' Also 'Theological'?" in *Perspectives on Ecclesiology and Ethnography*, ed. Pete Ward (Grand Rapids, MI: Eerdmans, 2012), 129–30.

[26] Michael Burawoy, "The Extended Case Method," in *Ethnography Unbound: Power and Resistance in the Modern Metropolis* (Berkeley, CA: University of California Press, 1991), 280–81.

especially to recover the pragmatic approach to ministry that current historiography is showing happily characterized our past, but that today seems to be ever more effectively smothered by the 'normative' or by some idealized model? . . . It is not our 'fidelity' that today needs testing, but our creativity."[27] In this quest toward creativity, I want to suggest that it is the anomaly—not the norm—that offers a path forward.

Anomalies in Ministry

To speak of an anomaly is to presume a common rule against which it stands as an exception. It is to posit a "normal," a mainstream, a dominant view or trajectory, and thus to introduce the issues of privilege and marginalization, domination and subordination, center and periphery. The argument here emerges from the privileged center: I take "norm" to refer to the broad consensus on ministry found in recent magisterial statements, in ecumenical documents, and among Catholic theologians in the United States.

Postconciliar treatments of ministry provide an apt illustration of the interplay between this (always evolving) norm and the anomaly. Theologians have generally described the rise of lay ministries over the past fifty years as an outcome of the Second Vatican Council, fully consonant with its teaching. This interpretation is understandable, given the desire to grant new ministerial forms credibility by grounding them in the authority of the council. It is also a fair interpretation, particularly when we consider the broader ecclesiological vision laid out in the council texts. This stress on continuity, however, overlooks the ways in which lay ministry was genuinely new. Already in 1970, Yves Congar would write: "It is astonishing how the post-conciliar period has so little to do with the Council. The post-conciliar questions are new and radical. *'Aggiornamento'* [now] means changes and adaptations to a new situation."[28] When we consider the council's fairly limited discussion of ecclesial offices open to the laity and its extensive treatment of the laity's "secular character," couldn't we say that lay ministry is less an *example* of Vatican II's teaching than it is an *exception*?

---

[27] O'Malley, "Priesthood, Ministry, and Religious Life," 257.

[28] Yves Congar to Thomas O'Meara, December 9, 1970, quoted in Thomas F. O'Meara, "Being a Ministering Church: Insights from History," in *Lay Ecclesial Ministry: Pathways Toward the Future,* ed. Zeni Fox (New York: Rowman & Littlefield, 2010), 53.

The point I want to make is that this exception has been theologically productive. The fact that lay ministry did not fit neatly within Vatican II's teaching on the laity led theologians to revisit this teaching in light of the fundamental *ecclesiological* claims of the council. Congar is a good example. In the context of expanding ministries after the council, Congar returned to his earlier work on the laity (so influential at Vatican II) and suggested a different starting point and framework—not the dividing-line paradigm of clergy over-against laity, but a concentric-circles model of various ministries within the church and at the service of its mission.[29] The anomalous nature of lay ministry led to theological insight. Over the course of Christian history, the anomaly has often served not only as an opportunity for theological discovery but also as a major impetus for the development of doctrine. What we assume to be moments marking the natural evolution of ministerial forms—the rise of ministries of residential care, the monoepiscopate, communal forms of monasticism, presbyteral authority, papal primacy, mendicant orders, active communities of women religious—were more often than not deeply contested innovations. What in retrospect appears as development was, at the time, experienced as disruption. These shifts introduced odd, unexpected forms that did not fit into the prevailing theories of ministry at the time but that nevertheless had to be taken seriously. What is interesting, in these cases at least, is that the mainstream theological tradition did not simply reject prior theory; it found ways to revise the theory in light of the exception.

A more specific recent example of ministerial anomaly is the role of parish life coordinator—a layperson, vowed religious, or deacon who is entrusted with the overall pastoral care of a parish in the absence of a resident priest-pastor.[30] Although canon law authorizes this ministry (c. 517.2) and a number of bishops have employed parish life coordinators in their dioceses, the role does not fit well into the prevailing theological consensus, which, following Vatican II's patristic model of church, presumes a link between the ability to preside over the Eucharist and the ability to preside over the community. Parish life coordinators preside over the community; but, because they are not ordained priests, do not preside over the Eucharist. Thus they are something of an exception—a

---

[29] Yves Congar, "My Path-Findings in the Theology of Laity and Ministries," *The Jurist* 32 (1972): 169–88.

[30] See Edward P. Hahnenberg, "Exceptional Ministers: Where Parish Life Coordinators Might Lead," *New Theology Review* 24, no. 4 (November 2011): 49–60.

"stopgap measure" which exists, according to the US bishops' conference, "simply because of the shortage of priests."[31]

The temptation for systematic accounts of ministry is always to resolve the anomaly, to argue that such exceptions represent an inappropriate deviation from the norm. For parish life coordinators, resolution has often meant removal, as dioceses increasingly turn to other models (such as closing or clustering parishes) to deal with the declining number of priests. The argument for eliminating these positions rests on the dominant theological assumption that every parish should be presided over by a priest-pastor. Parish life coordinators simply do not fit within this paradigm. Thus their positions should be terminated. A quite different suggestion emerges at the other end of the ecclesial spectrum. If every parish needs a priest-pastor, then those lay women and lay men currently leading communities should not be eliminated. They should be ordained! The conclusion is radically different, but the underlying theological motivation is the same: Anyone who presides over the community should preside over the Eucharist. No exceptions allowed.

But what if instead of rushing to resolve the anomaly, systematic theologians were to welcome the anomaly as a source for new theological insight? What if parish life coordinators were not regarded as a temporary solution but were received as an emerging form of leadership in the local church? Instead of reinforcing the standard theological account, could the anomaly initiate a process of creative theological reflection, inviting the theologian to revisit the standard account—to reimagine the meaning of ecclesial community, the celebration of Eucharist, or the framework for ordered ministries? Might the anomaly lead to theological development? If so, then our theological reflection will need to attend closely to the lived experience of parish life coordinators. Here the disciplined observation and thick description of ethnography can serve as useful tools to help lift up the particularity of parish life coordinators—or any other concrete ministerial reality.

The point of attending closely to ministerial anomalies through ethnography is not to invent some novel theory or to abandon established doctrine. The point of adopting methods such as participant observation or extended interviewing is to immerse oneself in a specific ecclesial

---

[31] United States Conference of Catholic Bishops, *Co-Workers in the Vineyard of the Lord: A Resource for Guiding the Development of Lay Ecclesial Ministry* (Washington, DC: USCCB Publishing, 2005), 11.

context in order to allow its unique particularities to speak. The theologian—like the social scientist—however, does not enter this context as a blank slate. She brings with her the questions, assumptions, understandings, and theory that led her to the field in the first place. By privileging the anomaly, she is searching for something more than confirmation of these prior understandings. The sociologist Michael Burawoy makes this point explicit in his own ethnographic method.[32] Burawoy insists that the ethnographer ought to be looking for the ways a theory *falls short* in the face of reality. "What is important is that to highlight the particularity of our social situation we self-consciously and deliberately draw on existing knowledge to constitute the situation as 'abnormal' or 'anomalous.' That is to say, in the first place we treat social phenomena not as instances of some potential new theory but as counterinstances of some old theory. Instead of an *exemplar* the social situation is viewed as an *anomaly*."[33] Such an approach encourages the theologian to look for what is "interesting" or "surprising" or "unexpected"—those aspects of the ecclesial situation that cannot be explained by the theological theory. Such anomalies create a crisis for the theory, sparking a reconsideration or revision of the theory. If the theory does not stand up to reconsideration, the theory fails. "But failure leads not to rejection but to rebuilding theory. . . . Instead of abandoning theory when it faces refutation, we try to 'refute the refutation' by making our theory stronger."[34]

Ecclesiology is not social theory. The church exists within a broader tradition that is not only *normal* but also *normative*. Thus Burawoy's insight can only be applied here analogously. If theology is the theory of ministry, the theologian does not come to the study of concrete ministerial realities innocent of the larger tradition of thinking about ministry conveyed by past theologians and church doctrine. He sets out to examine ministerial anomalies not in order to undermine these doctrines or to propose new ones but rather to ask how previous understandings are

---

[32] I am indebted to Luke Bretherton for introducing me to the work of Burawoy. See Luke Bretherton, "Coming to Judgment: Methodological Reflections on the Relationship Between Ecclesiology, Ethnography and Political Theory," *Modern Theology* 28, no. 2 (April 2012): 167–96.

[33] Michael Burawoy, "Reconstructing Social Theories," in *Ethnography Unbound: Power and Resistance in the Modern Metropolis* (Berkeley, CA: University of California Press, 1991), 9.

[34] Ibid., 9–10.

confronted or complicated by reality. The norm of past tradition is rarely abandoned, but it is often bent, as individuals and groups work creatively with the norm, applying, adapting, and transcending it—sometimes even transforming the anomaly into the exemplar.[35] For the theologian, acknowledging the anomaly does not *prove* earlier doctrines wrong, but it can *spark* new insight into the mystery of God's work in the world.

Practical Reason, Normativity, and Discernment

Anomalies are always *theologically* productive, but they do not always contribute to the development of doctrine. How do we determine if the new theological insight sparked by an anomaly leads in a faithful direction or down a false path? How do we know what is of the Spirit and what is not? Can the theologian contribute in any way to this judgment, or is this task the exclusive work of the church's authoritative magisterium? Attending to the diversity of ministry in both the past and the present raises the issue of normativity—now understood not in its descriptive sense but in its prescriptive, and even proscriptive, meaning. The question that looms over all postconciliar accounts is this: What normative value (if any) does the experience of ministry have?

The answer to this question depends on how you think. To put it more precisely, the answer depends on the kind of rationality at work in making such a determination. In this I appeal to the distinction—proposed by Aristotle and adapted by Aquinas—between theoretical reason and practical reason. Aquinas described one as treating necessary truths, the other as dealing with the realm of the contingent.[36] It would be simplistic, however, to conclude that he saw the two types of rationality as antagonistic, or that practical reason is merely the application of universal laws to particular cases.[37] Rather, practical reason *arises out of* the particular. It is less a separate operating system for the mind than it is a different way of understanding how we come to truth, namely, by a rational process that is inductive, variable, and oriented toward action.

[35] Ibid., 27.

[36] Thomas Aquinas, *Summa Theologiae*, II-II, q. 94, a. 4.

[37] See the helpful treatment in Jean Porter, *The Recovery of Virtue: The Relevance of Aquinas for Christian Ethics* (Louisville, KY: Westminster/John Knox Press, 1990), 156–62.

Recent decades have seen a revival of interest in practical reason in a variety of disciplines, driven by a desire to escape modernity's false dichotomy between theoretical (*theoria*) and technical (*techne*) rationality. Proponents argue that the turn to the aesthetic, to praxis, to the local, contingent, and particular is not a retreat into irrationality, but, as Roberto Goizueta describes it, a call "for an *expansion* of our criteria of rationality beyond the logical, theoretical criteria of modern Western thought."[38] In theology, the impact of this renewed interest has been felt in the emphasis on historical praxis within liberation theology, in the turn to virtue theory within ethics, in the attention to popular religiosity among Latino/a theologians, and in the direct ways that practical theology has grappled with the role of practical reason.[39] This renewed interest is beginning to be felt within ecclesiology as well.

I want to suggest that a systematic theology of ministry has much to gain *as systematic theology* by attending to the role of practical reason. Whenever ecclesiology ventures into evaluative judgments about the pragmatic, contingent, and context-dependent world of ministerial experience, echoes of an older deductive approach can be heard. A local experience or new development is assessed in light of an objective norm: Does this ministerial structure serve the reign of God that Jesus proclaimed? Does it contribute to the evangelizing mission of the church? Does it meet the recurring needs of the community? Does it foster the full human flourishing of women? Moreover, in addressing these questions, little attention is given to the difficult work of developing the skills, perspectives, and wisdom needed for the proper exercise of practical reason.

Once again, an analogy with the social sciences is helpful. The Danish sociologist Bent Flyvbjerg makes a compelling case that, in the analysis of human interaction, practical reason should have priority. Rather than try to mimic the explanatory, generalizable, and predictive methodology of the natural sciences, Flyvbjerg argues that the social sciences should

---

[38] Roberto S. Goizueta, *Caminemos con Jesús: Toward a Hispanic/Latino Theology of Accompaniment* (Maryknoll, NY: Orbis Books, 1995), 139. See also Isasi-Díaz, *En la Lucha*, 176–87.

[39] A helpful summary is Claire E. Wolfteich, "Hermeneutics in Roman Catholic Practical Theology," in *Opening the Field of Practical Theology: An Introduction*, ed. Kathleen A. Cahalan and Gordon S. Mikoski (Lanham, MD: Rowman and Littlefield, 2014), 133–52. See also Claire E. Wolfteich, ed., *Invitation to Practical Theology: Catholic Voices and Visions* (New York: Paulist Press, 2014).

claim their own strength: a methodology that encourages attention to the variable and context-dependent nature of human life, along with a reflexive analysis of goals, values, and interests.[40] If the natural sciences deride qualitative research and case studies for their failure to produce universal claims, the social sciences embrace them precisely for their ability to generate concrete, practical, and contextualized knowledge. The case study offers not proof but insight.

According to Flyvbjerg, coming to such insight requires the virtue that Aristotle knew as *phronesis* and that Aquinas called *prudentia*, usually translated as "practical wisdom" or "prudence." He calls for a "phronetic social science" in order to escape the modern methodological monopoly of the natural sciences.

The theologian Luke Bretherton picks up on Flyvbjerg's insight and applies it to his own field. Working at the intersection of ecclesiology and social ethics, Bretherton takes Flyvbjerg one step further. It is the process and discipline of closely studying particular cases that actually form the theologian in the virtue of *phronesis*—the virtue by which she is able to make wise judgments about the relationship of normative claims to specific ecclesial practices. Bretherton discusses his own research on community organizing. Through the close-to-the-ground ethnographic work of participant observation, Bretherton discovered that community organizing is a kind of craft knowledge—very different from the "rationally explicable technique that can be set out in a manual."[41] With the help of many mentors, he learned by doing. "Apprenticeship and the tacit knowledge it engenders is the only way to learn how to make evaluations about what constitutes a well- or poorly-executed sequence." Through the experience of organizing, he came to know (a judgment of practical reason) what good organizing is. He suggests that the same could be said of many forms of practice-based action, "from hospice care to priestcraft."[42]

The ethnographic method of participant observation may serve a systematic theology of ministry well. By entering into a particular local community, the theologian learns with that community and with its ministers—not so that she can *speak for them*, but so that she might learn

---

[40] Bent Flyvbjerg, *Making Social Science Matter: Why Social Inquiry Fails and How It Can Succeed Again*, trans. Steven Sampson (Cambridge, UK: Cambridge University Press, 2001).

[41] Bretherton, "Coming to Judgment," 187.

[42] Ibid., 188.

how to *speak for herself with them*, having been cultivated in the practical wisdom that the community and its ministers already enact. Through her research, the theologian develops the experience, insight, and virtue necessary to make wise theological judgments—judgments rooted in the community and accountable to the community.

As an exercise of practical reason, such judgments depend on a particular context, without despairing of the possibility of universal meaning. The fact that theological judgments are contextual and contingent does not necessarily make them subjective or relative.[43] For, to borrow an insight from Alasdair MacIntyre, such judgments of practical reason are part of a living tradition, understood as "an historically extended, socially embodied argument, and an argument precisely in part about the goods which constitute that tradition."[44] Maria Pilar Aquino points out that this argument is not just about particular goods; it is the attempt to communicate among different *rationalities*. She sees the possibility for shared truths emerging out of the distinctive voices brought to an intercultural dialogue that is not "about" specific topics but is rather "a theological dialogue 'with' and 'from' the limitations and possibilities opened by the historicity proper to each engaged rationality."[45] Each voice contains "parcels of reason," because every subject "assumes his or her human existence as such, from it constructs a personal mode of arriving at knowledge, and creates *conceptual frameworks for grounding visions of the world with valid claims to universality*."[46] Within the church, the "whole" of truth occurs in "the very process of exchange among culturally plural 'truths'" that together constitute the community of disciples striving to witness, celebrate, and serve the mission of Christ.[47]

This conversation about the church's mission (within which its very identity becomes known) demands the cultivation of people able to make good judgments. It demands not only theoretical knowledge but also practical wisdom, *phronesis*. Like any virtue, *phronesis* develops through

---

[43] Ibid., 177.

[44] Alasdair MacIntyre, *After Virtue: A Study in Moral Theory*, 2nd ed. (Notre Dame, IN: University of Notre Dame Press, 1984), 222.

[45] María Pilar Aquino, "Theological Method in U.S. Latino/a Theology: Toward an Intercultural Theology for the Third Millennium," in *From the Heart of Our People: Latino/a Explorations in Catholic Systematic Theology*, ed. Orlando O. Espin and Miguel H. Diaz (Maryknoll, NY: Orbis Books, 1999), 11.

[46] Pilar Aquino, "Theological Method in U.S. Latino/a Theology," 10 (emphasis in original).

[47] Ibid., 21.

practice, the formation of habits that come through life lived within particular narratives and particular communities. In the fragmented world of postmodernity, the development of this virtue requires intentionality. It is precisely the cultivation of practical wisdom that recommends greater use of ethnographic methods among Catholic theologians of ministry. Close, on-the-ground attention to the concrete, local particularities of ministerial experience not only offers a more credible description of that reality; it also provides a kind of formation for the theologian. As Bretherton concludes, "Recourse to ethnographic methods is not simply in order to describe practices and interpret their meanings. Rather, on my account, theology is a constructive judgment that can utilize ethnographic modes of attention as ways of engaging not in abstract judgments but listening up close and participating so as to make judgments based on practical reason. Such judgments are in the service of better, that is to say more faithful, action."[48]

The Christian tradition has a name for the kind of particular, embedded, and practical judgment proposed here: *discernment*. Over the centuries, various schools of spirituality have fostered a variety of ways for individuals and communities to reflect on the movement of the Spirit in their hearts and in their lives.[49] Discernment is not a logical application of universal principles to a concrete situation. Instead, it is the discovery of our response to God's always unprecedented and unique love for us in this place, at this time.[50] Such discernment is not a technique mastered in graduate school or a heavenly gift granted at ordination but a craft cultivated within community through careful attention, genuine listening, shared practice, and intellectual conversion. The theologian of ministry learns to discern as an apprentice, and the experience of ministry serves as mentor. We learn not *what* to think but *how* to think—the lesson of every good teacher.

---

[48] Bretherton, "Coming to Judgment," 190.

[49] Marc H. Lavallee, "Discernment, Practical Wisdom, and Christian Spirituality: A Study in Practical Theological Method" (PhD diss., Boston University, 2013).

[50] See Karl Rahner, "The Logic of Concrete Individual Knowledge in Ignatius Loyola," in *The Dynamic Element in the Church*, trans. W. J. O'Hara (New York: Herder and Herder, 1964), 84–170; and Edward P. Hahnenberg, *Awakening Vocation: A Theology of Christian Call* (Collegeville, MN: Liturgical Press, 2010).

For Further Reading

Bretherton, Luke. "Coming to Judgment: Methodological Reflections on the Relationship between Ecclesiology, Ethnography and Political Theory." *Modern Theology* 28, no. 2 (April 2012): 167–96.

Cahalan, Kathleen A., and Gordon S. Mikoski, eds. *Opening the Field of Practical Theology: An Introduction*. Lanham, MD: Rowman and Littlefield, 2014.

Hahnenberg, Edward P. *Awakening Vocation: A Theology of Christian Call*. Collegeville, MN: Liturgical Press, 2010.

———. *Ministries: A Relational Approach*. New York: Crossroad Publishing, 2003.

———. *Theology for Ministry: An Introduction for Lay Ministers*. Collegeville, MN: Liturgical Press, 2014.

Isasi-Díaz, Ada María. *En la Lucha, In the Struggle: Elaborating a Mujerista Theology*. 10th anniversary ed. Minneapolis, MN: Fortress Press, 2004.

Komonchak, Joseph A. *Foundations in Ecclesiology*. Supplementary issue of the *Lonergan Workshop*, vol. 11. Boston: Boston College, 1995.

Scharen, Christian B., ed. *Explorations in Ecclesiology and Ethnography*. Grand Rapids, MI: Eerdmans, 2012.

O'Meara, Thomas F. *Theology of Ministry*. Rev. ed. New York: Paulist Press, 1999.

Ormerod, Neil. *Re-Visioning the Church: An Experiment in Systematic-Historical Ecclesiology*. Minneapolis, MN: Fortress Press, 2014.

Ward, Pete, ed. *Perspectives on Ecclesiology and Ethnography*. Grand Rapids, MI: Eerdmans, 2012.

Wolfteich, Claire E., ed. *Invitation to Practical Theology: Catholic Voices and Visions*. New York: Paulist Press, 2014.

CHAPTER 9

A Promising New Thrust in Ecumenical Theology

Michael A. Fahey, SJ

In modern usage, the word "ecumenical," especially when combined with the noun "movement," denotes various activities designed to overcome the divisions among Christian churches. Its other theological usage, as in "ecumenical council," refers to a geographical concept, a reality involving representatives from different parts of the inhabited world (the *oikoumenè*).[1] Ecumenical attitudes are distinguished from polemic or apologetic contacts between various confessional churches. The ecumenist is one who has an acute sense of the scandal of Christian disunity and who seeks to eliminate religious divisions by prayer, study, and personal involvement. In modern times there have been two main strands of ecumenists: the spiritual ecumenists whose principal vocation is prayer for unity, and the theological ecumenists who, in addition to prayer, rely on study, historical investigation, teaching, and mutual discussion. These theological ecumenists explore the reasons why churches separated in order to propose paths to reconciliation. They share in the pursuit of love and appreciation of other Christians and are embarked on a search for understanding and respect. Ecumenists are not only found among professional theologians and church historians but also among preachers, diocesan or denominational leaders, and Christians involved directly in pastoral and social ministries. In addition, thousands of others live the ecumenical agenda in their marriages, private lives, hopes, and dreams.

---

[1] The same word is used in Luke 2:1 and in Matt 28:14, 19.

Ecumenists have come to recognize the importance of context for their work. In South America, ecumenism is embedded in the serious concerns about social justice, poverty, and conscientization that emerge from base ecclesial communities. Ecumenists in Africa and the Caribbean resist being drawn into European, post-Reformation debates that they did not initiate and that are disconnected from their own local concerns. In Asia, Christian ecumenism cannot be separated from a broader engagement with culture or considered apart from "interreligious" dialogue with the great religious traditions that define the continent.

Modern Beginnings of Ecumenism

The history of the modern ecumenical movement is traditionally traced back to 1910, the year of the First World Missionary Conference, held in Edinburgh, Scotland. But that missionary conference did not emerge from nowhere. Leading up to the Edinburgh meeting were various events that drew Christians into conversation. These included the evangelical revivals beginning in the eighteenth century; the missionary expansion of the nineteenth century, with its gradual emphasis on interdenominational cooperation; the work of international Bible societies, which drew on the resources of numerous churches; and the student Christian movement, which was interdenominational in membership.

In 1895, the American John R. Mott (1865–1955) founded the World Student Christian Federation, which sprang from the Christian Association of Young People in the United States. The federation had for its purpose forming students into followers of Jesus Christ, "the only Savior and Lord." The young people from the different denominations thus came to realize that there were disciples of Christ in other churches. In 1911, Mott convened a conference of the World Student Christian Federation at Constantinople and invited representatives of the Eastern churches to attend. This meeting was of decisive importance for the history of the ecumenical movement, for it led to a recognition that the movement could not be simply Western or exclusively Protestant. The recognition was mutual. In 1920 the Ecumenical Patriarchate of Constantinople issued an encyclical letter appealing to "all the churches of Christ for closer cooperation."[2] The contacts and friendships begun at

---

[2] "Unto the Churches of Christ Everywhere," in *The Orthodox Church in the Ecumenical Movement (1902–76)*, ed. Constantin Patelos (Geneva: World Council of Churches, 1978), 18.

the Constantinople meeting made it possible later on for the Russian émigrés who fled the Revolution of October 1917 to find support in their newly adopted countries. As a result of that support, they would be able to establish the Institut Saint Serge and the YMCA publishing house in Paris, the Fellowship of St. Alban and St. Sergius in London, and the St. Vladimir Institute in New York.

Mott became known chiefly for his zealous propaganda on behalf of the missions and for acting as chairman of the First International Missionary Conference in 1910. But Mott was not the only early ecumenist. One could also point to William Temple (1881–1944), archbishop of Canterbury from 1942 to 1944. There was also an important event in the 1920s known as the Malines Conversations, held in the Archdiocese of Malines (Mechelen) in Belgium. Cardinal Désiré Mercier of Malines hosted a series of five exchanges between continental Catholics and English Anglicans. These meetings were organized by Fernand Portal (1855–1926), a French priest, and the Anglican Charles Lindley Wood (1839–1934), the Second Viscount Halifax and a committed member of the Oxford Movement.

In the years following the Edinburgh World Missionary Conference of 1910, three ecumenical groups, with three distinct areas of concern— (1) missionary work, (2) the life and work of the churches, and (3) faith and order—eventually merged. They became part of an umbrella organization known as the World Council of Churches (WCC). In 1948, in the aftermath of the Second World War, the WCC met in Amsterdam to hold its first World Assembly.

Catholic Awakening

For the first half of the twentieth century, the leadership of the Roman Catholic Church looked askance on the ecumenical movement. Pope Leo XIII had published *Apostolicae Curae* in 1896, stating that Anglican orders were "absolutely null and thoroughly void." Pope Pius XI, in his 1928 encyclical *Mortalium Animos*, called Protestants who proposed theological exchanges "Pan-Christians." He went on to state:

> It is clear why this Apostolic See has never allowed its subjects to take part in the assemblies of non-Catholics. There is but one way in which the unity of Christians may be fostered, and that is by furthering the return to the one true Church of Christ of those who are separated from it; for from that one true Church of Christ they have in the past fallen away. The one Church of Christ is visible to

all, and will remain, according to the will of its Author, exactly the same as He instituted it. The mystical Spouse of Christ has never in the course of centuries been contaminated, nor in the future can she ever be.[3]

Such a bleak assessment is sobering but instructive. Its model for church unity was basically what might be called "the Prodigal Son paradigm": Orthodox and Protestants were to recognize their errant ways, return to Rome in humility, and confess to the parent: "I have sinned against heaven and before you."

In that period, Catholics felt obliged to remain aloof from ecumenical contacts in order to avoid the impression of indifferentism, false irenicism, or even syncretism. Official church documents fostered this attitude. Thanks, however, to the courageous work of pioneering individuals who had to bear the brunt of criticism, suspicion, and even silencing from officials in the Catholic Church, Catholics eventually became participants in the modern ecumenical movement. Catholics learned to see other Christians as partners in dialogue, persons with whom they already enjoyed a communion of fellowship, but with whom they needed to work toward full visible communion. One of the principal voices calling for such a shift in Roman Catholic consciousness was the Dominican Yves Congar who, at the age of thirty-three, published his pioneering work *Chrétiens Désunis* (*Divided Christendom*)—a work that launched what one writer described as "the Catholic rediscovery of Protestantism."[4]

The shift from grudging tolerance to mutual dialogue was facilitated by the shared trauma of World War II, by population shifts after the war, and by the adoption among Catholics of historical-critical methods for interpreting Sacred Scripture (and eventually for interpreting later church teaching as well). Attention to the historical context of the Bible helped Catholics recognize complementary but distinct theologies in the New Testament itself concerning the mission of Jesus Christ, salvation, and apostolic ministry. Some Catholics began to suggest that denominational differences could be seen, at least in part, as reflecting different

[3] Pius XI, *Mortalium Animos*, 10, http://www.vatican.va/holy_father/pius_xi /encyclicals/documents/hf_p-xi_enc_19280106_mortalium-animos_en.html, accessed November 26, 2014.

[4] Yves Congar, *Chrétiens désunis: principes d'un "oecuménisme" catholique* (Paris: Cerf, 1937); in English, *Divided Christendom: A Study of the Problem of Reunion* (London: C. Bles, 1939).

currents of spirituality that were firmly rooted in the New Testament. It is not surprising that one of the individuals who advanced the early Catholic cause of ecumenism during Vatican II was the German Jesuit Augustin Bea, who had worked with Protestant exegetes in the study of Scripture.

The theological basis for this new openness was the belated appreciation among Christians that what binds together Protestant and Catholic, Anglican and Orthodox, is far richer than what separates. All Christians are bound together by an appreciation of Jesus' ministry, by commitment to worship God the Father of Jesus Christ, by baptism, by the desire to celebrate the Lord's Supper, and by a shared aspiration to respond to the challenge of the Sermon on the Mount in modern society. Real communion, based on the Holy Spirit's indwelling in the baptized, already existed—but this invisible communion needed to become visibly expressed and expanded.

Individuals continued to make a difference. Angelo Roncalli, who became Pope John XXIII, had been a papal delegate in Bulgaria, Turkey, and Greece, where he enjoyed cordial relations with the Orthodox. He got to know personally Orthodox Church leaders who, to the Roman Curia, were mere names. In 1959 he announced his plan to call a general council for Catholics and invited observers from other churches. He established the Secretariat for Promoting Christian Unity and appointed Bea as its first president. The council produced *Unitatis Redintegratio* (The Decree on Ecumenism), which was promulgated in 1964. One year later, in a ceremony marking the conclusion of the Second Vatican Council, Pope Paul VI and the Ecumenical Patriarch Athenagoras I simultaneously lifted the mutual excommunications that had stood as a sign of division for a millennium. Following these historic events, the Vatican established various international bilateral consultations to explore church unity. A particularly dramatic moment came on December 14, 1975, when, standing together in the Sistine Chapel, Metropolitan Meliton unexpectedly informed Pope Paul VI that the Orthodox wanted official dialogue with Rome. The pope fell to his knees and kissed the feet of Meliton, citing Romans 10:15: "How beautiful are the feet of those who bring the good news." As genuine ecumenical progress was made at the highest official levels, a variety of efforts developed and spread rapidly at the national, regional, and local levels.

The Decree on Ecumenism stated that all of the baptized "have a right to be called Christians, and with good reason are accepted as sisters and brothers in the Lord by the children of the Catholic Church" (UR 3).

Catholics were now ready to recognize explicitly the charisms, graces, and inspirations given to individuals in different historical communities of Christian faith. They were also able to recognize churches which, from a Roman Catholic viewpoint, might be lacking in elements considered crucial to the fullness of church. Catholics came to see the authentic character of other parts of the Christian family because they began to see themselves as a searching, sojourning "pilgrim church" in need of reform. They came to view the Reformers not as disobedient rebels but as pious persons burning with a fervor to eliminate abuses or ambiguities in earlier historical embodiments of the Church Catholic.

The Decree on Ecumenism is less than thirty short pages. It merits close reading even today, especially since many aspects of its teachings have not yet filtered down into our daily lives. Some of its teaching includes, for instance, the frank admission that present-day Roman Catholics, and those who preceded them, share the blame for the divisions that still exist in Christianity and stand as a barrier to effective preaching of the Gospel in the world. The decree asks for forgiveness and offers pardon and reconciliation to those who have persecuted the Catholic Church. It states boldly the need to recognize the necessity of reform at all levels of church life. The decree also affirms that unity does not mean uniformity and issues a fervent call to all Christians to work together for the promotion of social justice and peace.

What was really new in the council's document? After fifty years it is hard to appreciate what was so different: (a) the elevation of Christian unity as one of the major concerns of Vatican II, and thus of the church in contemporary times; (b) the tone of the document, which spoke no longer of "non-Catholics," "heretics," or "schismatics" but rather of separated brothers and sisters with whom we share a real communion of faith; (c) the assertion that other groups of Christians are to be referred to as "churches and ecclesial communities" (UR 19); and (d) the teaching that the one, holy, catholic, and apostolic church "subsists in" (UR 4) the Catholic Church but is not limited or simply coterminous to it. I single out for reflection three particular elements from the teaching of the Decree on Ecumenism: the role of the Holy Spirit in bringing about greater church unity, the role to be played by every member of the church in the work of ecumenism, and the need for personal self-examination to see whether in any possible way, through harmful language, prejudice, or laziness, Catholics themselves stand as an obstacle to greater church unity.

Inspired by the pioneering efforts of individual Catholic ecumenists and the teachings of Vatican II, a growing number of individual Catholic theologians devoted their research to aspects of church unity. In the

United States, beginning in the 1960s, Dominican Thomas O'Meara published an impressive list of studies on the need for ecumenism.[5] In Europe, perhaps the leading Catholic ecumenist is the German cardinal Walter Kasper, who both as president of the Pontifical Council for Promoting Christian Unity and as a private theologian has produced an extensive collection of ecumenical studies.[6]

Emerging Consensus Statements

In the last thirty or so years, a significant number of official international bilateral (or multilateral) consensus statements have been published. Among the most important I would list the following:

- Anglican/Roman Catholic International Commission (ARCIC I), *The Final Report* (1981);

- World Council of Churches, Faith and Order Commission, *Baptism, Eucharist and Ministry* [*The Lima Report*], Faith and Order Paper No. 111 (1982);

- The Joint Commission for Theological Dialogue between the Roman Catholic Church and the Orthodox Church, *The Mystery of the Church and of the Eucharist in the Light of the Mystery of the Holy Trinity* (1982);

- Anglican/Roman Catholic International Commission (ARCIC II), *Church as Communion: An Agreed Statement* [*The Dublin Report*] (1991);

- Groupe des Dombes, *Pour la conversion des Eglises* (1991), English translation: *For the Conversion of the Churches* (1993);

- Lutheran World Federation & Pontifical Council for Promoting Christian Unity, *Joint Declaration on the Doctrine of Justification* (1999);

- World Council of Churches, *The Nature and Mission of the Church*, Faith and Order Paper No. 198 (2005);

---

[5] See, at the end of this book, the entries from the official list of O'Meara's published works that directly discuss ecumenism: nos. 5, 6, 8, 15, 16, 17, 20, 24, 29, 55, 70, 117, 145, 167, as well as his studies on Martin Luther, Friedrich Schelling, Max Müller, and Paul Tillich.

[6] See, among other books, Walter Kasper's *That They May All Be One: The Call to Unity Today* (New York: Burns and Oates, 2003). For an overview of his contributions, see Brian E. Daley, "Dialogue, Communion, and Unity," in *The Theology of Cardinal Walter Kasper: Speaking Truth in Love* (Collegeville, MN: Liturgical Press, 2014), 139–53.

- *The Church of the Triune God: The Cyprus Statement Agreed by the International Commission for Anglican-Orthodox Theological Dialogue* (2006);

- World Council of Churches, *The Church: Towards a Common Vision*, Faith and Order Paper No. 214 (2013);

- The Joint Working Group between the Roman Catholic Church and the World Council of Churches, *Reception: A Key to Ecumenical Progress* (2014).

These consensus statements have explored a wide variety of topics, including the presence of Christ in the celebration of the Lord's Supper, the significance of ordination, whether *episkopē* can exist apart from bishops, papal primacy, and the significance of justification.

Yet despite growing consensus on a number of issues, the ecumenical journey is still ongoing. Authorities in various churches remain unwilling to permit canonical adjustments to allow for eucharistic sharing, even when agreed-on doctrinal positions regarding the Eucharist, the nature of ordination, and the effects of baptism illustrate that what have been considered church-dividing issues are in fact different theological emphases that do not of themselves warrant denial of eucharistic hospitality. Similarly, the way consensus statements have described ecclesial ministry, both ordained and lay, is a major advancement. The mainline churches all follow the same methodology in describing ministry: begin with the ministry of Jesus during his public life, move on to the roles assigned to the Twelve, and then consider the emergent ministry of the early church. Although various churches and their theologians articulate differently the number of the sacraments in the church, there is shared conviction that the two principal sacraments are baptism and the Lord's Supper.

While there is obvious hesitation among non-Catholics to agree to the terminology and mindset of Vatican I regarding papal jurisdiction and infallibility, there is openness to the possibility that one church office could bear the responsibility of *sollicitudo omnium ecclesiarum* (care for all churches), a primacy of honor that does not exclude other "primacies." At one point, a creative shift of terminology was launched by Pope Paul VI and Cardinal Johannes Willebrands when they described the Second Council of Lyons (1274) not as a truly "ecumenical" council but as a "general council of the West." Force of habit soon squelched this promising shift of terminology, however. Liturgical renewal in many of the churches has sought greater compatibility in language and structure.

But the recent Vatican revision of liturgical language, at least in English, has eliminated that advantage.[7]

Thus the postconciliar period of ecumenical interchange has seen both healing advances and painful frustrations. Given the labor-intensive process of reaching an agreement on these complex and longstanding controversial topics, one has to ask why these remarkable statements have had so little impact on contributing to full, visible unity within the churches. Among the many reasons, one would have to include the following:

- The texts are not widely known except among specialists in ecumenical theology and are often available only in specialized publications;

- The language of most of these texts is probably too technical for even the well-disposed churchgoer;

- The sponsoring ecclesial authorities that mandated the commissions have generally not responded to them competently, much less ever cited their conclusions in the life of their respective churches;

- Even in divinity schools for the training of clergy and religious educators, the texts are rarely incorporated into the core curriculum;

- With rare exception (e.g., *The Nature and Mission of the Church*), the texts have not been reworked or revised once they have been usefully critiqued.

In her chapter in *Receiving the Nature and Mission of the Church*, the Romanian Catholic theologian Korinna Zamfir describes the "non-reception" of ecumenical consensus statements as one of the most serious challenges facing the modern ecumenical movement. She is concerned principally with non-reception by church leaders who are slow to "receive" documents written in collaboration with Christians of other churches.

---

[7] For further reflections on ecumenical achievements from 1970 to 2010, I refer readers to several of my publications: Michael Fahey, *Ecumenism: A Bibliographical Overview*, Bibliographies and Indexes in Religious Studies (Westport, CT: Greenwood Press, 1992); Michael Fahey, "Ecumenical Ecclesiology," in *The Gift of the Church: A Textbook on Ecclesiology*, ed. Peter C. Phan, 111–27 (Collegeville, MN: Liturgical Press, 2000); Michael Fahey, "The Ecumenical Movement Inspired by the Holy Spirit," in *The Holy Spirit, the Church, and Christian Unity*, ed. Doris Donnelly et al. (Leuven, Belgium: Peeters Press, 2005), 119–36; and Michael Fahey, "Shifts in Roman Catholic, Orthodox, Anglican and Protestant Ecclesiology from 1965 to 2006," *Ecclesiology* 4, no. 2 (2008): 134–47.

But the non-reception is also a factor among theologians and the faithful at large.[8]

Challenges Facing Ecumenism

What about the continuing neuralgic areas of unresolved ecumenical investigations? As indicated above, despite the accuracy, comprehensiveness, and pertinence of the conciliar decrees and the agreed-on ecumenical consensus statements, as well as monographs from the same period, little of this material has had an impact on the daily life and attitudes of the faithful in the churches. The Roman Catholic Church, at least its higher authorities, typically cites only papal statements and conciliar documents, not the work of ecumenical consultations or individual theologians. Even though the consensus statements are more and more written in an accessible style, they are neither read nor studied by the faithful. They circulate only among a tiny elite, and rarely attract the attention even of graduate theological students. The BEM Lima statement (1982) did receive a number of "official" reactions (edited by Max Thurian as *Churches Respond to BEM* in several volumes), but few practical conclusions emanated from the process. The only Roman Catholic episcopal conferences I know of that cite in a footnote a consensus statement are the three Catholic Bishops' Conferences of England and Wales, Ireland, and Scotland, in their joint document on the Eucharist, *One Bread, One Body* (1998).

Ecclesiology remains by and large a Eurocentric/North Atlantic dominated realm, despite some efforts to broaden it to include Latin America, Africa, and Asia. Church leaders and the faithful in these marginalized areas of the world are acutely aware of this and resent their being ignored. Although there has been some progress in theological globalization, there has also been a regrettable decline in theological reading, a dearth of theological or religious bookshops (even in large cities), a dramatic decline in the number of translations from foreign languages (even French, German, and Spanish), and a decline in church attendance. English-speaking Christians are not well informed about the thinking and practices of other countries. Even the hoped-for renewal of interest in biblical studies has generally been minimal.

---

[8] Korinna Zamfir, "Is There a Future for the Catholic-Protestant Dialogue? Non-Reception as Challenge for Ecumenical Dialogue," in *Receiving the Nature and Mission of the Church*, ed. Paul Collins and Michael Fahey (London: Continuum/T. & T. Clark, 2008), 85–102.

Nowadays several of the major churches are hindered because of a credibility crisis (pedophilia among the clergy and the negligent response of bishops to sexual abuse by priests), or because of internal divisions (tensions regarding the ordination of women, and the appointment to the episcopate of persons in same-sex partnerships/marriages are just two examples). Church leaders are sometimes more inclined to consult lawyers or bankers than theologians. A kind of ennui has set in that colors the ecclesiological environment.

Despite the theoretical force of Vatican II's teaching about charisms understood as gifts bestowed on the faithful by the Holy Spirit for the building up of the church, very few effective ways of putting that conviction into practice exist. Hopes for an enhancement of the synodal life of the hierarchically structured churches, as well as greater coresponsibility, have come to be seen as utopian. Some churches are extremely reluctant to permit the reality of change in doctrinal formulations or ecclesiastical practices. A burning question remains how believers, whatever their confessional allegiance, can be educated on a continuing basis about the origin, significance, and nature of the church.

From what I observe, many teachers are attempting to theologize about the church without sufficiently relating it to Christology or Pneumatology. Efforts to describe the church as the *Ur-Sakrament*, the primordial sacrament of Christ's presence, have not been sufficiently stressed. Controverted ethical issues are rarely mentioned.

What can be done to ameliorate the situation? Ecclesiologists, especially those who are actively involved in ecumenical discussions, must continue to speak out, narrating the history of Christian practices, highlighting legitimate diversity in the church, and translating research into pastoral practices. Those in the church who are frightened by change should not be allowed to demonize responsible loyal opposition by labeling it as dissent. Many departments of theology in university or divinity school settings remain isolated. Theologians need to deghettoize themselves academically and find new ways to communicate pastorally for the good of the church worldwide.

Receptive Ecumenism and the Future

Reflection on the stalemate surrounding consensus statements has promoted the gradual emergence of what has come to be known as "receptive ecumenism." This movement is based on the recognition—not totally new—that among the participating churches there still lurks the persistent, self-referential attitude that assumes it is the *other* churches that are to blame, that *other* Christians are in error, that *they* have an inadequate understanding of the proper nature of the church. Receptive ecumenism begins not with these assumptions but with a stance of appreciative openness toward "the other." It looks to other Christian churches not for errors to correct but for the gifts these churches have to offer.

Before explaining this promising thrust, one needs to review how the term "reception" has traditionally been used in theology.

In the theology of grace it has consistently been taught that, whereas God through revelation takes the initiative in offering to individuals the gift of faith, still, for this offer to be accepted, it must be freely "received" or welcomed by each individual person. By its very nature, faith in divine revelation cannot be imposed or forced on a person but must be willingly ratified. Thus, in the context of an act of faith, an individual's "coopera-tion" needs to come into play. Of course, the mysterious interplay be-tween grace and free will is one of the most complex relationships in the process of salvation.

In a different context, the term "reception" has long been associated with a local church's (or even an individual's) acceptance of a teaching or a mandate issuing forth from, in the first instance, an ecumenical council. Conciliar teaching is assimilated in two stages: the promulgation of various formulations articulated by the council itself, followed by the subsequent "reception" or willing assimilation by individuals, dioceses, and national and international communities of faith. This reception of a conciliar teaching rests on a number of factors. The teaching of Vatican I in its decree *Pastor Aeternus*, concerning the primacy and teaching au-thority of the pope, came to be generally "received" by the Catholic community once the technical language and stated limits of the teaching were clarified and understood. At the time of Vatican I, however, certain theologians within the Catholic Church, such as Ignaz von Döllinger, did not "receive" the teaching on papal prerogatives and ultimately found themselves outside the Catholic community. In the case of various documents of Vatican II, the well-known opposition by the French arch-bishop Marcel Lefebvre (founder of the Society of St. Pius X) to various conciliar teachings, including his rejection of ecumenism in favor of exclusivism, is a more recent example of "non-reception" of conciliar teachings.

While this form of reception or non-reception is applied primarily to the teachings of an ecumenical council, it is sometimes used in regard to the acceptance or rejection of other magisterial teaching, whether papal or episcopal, even in the form of an encyclical. As is widely recognized, the majority of Roman Catholics have not "received" the teaching of Pope Paul VI in *Humanae Vitae* (1968) where it is stated that "each and every marital act must of necessity retain its intrinsic relationship to the procreation of human life."[9]

The non-reception of a particular teaching of an ecumenical council (or a magisterial document) by the faithful does not necessarily imply error or ill will on their part. On the contrary, it may illustrate that, drawing on the Holy Spirit's gift of the *sensus fidelium*, the community as a whole or in part has appropriately discerned that the formulation of a particular teaching is inadequate because it fails to include some crucial additional factor. Therefore, to label every form of such non-reception as "dissent" is tendentious.

The new term "receptive ecumenism" is described as follows: "The essential principle behind Receptive Ecumenism is that the primary ecumenical responsibility is to ask not 'What do the other traditions first need to learn from us?' but 'What do we need to learn from them?' The assumption is that if all were asking this question seriously and acting upon it then all would be moving in ways that would both deepen our authentic respective identities and draw us into more intimate relationship."[10] This specific method of promoting church unity has been newly and actively fostered by Professor Paul D. Murray of the Centre for Catholic Studies at the University of Durham (UK), who organized at his university two international conferences on the theme in 2006 and 2009.[11] With the assistance of Professor Paul Lakeland of Fairfield University in Connecticut, a third conference, drawing some 125 participants from twenty countries and five continents, was held in June 2014 at Fairfield on the theme: "Receptive Ecumenism in International Perspective: Contextual Ecclesial Learning."

Avery Dulles was among the first Americans to insist that "in our ecumenical contacts we should assume that all Christian communities have something valuable to give and that God may wish to say something

---

[9] Paul VI, *Humanae Vitae*, 11, http://www.vatican.va/holy_father/paul_vi /encyclicals/documents/hf_p-vi_enc_25071968_humanae-vitae_en.html, accessed November 26, 2014.

[10] "Receptive Ecumenism," https://www.dur.ac.uk/theology.religion/ccs/projects /receptiveecumenism/, accessed November 26, 2014.

[11] Already published are the *acta* of the first conference: Paul D. Murray and Luca Badini Confalonieri, eds., *Receptive Ecumenism and the Call to Catholic Learning: Exploring a Way for Contemporary Ecumenism* (Oxford: Oxford University Press, 2008). The papers delivered at the second conference in 2009 are in the process of being edited as *Receptive Ecumenism and Ecclesial Learning: Learning to Be Church Together*.

to us through them" and that "the surest path to Christian unity consists in mutual giving, mutual receptivity, and progressive convergence."[12]

To be sure, ecumenists will recognize in receptive ecumenism echoes of the so-called "spiritual ecumenism" promoted by Abbé Paul Couturier in the early twentieth century. It is also aligned with the insights of the French "Groupe des Dombes" in their joint appeal "for the conversion of the churches."[13] The late Toronto theologian Margaret O'Gara also adumbrated this emphasis in her book *The Ecumenical Gift Exchange*, as well as in her posthumous *No Turning Back: The Future of Ecumenism*.[14] Another American theologian, Lorelei Fuchs, has developed similar emphases in her Leuven doctoral dissertation.[15]

As its name implies, "receptive ecumenism" deals only with exchanges between Christian communities, although it has been argued that inter-religious dialogue could likewise profit from the same openness.[16]

Pope John Paul II described ecumenical dialogue as "an exchange of gifts" in his encyclical *Ut Unum Sint* (28). Pope Francis, in his 2013 post-synodal apostolic exhortation *Evangelii Gaudium* took this a step further, inviting an active attentiveness to gifts in the other churches as potential areas of learning about our own ecclesial needs. "If we really believe in the abundantly free working of the Holy Spirit, we can learn so much from one another! It is not just about being better informed about others but rather about reaping what the Spirit has sown in them, which is also meant to be a gift for us. . . . Through an exchange of gifts, the Spirit can lead us ever more fully into truth and goodness."[17]

The Canadian Conference of Catholic Bishops, in its pastoral letter *Celebrating the 50th Anniversary of the Second Vatican Council's Decree on*

---

[12] Originally published as Avery Dulles, "Principles of Catholic Ecumenism," *Ecumenical Trends* 2, no. 9 (December 1973): 2.

[13] See Richard R. Gaillardetz, "The Groupe des Dombes Document 'One Teacher' (2005): Toward a Postconciliar Catholic Reception," *Theological Studies* 74 (2013): 20–47.

[14] Margaret O'Gara, *The Ecumenical Gift Exchange* (Collegeville, MN: Liturgical Press, 1998); Margaret O'Gara, *No Turning Back: The Future of Ecumenism* (Collegeville, MN: Liturgical Press, 2014).

[15] Lorelei F. Fuchs, *Koinonia and the Quest for an Ecumenical Ecclesiology: From Foundations through Dialogue to Symbolic Competence for Communionality* (Grand Rapids, MI: Eerdmans, 2008).

[16] See, for instance, J. Philip Wogaman, *What Christians Can Learn from Other Religions* (Louisville, KY: Westminster John Knox, 2014).

[17] Francis, *Evangelii Gaudium* (On the Joy of the Gospel), 246, http://w2.vatican.va /content/francesco/en/apost_exhortations/documents/papa-francesco_esortazione -ap_20131124_evangelii-gaudium.html, accessed November 4, 2014.

Ecumenism, Unitatis Redintegratio, 1964–2014, stated: "We can learn and receive from the insights and experiences of other Christian communities as we seek to renew the life of the Catholic Church in fidelity to the gospel."[18]

In summary, receptive ecumenism denotes a personal or denominational conviction of Christians, when engaged informally or officially in dialogue with members of other Christian denominations, that the "others" possess theoretical or practical spiritual qualities that would enrich one's own church. It refers to an attitude anterior to or concurrent with discussions with other Christians, a prerequisite based on a firm commitment regarding the values of one's own denominational allegiance, but with the understanding that one's ecclesial assimilation may in some way be wanting. It presupposes discerning humility. Such an attitude is based in part on one's understanding that the New Testament contains a certain amount of diversity even in its conception of church structures. This originates in a variety of spiritual charisms, bestowed by the Holy Spirit, intended to aid in the building up of church life. St. Paul's teaching on charisms focuses on gifts to individuals, but one may legitimately extrapolate from that reality to recognize corporate or ecclesial charisms with their own emphases. Perhaps another name for this new emphasis in ecumenical dialogue could be "receptors' or receptor's ecumenism." This places emphasis on the doer(s) and their personal or corporate dispositions.

In no way does receptive ecumenism diminish or eliminate the need for continued mutual study of the history and doctrine of controverted teachings, nor does it permit neglect of the already rich accumulation of consensus statements. As Catherine Clifford argues: "This is a moment to learn from the methods and achievements of the dialogues to date, to build upon them rather than discard their accomplishments."[19]

The following questions still need to be addressed by professional theologians, especially those involved in university and divinity school settings: How can the academic community rekindle the level of enthusiasm and commitment toward promoting Christian unity that existed in the early twentieth century, especially among the younger generation?

---

[18] Canadian Conference of Catholic Bishops, *Celebrating the 50th Anniversary of the Second Vatican Council's Decree on Ecumenism,* Unitatis Redintegratio, *1964–2014* (Ottawa: CCCB, 2014), 3.

[19] Catherine E. Clifford, "Lonergan's Contribution to Ecumenism," *Theological Studies* 63, no. 3 (2002): 522.

How can the real but limited achievements produced by the principal consensus statements of the bilateral and multilateral ecumenical consultations be preserved and disseminated in academic and ecclesial settings? What additional activities besides study and instruction can be undertaken by teachers to promote the central goals of receptive ecumenism, especially its stress on reform? And finally, how can the academic community of theologians contribute to fostering greater exchange of ideas with bishops and other community leaders?

For Further Reading

Canadian Conference of Catholic Bishops. *Celebrating the 50th Anniversary of the Second Vatican Council's Decree on Ecumenism*, Unitatis Redintegratio, *1964–2014*. Ottawa: CCCB, 2014.

Donnelly, Doris, Adelbert Denaux, and Joseph Famerée, eds. *The Holy Spirit, the Church, and Christian Unity*. Leuven, Belgium: Peeters Press, 2005.

Fuchs, Lorelei F. *Koinonia and the Quest for an Ecumenical Ecclesiology: From Foundations through Dialogue to Symbolic Competence for Communionality*. Grand Rapids, MI: Eerdmans, 2008.

Kasper, Walter. *That They May All Be One: The Call to Unity Today*. New York: Burns and Oates, 2003.

Kinnamon, Michael. *Can a Renewal Movement Be Renewed? Questions for the Future of Ecumenism*. Grand Rapids, MI: Eerdmans, 2014.

Murray, Paul D., and Luca Badini Confalonieri, eds. *Receptive Ecumenism and the Call to Catholic Learning: Exploring a Way for Contemporary Ecumenism*. Oxford: Oxford University Press, 2008.

O'Gara, Margaret. *The Ecumenical Gift Exchange*. Collegeville, MN: Liturgical Press, 1998.

Reiser, Konrad. *Ecumenism in Transition: A Paradigm Shift in the Ecumenical Movement?* Translated by Tony Coates. Geneva: World Council of Churches, 1991.

Routhier, Gilles. *Cinquante ans après Vatican II: Que reste-t-il à mettre en oeuvre?* Paris: Cerf, 2014.

Rusch, William G. *Ecumenical Reception: Its Challenge and Opportunity*. Grand Rapids, MI: Eerdmans, 2007.

Thomas F. O'Meara, OP, Bibliography of Publications

Compiled by Michael A. Fahey, SJ

1960

1. "The Bee: Instinct or Intelligence." *Reality* 8 (1960): 87–106.

1961

2. "The Second Spring." *Worship* 35 (1961): 270–75.

1962

3. "Lacordaire, the Dominican." *The Dominican Tertiary* 2 (1962): 121–23.
4. "The Liturgy of Taizé." *Worship* 36 (1962): 638–44.
5. "Mary and the Ecumenical Era." *The Marian Era* 3 (1962): 26–31.
6. "Paul Tillich and Ecumenism." *Reality* 10 (1962): 151–80.
7. "St. Thérèse of Lisieux and St. Thomas Aquinas." Translation of André Combes. *Cross and Crown* 14 (1962): 295–310.

1963

8. "Dominicans and the Ecumenical Movement." *Dominican Educational Bulletin* 4 (1963): 34.
9. "The Rule of Taizé." *Review for Religious* 22 (1963): 318–26.

1964

10. "Introduction." In *Paul Tillich in Catholic Thought*, edited by Thomas F. O'Meara and Celestin D. Weisser, xvii–xxiii. Chicago: Priory Press, 1964; Garden City, NY: Image Books, 1969.
11. "Marian Theology and the Contemporary Problem of Myth." *Marian Studies* 8 (1964): 127–56.

12. "Paul Tillich and Ecumenism." In *Paul Tillich in Catholic Thought*, edited by Thomas F. O'Meara and Celestin D. Weisser, 273–300. Chicago: Priory Press, 1964; Garden City, NY: Image Books, 1969.

13. *Paul Tillich in Catholic Thought*. Edited by Thomas F. O'Meara and Celestin D. Weisser. Chicago: Priory Press, 1964; London: Darton, Longman and Todd, 1965; Garden City, NY: Image Books, 1969.

1965

14. *Aspects of the Church*. Translation of Heinrich Fries. Westminster, MD: Newman Press, 1965; Dublin: Gill and Son, 1965.

15. "Is Christian Unity a Utopia?" Translation of Heinrich Fries. *Cross and Crown* 17 (1965): 152–61.

16. "Towards a Pastoral Ecumenism." *Worship* 39 (1965): 96–105.

1966

17. "Cinq années d'oecuménisme aux États-Unis: Dubuque, Iowa." *Vers L'Unité Chrétienne* 19 (1966): 42–43.

18. "Interview with Hans Küng." Translation. *Listening* 1 (1966): 172–82. [An interview in *Der Spiegel*: "Die neue Freiheit ist nicht mehr auszulöschen," January 1, 1966].

19. "Karl Rahner on Priest, Parish, and Deacon." *Worship* 40 (1966): 103–10.

20. "Liturgy of the Word: Ecumenical Perspectives." *Cross and Crown* 18 (1966): 146–52.

21. "Liturgy of the Word: Theological Perspectives." *Cross and Crown* 18 (1966): 321–30.

22. *Mary in Protestant and Catholic Theology*. New York: Sheed and Ward, 1966.

23. "The Speculative Church and the Practical Church." *Herder Correspondence* 3 (1966): 214–16.

1967

24. "Five Years of Ecumenism in Dubuque, Iowa." *Faith and Unity* 11 (1967): 85–86.

25. "Karl Rahner, Theologian." *Doctrine and Life* 17 (1967): 31–37.

26. "The Pathway." Translation of Martin Heidegger. *Listening* 2 (1967): 88–91. Reprinted in *Listening* 8 (1973): 32–39; Thomas Sheehan, ed., *Heidegger: The Man and the Thinker*. Chicago: Precedent Publishing Company, 1981, 69–72; Thomas Frick, ed., *The Sacred Theory of the Earth*. Berkeley: North Atlantic Books, 1986, 45–48; Manfred Stassen, ed., *Martin Heidegger, Philosophical and Political Writings*. New York: Continuum, 2003, 77–79.

27. "Rudolf Bultmann's Theology of God." *Irish Theological Quarterly* 34 (1967): 38–60.

28. "Theology: Made in the USA." *The Catholic World* 205 (1967): 231–37. Reprinted in *Guide* 221 (October 1967): 12–16.

1968

29. "Always Ecumenism, Sometimes Merger." *Great Plains Observer* 2 (1968): 12–13.
30. "The Apostolate and Community." In *Renewal through Community and Experimentation*, 69–78. Canon Law Society of America Workshop, 1968.
31. "Bultmann and the Future of Theology." In *Rudolf Bultmann in Catholic Thought*, edited by Thomas F. O'Meara and Donald M. Weisser, 222–50. New York: Herder and Herder, 1968.
32. "Heidegger on God." *Continuum* 5 (1968): 686–98.
33. "Introduction." In *Rudolf Bultmann in Catholic Thought*, edited by Thomas F. O'Meara and Donald M. Weisser, 15–28. New York: Herder and Herder, 1968.
34. "Liturgy Hot and Cool." *Worship* 42 (1968): 215–23. Reprinted in *Encounter* 16 (1968): 8–10.
35. *Rudolf Bultmann in Catholic Thought*. Edited by Thomas F. O'Meara and Donald M. Weisser. New York: Herder and Herder, 1968.
36. *Superstition and Irreverence. Summa Theologiae*, II-II, qq. 92–100. Translation of Thomas Aquinas. *Summa Theologiae*, vol. 40. New York: McGraw-Hill, 1968; London: Eyre and Spottiswoode, 1968.
37. "Thomas Aquinas: Friar, Theologian and Mystic." Translation of Karl Rahner. *Cross and Crown* 20 (1968): 5–9.
38. "Tillich and Heidegger: A Structural Relationship." *Harvard Theological Review* 61 (1968): 249–61.

1969

39. "Apostolate and Community: Secularization and Revolution." *Sisters Today* 40 (1969): 335–46.
40. "Community and Commitment." *Review for Religious* 28 (1969): 541–51.
41. Foreword to *Kerygma and Dogma* by Karl Rahner and Karl Lehmann, 7–10. New York: Herder and Herder, 1969.
42. Foreword to *Revelation* by Heinrich Fries, 7–11. New York: Herder and Herder, 1969.
43. "Paul Tillich and the Problem of God." *Communio* 2 (1969): 123–42.
44. "Where is Theology Going?" *Thought* 44 (1969): 53–68.

1970

45. "Afterword: The End of Theology?" In *Projections: Shaping an American Theology for the Future*, edited by Thomas F. O'Meara and Donald M. Weisser, 217–28. New York: Doubleday, 1970.
46. "The Encounter with God." *Spiritual Life* 16 (1970): 72–80.
47. *Holiness and Radicalism in Religious Life*. New York: Herder and Herder, 1970.
48. "Is There a Common Authority for Christians?" *The Ecumenical Review* 22 (1970): 16–28.

49. "Justification and Sanctification." *Cross and Crown* 22 (1970): 160–70.

50. *Paul Tillich's Theology of God*. Dubuque, IA: Listening Press, 1970.

51. *The Presence of the Spirit of God*. Washington, DC: Corpus Books, 1970.

52. *Projections: Shaping an American Theology for the Future*. Edited by Thomas F. O'Meara and Donald M. Weisser. New York: Doubleday, 1970.

53. "Radicalism and Renewal." *exChange* 2 (1970): 11.

54. "Radicalism in the Religious Life." *Sign* 49 (1970): 21–25.

55. "Responsibility to Others." *Chicago Studies* 9 (1970): 183–201. Reprinted in *Shared Responsibility in the Local Church*, edited by Charles E. Curran and George J. Dyer, 71–89. Chicago: Catholic Theological Society of America, 1970.

56. "Roman Catholicism: The Authority Crisis." *McCormick Quarterly* 23 (1970): 168–80.

57. "Shaping an American Theology for the Future." In *Projections: Shaping an American Theology for the Future*, edited by Thomas F. O'Meara and Donald M. Weisser, 1–17. New York: Doubleday, 1970.

58. "Theological Reflection on Institutional Renewal in the Church." *Proceedings of the 32nd Annual Convention of the Canon Law Society of America* 32 (1970): 1–14.

59. "Towards a Roman Catholic Theology of the Presbytery." *The Heythrop Journal* 10 (1970): 390–404.

1971

60. "Christian Belief and Today's Image of Man." *Cross and Crown* 23 (1971): 24–38.

61. "The Cultural Crisis of Christian Faith." In *Faith and Religious Life*. Donum Dei, no. 17, 55–66. Ottawa: Canadian Religious Conference, 1971.

62. "Emergence and Decline of Popular Voice in the Selection of Bishops." In *The Choosing of Bishops: Historical and Theological Studies*, edited by William W. Bassett, 21–32. Hartford, CT: Canon Law Society of America, 1971.

63. "The End of Liberal Theology." *The Lutheran Quarterly* 23 (1971): 268–73.

64. "Homeland." Translation of Martin Heidegger. *Listening* 6 (1971): 231–38.

65. Introduction to *The Virgin Mary in Evangelical Perspective* by Heiko Oberman, v–xvi. Philadelphia: Fortress Press, 1971.

66. "Life beyond Polarization." *Review for Religious* 30 (1971): 235–44.

67. "The National Pastoral Council of a Christian Church: Ecclesiastical Accessory or Communal Voice?" In *A National Pastoral Council: Pro and Con*, 21–34. Washington, DC: USCC, 1971.

68. "Was Jesus in an Underground?" *Listening* 6 (1971): 104–8.

1972

69. "Christian Ministry and Health Service." *Hospital Progress* 51 (1972): 48–55.

70. "The Ecumenical Evolution in the United States: From Confession to Politics." In *Begegnung: Beiträge zu einer Hermeneutik des theologischen Gesprächs*, edited by Max Seckler et al., 559–66. Vienna: Styria, 1972.
71. "Ministries." *Bulletin (Sister Formation Conference)* 18 (1972): 12.
72. "Optional Ministerial Celibacy: Its Effect on Religious Life." *American Ecclesiastical Review* 166 (1972): 587–96.
73. "Religious Life and Social Crisis." *Sisters Today* 43 (1972): 420–27. Reprinted in *Religious Life in the 1970's*, edited by Kevin O'Rourke. Dubuque, IA: Aquinas Institute, 1971.
74. *Rudolf Bultmann en el pensamiento catolico*. Barcelona: Sal Terrae, 1972. Translation of Thomas F. O'Meara and Donald M. Weisser, eds. *Rudolf Bultmann in Catholic Thought*. New York: Herder and Herder, 1968.
75. "Towards a Theology of Ministry for Sisters." *Sisters Today* 44 (1972): 119–26.
76. "The Trial of Jesus." *Theology Today* 28 (1972): 451–65.

1973

77. "Art and Music as Illustrators of Theology." *Anglican Theological Review* 55 (1973): 267–79.
78. "Clerical Culture and Feminine Ministry." *Commonweal* 98 (1973): 523–26.
79. "Pastoral Councils in the Catholic Church." *New Catholic World* 216 (1973): 212–16.
80. "Poverty and Time." *Sisters Today* 45 (1973): 141–49.
81. "Religious Education for Maturity: The Presence of Grace." *Religious Education* 68 (1973): 454–64.
82. "Teilhard de Chardin in China." *Worldview* 16 (1973): 31–34.
83. "Theologies and Liberations." *Link* (1973): 1–6.

1974

84. "Adult Religious Education." *The Lamp* 72 (1974): 6–9.
85. *Loose in the World*. New York: Paulist Press, 1974.
86. "Ministry Anyone? Ministry Everyone!" *New Catholic World* 217 (1974): 110–13.
87. "Ministry to Presence: The Hospital and the Spirit." *Hospital Progress* 55 (1974): 62–65.
88. "A New Look at Orders: Ministry for the Many." In *Women and Orders*, edited by Robert Heyer, 75–86. New York: Paulist Press, 1974.
89. "Paris as the Cultural Milieu for Thomas Aquinas." *The Thomist* 38 (1974): 689–722.

1975

90. "Bright Continent." *Provincial Newsletter, Dominican Province of St. Albert the Great* (Spring 1975): 15, 22.

91. "Decision-Making for America: Political-Theological Influences." *Proceedings of the Catholic Theological Society of America* 30 (1975): 49–62.

92. "Did Anyone Call? A Theology of Vocation." *New Catholic World* 218 (1975): 57–59.

93. "Towards a Subjective Theology of Revelation." *Theological Studies* 36 (1975): 401–27.

1977

94. "F. W. J. Schelling: A Bibliographical Essay." *The Review of Metaphysics* 31 (1977): 283–309.

1978

95. "The Crisis in Ministry Is a Crisis of Spirituality." *Spirituality Today* 30 (1978): 14–23.

96. "An Eckhart Bibliography." In *Meister Eckhart of Hochheim (1228–1978)*, edited by Thomas F. O'Meara. Special issue, *The Thomist* 42 (1978): 313–36. Reprinted in Jeanne Ancelet-Hustache, ed., *Maître Eckhart Sermons*, vol. 3, 187–214. Paris: Éditions du Seuil, 1979.

97. "Health Care amid Religion and Revelation." *Hospital Progress* 59 (1978): 68–72. Reprinted in *Camillian* 18 (1979): 13–21.

98. "Meister Eckhart's Destiny (I, II)." *Spirituality Today* 30 (1978): 250–62, 348–59.

99. *Meister Eckhart of Hochheim (1228–1978)*. Edited by Thomas F. O'Meara. Special issue, *The Thomist* 42 (1978).

100. "Philosophical Models in Ecclesiology." *Theological Studies* 39 (1978): 3–21. Reprinted in *Selecciones de teologia* (1980): 80–91.

101. "The Presence of Meister Eckhart." In *Meister Eckhart of Hochheim (1228–1978)*, edited by Thomas F. O'Meara. Special issue, *The Thomist* 42 (1978): 171–81.

1979

102. "Process and God in Schelling's Early Thought." *Listening* 14 (1979): 223–36.

1980

103. "Albert the Great and Martin Luther on Justification." In *Albert the Great, Theologian: Essays in Honor of Albertus Magnus (1280–1980)*, edited by Thomas F. O'Meara. Special issue, *The Thomist* 44 (1980): 539–59.

104. "Albert the Great: A Bibliographical Guide." In *Albert the Great, Theologian: Essays in Honor of Albertus Magnus (1280–1980)*, edited by Thomas F. O'Meara. Special issue, *The Thomist* 44 (1980): 597–98.

105. *Albert the Great, Theologian: Essays in Honor of Albertus Magnus (1280–1980)*. Edited by Thomas F. O'Meara. Special issue, *The Thomist* 44 (1980).

106. "Did Anyone Call? A Theology of Vocation." In *Young Adult Living*, edited by Jean Marie Hiesberger, 17–25. New York: Paulist Press, 1980.

107. "A History of Grace." In *A World of Grace: An Introduction to the Themes and Foundations of Karl Rahner's Theology*, edited by Leo J. O'Donovan, 76–91. New York: Seabury, 1980; Washington, DC: Georgetown University Press, 1995.

108. "How Secular Are We?" *New Catholic World* 223 (1980): 88–91.

109. "The Spirituality of the Sixteenth Century." In *450th Anniversary of the Augsburg Confession*. Dubuque: Wartburg Theological Seminary, 1980.

1981

110. "Catholic Science Fiction, 1900." *America* 144 (1981): 525–27.

111. "Creative Imagination: The Aesthetic Horizon in Theology." Presidential Address. *Proceedings of the Catholic Theological Society of America* 36 (1981): 83–95.

112. "Lutheran Spirituality." Translation of Georges Casalis and Jean-Louis Klein. *Spirituality Today* 33 (1981): 218–39.

113. "Of Art and Theology: Hans Urs von Balthasar's Systems." *Theological Studies* 42 (1981): 272–76.

1982

114. "The Presence of Meister Eckhart." *Dominican Ashram* 1 (1982): 115–21.

115. *Romantic Idealism and Roman Catholicism: Schelling and the Theologians*. Notre Dame, IN: University of Notre Dame Press, 1982.

116. "Schelling's Philosophy of Revelation." In *Meaning, Truth, and God*, edited by Leroy S. Rouner, 216–36. Notre Dame, IN: University of Notre Dame Press, 1982.

1983

117. "Aquinas Institute in Dubuque: An Ecumenical Recollection." *Provincial Newsletter, Dominican Province of St. Albert the Great* (September 1983): 11–13.

118. *Theology of Ministry*. New York: Paulist Press, 1983.

119. "Thomas Aquinas, Vatican II, and Contemporary Theology." Translation of C. J. Pinto de Oliveira. *Nova et Vetera* 56 (1983): 161–80.

1984

120. "The Aesthetic Dimension in Theology." In *Art, Creativity, and the Sacred: An Anthology in Religion and Art*, edited by Diane Apostolos-Cappadona, 205–18. New York: Crossroad, 1984.

121. "Lutheranism: A School of Spirituality." *Dialog* 23 (1984): 126–34.

122. "The Providential Event: Sermon on the 450th Anniversary of the Birth of Martin Luther." *Dialog* 23 (1984): 223–26.

123. "Response to John Clayton." *Papers of the Nineteenth Century Theology Working Group* 10 (1984): 13–17.

1985

124. "Martin Heidegger and Liturgical Time." *Worship* 59 (1985): 126–33.
125. "The Ministry of the Priesthood and Its Relationship to the Wider Ministry in the Church." *Seminaries in Dialogue* 11 (1985): 1–8.
126. "The Origins of the Liturgical Movement and German Romanticism." *Worship* 59 (1985): 326–42.
127. "Paul Tillich and the Catholic Substance." In *The Thought of Paul Tillich*, edited by James Luther Adams, Wilhelm Pauck, and Roger Lincoln Shinn, 290–306. San Francisco: Harper and Row, 1985.
128. "Schelling Studies: A Bibliographical Report." *Owl of Minerva* 2 (1985): 300–301.
129. "The Trouble with Seminaries." *Church* 1 (1985): 18–22.

1986

130. "Between Idealism and Neo-Scholasticism: The Fundamental and Apologetic Theology of Alois Schmid." *Église et théologie* 17 (1986): 335–54.
131. "Christ in Schelling's Philosophy of Revelation." *Heythrop Journal* 27 (1986): 275–89.
132. "The Future of Catholicism." Inaugural Lecture as the William K. Warren Professor of Catholic Theology at the University of Notre Dame (October 15, 1986).
133. "Heidegger and His Origins: Theological Perspectives." *Theological Studies* 47 (1986): 205–26.
134. *Karl Rahner in Dialogue: Conversations and Interviews, 1965–1982.* Translation of Karl Rahner (various sections). Edited by Harvey Egan. New York: Crossroad, 1986.
135. "Modern Art and the Sacred: The Prophetic Ministry of Alain Couturier, O.P." *Spirituality Today* 38 (1986): 31–40.

1987

136. "Eckhart, Johannes." In *The Encyclopedia of Religion*, edited by Mircea Eliade, 4:580–81. New York: Macmillan, 1987.
137. "Grace." In *The Encylopedia of Religion*, edited by Mircea Eliade, 6:84–88. New York: Macmillan, 1987.
138. "The Identity of the Priest and the Wider Ministry." *The Serran* (August 1987): 10–13.
139. "Ministry." In *The New Dictionary of Theology*, edited by Joseph A. Komonchak, Mary Collins, and Dermot A. Lane, 657–61. Wilmington, DE: Michael Glazier, 1987.

140. "Orders and Ordination." In *The New Dictionary of Theology*, edited by Joseph A. Komonchak, Mary Collins, and Dermot A. Lane, 723–27. Wilmington, DE: Michael Glazier, 1987.

141. "The Presence of Schelling in the Third Volume of Paul Tillich's *Systematic Theology*." In *Religion et Culture*, edited by Michel Despland, Jean-Claude Petit, and Jean Richard, 187–206. Paris: Cerf, 1987.

142. "Revelation and History: Schelling, Möhler and Congar." *Irish Theological Quarterly* 53 (1987): 17–35.

143. "Schelling, Friedrich." In *The Encyclopedia of Religion*, Mircea Eliade, 13:97–98. New York: Macmillan, 1987.

144. "Thomas Aquinas and German Intellectuals: Neoscholasticism and Modernity in the Late 19th Century." *Gregorianum* 68 (1987): 719–36.

1988

145. "Ecumenist of Our Times: Yves Congar." *Mid-Stream* 27 (1988): 67–73.

146. "Fundamentalism and the Christian Believer." *The Priest* 44 (1988): 39–46.

147. "Grace as a Theological Structure in the *Summa Theologiae* of Thomas Aquinas." *Recherches de théologie ancienne et médiévale* 55 (1988): 130–53.

148. "Pope and Bible: The Search for Authority." William K. Warren Lecture, University of Tulsa (October 1988).

149. "Revelation in Schelling's *Lectures on Academic Study*." In *Los comienzos filosoficos de Schelling*, edited by Ignacio Falgueras, 121–31. Malaga: Servicio de Publicaciones de la Universidad de Malaga, 1988.

1989

150. "Between Berlin and Rome in 1900: Roman Catholic Reform Programs for the 20th Century." Anaheim, CA: American Academy of Religion, 1989.

151. "Doctoral Education in Theology in Catholic Universities." *America* 160 (1989): 434–36.

152. "Expanding Horizons: A World of Religions and Jesus Christ." In *Faithful Witness: Foundations of Theology for Today's Church*, edited by Leo J. O'Donovan and T. Howland Sanks, 151–66. New York: Crossroad, 1989.

153. "The Teaching Office of Bishops in the Ecclesiology of Charles Journet." *The Jurist* 49 (1989): 23–47.

154. "Thomas Aquinas and Modernity." In *Thomas Aquinas and Contemporary Thought*, edited by Richard Woods, 1–23. Chicago: Dominican Publications, 1989.

1990

155. *Faith in a Wintry Season: Conversations and Interviews with Karl Rahner in the Last Years of His Life*. Translation of Karl Rahner (various sections). Edited by Harvey Egan. New York: Crossroad, 1990.

156. *Fundamentalism: A Catholic Perspective*. New York: Paulist Press, 1990.

157. "A Visit to the Novitiate." *Provincial Newsletter, Dominican Province of St. Albert the Great* (April 1990): 14–15. Translated into French, Italian, German and Spanish for *IDI*, the international newsletter of the Dominican Order.

1991

158. *The Basilica of the Sacred Heart at Notre Dame: A Theological Guide to the Paintings and Windows.* Notre Dame, IN: Hammes University of Notre Dame Bookstore, 1991.

159. *Church and Culture: German Catholic Theology, 1860 to 1914.* Notre Dame, IN: University of Notre Dame Press, 1991.

160. "The Dominican School of Salamanca and the Spanish Conquest of America: Some Bibliographical Notes." *Provincial Newsletter, Dominican Province of St. Albert the Great* (Fall 1991): 68–69.

161. "Field of Grace." *Notre Dame Magazine* 20 (1991): 12–13.

162. "Karl Rahner: Some Audiences and Sources for His Theology." *Communio* 18 (1991): 237–51.

1992

163. "The Dominican School of Salamanca and the Spanish Conquest of America: Some Bibliographical Notes." *The Thomist* 56 (1992): 555–82.

164. "Exploring the Depths: A Theological Tradition in Viewing the World Religions." In *Verantwortung für den Glauben: Beiträge zur Fundamentaltheologie und Ökumenik: Für Heinrich Fries,* edited by Peter Neuner and Harald Wagner, 375–90. Freiburg: Herder, 1992.

165. "Katolicky pohled na fundamentalismus." *Salve* 2 (1992): 17–22.

166. "Theologians and Native Americans." *Providence* (Winter 1992): 18–24.

1993

167. "Ecumenical Beginnings in the Midwest." *Lutheran Partners* (January/February 1993): 11–13.

168. "Fundamentalism: A Catholic Perspective." In *Reasoned Faith: Essays on the Interplay of Faith and Reason,* edited by Frank T. Birtel, 196–217. New York: Crossroad, 1993.

1994

169. "The Department of Theology at a Catholic University." In *The Challenge and Promise of a Catholic University,* edited by Theodore Hesburgh, 243–56. Notre Dame, IN: University of Notre Dame Press, 1994.

170. "Paul Tillich in Catholic Thought: The Past and the Future." In *Paul Tillich: A New Catholic Assessment,* edited by Raymond F. Bulman and Frederick J. Parella, 9–32. Collegeville, MN: Liturgical Press, 1994.

171. "Raid on the Dominicans: The Repression of 1954." *America* 170 (1994): 8–16. Abbreviated as "The Dominican Repression of 1954." *Linkup* 65 (1994): 12–14.

172. "Schelling's Religious Aesthetic." In *Reform and Counterreform: Dialectics of the Word in Western Christianity Since Luther*, edited by John C. Hawley, 119–38. Berlin: Mouton de Gruyter, 1994.
173. "The School of Thomism at Salamanca and the Presence of Grace in the Americas." *Angelicum* 71 (1994): 321–70.
174. "What a Bishop Might Want to Know." *Worship* 68 (1994): 55–63.

1995

175. "The History of Being and the History of Doctrines: An Influence of Heidegger on Theology." *American Catholic Philosophical Quarterly* 69 (1995): 351–74.
176. "Romano Guardini's *Akademische Feier* in 1964." In *Romano Guardini: Proclaiming the Sacred in a Modern World*, edited by Robert A. Krieg, 98–103. Chicago: Liturgy Training Publications, 1995.

1996

177. "Fundamentalism and Catholicism: Some Cultural and Theological Reflections." *Chicago Studies* 35 (1996): 68–81.
178. "Leaving the Baroque: The Fallacy of Restoration in the Postconciliar Era." *America* 174 (1996): 10–12, 14, 25–28.

1997

179. "Beyond 'Hierarchology': Johann Adam Möhler and Yves Congar." In *The Legacy of the Tübingen School: The Relevance of Nineteenth-Century Theology for the Twenty-First Century*, edited by Donald J. Dietrich and Michael J. Himes, 173–91. New York: Crossroad, 1997.
180. "The Expansion of Ministry: Yesterday, Today, and Tomorrow." In *The Renewal that Awaits Us*, edited by Eleanor Bernstein and Martin F. Connell, 91–103. Chicago: Liturgical Training Publications, 1997.
181. "A French Resistance Hero." *America* 175 (1997): 12–17.
182. "The Presence of Grace Outside of Evangelization, Baptism and Church in Thomas Aquinas' Theology." In *That Others May Know and Love: Essays in Honor of Zachary Hayes O.F.M., Franciscan, Educator, Scholar*, edited by Michael F. Cusato and F. Edward Coughlin, 91–132. St. Bonaventure, NY: Franciscan Institute, 1997.
183. *Seeing Theological Forms.* Monograph Number Six. Belmont, CA: The Archives of Modern Christian Art, 1997.
184. *Thomas Aquinas, Theologian.* Notre Dame, IN: University of Notre Dame Press, 1997.
185. "Virtues in the Theology of Thomas Aquinas." *Theological Studies* 58 (1997): 254–85.

1998

186. "Ministry in the Catholic Church Today: The Gift of Some Historical Trajectories." In *Together in God's Service: Toward a Theology of Ecclesial Lay Ministry*, edited by NCCB Subcommittee on Lay Ministry, 70–86. Washington, DC: USCC, 1998.
187. "Tarzan, Las Casas, and Rahner: Aquinas's Theology of Wider Grace." *Theology Digest* 45 (1998): 319–28.
188. "Teaching Karl Rahner." *Philosophy and Theology* 11 (1998): 191–205.
189. "Thomas Aquinas and Today's Theology." *Theology Today* 55 (1998): 46–58.
190. "The Witness of Engelbert Krebs." In *Continuity and Plurality in Catholic Theology: Essays in Honor of Gerald A. McCool, S.J.*, edited by Anthony Cernera, 127–54. Fairfield, CT: Sacred Heart University Press, 1998.

1999

191. "Christian Theology and Extraterrestrial Intelligent Life." *Theological Studies* 60 (1999): 3–30.
192. "Karl Rahner." In *Dictionary of Existentialism*, edited by Haim Gordon, 189–93. Westport, CT: Greenwood Press, 1999.
193. "Reflections on Yves Congar and Theology in the United States." *U.S. Catholic Historian* 17 (1999): 91–105.
194. *Theology of Ministry*. Revised edition. New York: Paulist Press, 1999.

2000

195. "The Ministry of Presbyter and the Many Ministries in the Church." In *The Theology of Priesthood*, edited by Donald J. Goergen and Ann Garrido, 67–86. Collegeville, MN: Liturgical Press, 2000.
196. "Recollections of Thomas Donlon, O.P." *Provincial Newsletter, Dominican Province of St. Albert the Great* (November 2000): 9–10.

2001

197. "A Center of Dominican Studies and the Theology of Thomas Aquinas." In *Conversation and Collaboration: A Vision for Dominican Mission in the New Century*, 7–21. Miami: Center for Dominican Studies, 2001.
198. "The Heirs of the Clergy? The New Pastoral Ministries and the Reform of the Minor Orders." Translation of Winfried Haunerland. *Worship* 75 (2001): 305–20.
199. "Jean-Pierre Torrell's Research on Thomas Aquinas." *Theological Studies* 62 (2001): 787–801.
200. "Loving Openness Toward Every Truth: A Letter from Thomas Aquinas to Karl Rahner." Translation of Yves Congar. *Philosophy and Theology* 12 (2001): 213–19.

201. "Le ministère dans l'église catholique d'aujourd'hui: Les données de quelques trajectoires historiques." In *Des ministres pour l'église*, edited by Joseph Doré and M. Maurice Vidal, 152–70. Paris: Cerf, 2001.

2002

202. *Erich Przywara: His Theology and His World*. Notre Dame, IN: University of Notre Dame Press, 2002.
203. "Interpreting Thomas Aquinas: Aspects of the Dominican School of Moral Theology in the Twentieth Century." In *The Ethics of Aquinas*, edited by Stephen Pope, 355–74. Washington, DC: Georgetown University Press, 2002.
204. "Onkraj Granica." In *Vjesnik. Hrvatske Dominikanske Provincije* 39 (2002): 34–36. Croatian Translation of "Beyond Boundaries," an Address Given at the Granting of the Degree STM in the Province of St. Albert the Great.
205. "Recollections of a Theologian: Dialogue with Newman." Translation of Heinrich Fries. *Irish Theological Quarterly* 67 (2002): 251–64.
206. *A Theologian's Journey*. New York: Paulist Press, 2002.
207. *Thomas Aquinas, Theologian*. Korean translation. Seoul: Catholic Publishing House, 2002.

2003

208. "Autobiography in Dialogue with Cardinal Newman: Recollections of a Theologian." Translation of Heinrich Fries. *Irish Theological Quarterly* (2002): 251–64.
209. "Divine Grace and Human Nature as Sources for the Universal Magisterium of Bishops." *Theological Studies* 64 (2003): 683–706.
210. "Dominican Studies and the Theology of Thomas Aquinas." *Listening* 38 (2003): 212–24.
211. "The End!" *Celebration* 32 (2003): 468.
212. Foreword to *Creating Communion: The Theology of the Constitutions of the Church* by John J. Markey, v–xviii. Hyde Park: New City Press, 2003.
213. "Pastor, Lay Ministers, and Community . . . amid the Changes of History." In *What Is Good Ministry? Resources to Launch a Discussion*, edited by Jackson W. Carroll and Carol E. Lytch, 28–31. Durham: Pulpit and Pew Research Reports, 2003.
214. "Paul Tillich und Erich Przywara in Davos." *Davoser Revue* 78 (2003): 18–22.
215. "Religion in History. Schelling and Molitor." In *Études sur Schelling en homage à Xavier Tilliette*. Special issue, *Iris: Annales de philosophie* 24 (2003): 199–213.

2004

216. "Ambition in the Church." *Spirituality* 10 (2004): 111–18.
217. "Christ Died for Our Sins." *The Catechist's Connection* 22 (2004): 6.

218. "Concerning the Mystery and Gift of Teaching." In *For the Love of Teaching*, edited by George Howard, 210–19. Notre Dame, IN: Academic Publications, 2004.

219. "Faith in Color." *ParishWorks* 7 (2004): 8.

220. "Paul Tillich and Erich Przywara at Davos." *Bulletin of the North American Paul Tillich Society* 30 (2004): 8–9.

221. "Theological Method according to John Henry Newman and Karl Rahner." Translation of Heinrich Fries. *Philosophy and Theology* 16 (2004): 163–93.

222. "What Can We Learn from the Tridentine and Baroque Church?" In *The Catholic Church in the 21st Century: Finding Hope for Its Future in the Wisdom of the Past*, edited by Michael Himes, 56–64. Liguori: Liguori Press, 2004.

2005

223. "Christmas." *Celebration* 34 (2005): 3–4.

224. *The Future of the Church: Insights from Three Dominicans*. Columbus: Ohio Dominican University, 2005.

225. "Lay Ecclesial Ministry—What It Is and What It Isn't." In *Lay Ministry in the Catholic Church*, edited by Richard W. Miller, 67–78. Liguori, MO: Liguori Press, 2005.

226. "Schelling, Drey, Möhler und die nachkonziliare Zeit: Kunst und Organismus im Kirchenverständnis." In *Theologie als Instanz der Moderne: Beiträge und Studien zu Johann Sebastian Drey und zur Katholischen Tübinger Schule*, edited by Michael Kessler and Ottmar Fuchs, 207–16. Tübingen: Francke, 2005.

227. "Theologies on the Boundary." *Veritas* (September 2005): 19–20.

228. "Theology of Church." In *The Theology of Thomas Aquinas*, edited by Rik van Nieuwenhove and Joseph Wawrykow, 303–25. Notre Dame, IN: University of Notre Dame Press, 2005, 2010.

229. "Yves Congar, Theologian of Grace in a Vast World." In *Yves Congar: Theologian of the Church*, edited by Gabriel Flynn, 371–400. Leuven: Peeters, 2005.

2006

230. "The Church Is Active in Ministry." In *The Many Marks of the Church*, edited by William Madges and Michael J. Daley, 65–68. New London: Twenty-Third Publications, 2006.

231. "French Baroque Thomism: The Theological System of Vincent de Contenson, O.P." *Science et Esprit* 58 (2006): 23–41.

232. "Neo-Thomism." In *The Edinburgh Dictionary of Continental Philosophy*, edited by John Protevi, 424–25. Edinburgh: Edinburgh University Press, 2005; New Haven, CT: Yale University Press, 2006.

233. "Paul Tillich and Erich Przywara." *Gregorianum* 87 (2006): 227–38.

234. "Paul Tillich in Japan." Translation of Eiko Hanaoka. *Bulletin of the North American Paul Tillich Society* 323 (2006): 6–9.

235. "A Pioneer in Pastoral Theology: Constantin Noppel, S.J." In *In God's Hands: Essays on the Church and Ecumenism in Honour of Michael A. Fahey, S.J.*, edited by Jaroslav Skira and Michael Attridge, 75–87. Leuven: Leuven University Press, 2006.

236. "Preaching and Ministry in a Time of Expansion." In *The Grace and Task of Preaching*, edited by Michael Monshau, 255–69. Dublin: Dominican Publications, 2006.

237. "The Priest Preaching in a World of Grace." In *Priests for the 21st Century*, edited by Donald Dietrich, 66–76. New York: Rowman and Littlefield, 2006.

238. "Schelling." In *Encyclopedia of Religion*, 2nd ed., edited by Lindsay Jones, 8148–49. New York: Thomson Gale, 2006.

239. "Thomas Aquinas in Africa." *America* 194 (2006): 13–17. Reprinted in *International Dominican Information* 440 (March 2006): 71–73.

2007

240. "Between Apologetics and Ecclesiology. Sertillanges on the Church." In *Dominikanische Beiträge zur Ekklesiologie und zum kirchlichen Leben im Mittelalter*, edited by Thomas Prügl and Marianne Schlosser, 403–20. Paderborn: Schöningh, 2007.

241. *God in the World: A Guide to Karl Rahner's Theology.* Collegeville, MN: Liturgical Press, 2007.

242. "Power and Display in the Church: Yves Congar's Critique." *Dominican Studies* 1 (2007): 26–36.

243. "Wilhelm von Tripoli." *Wort und Wahrheit* 48 (2007): 131–35.

244. "Yves Congar, théologien de la grâce dans un vaste monde." In *Yves Congar, théologien de l'église*, 329–46. Paris: Éditions du Cerf, 2007.

2008

245. "Events Dramatic and Violent. . . ." *Light and Life: The Magazine of Weston Jesuit School of Theology* (Spring 2008): 5.

246. "A Note on Ministry in the Theology of J.-M. R. Tillard." *Science et Esprit* 61 (2009): 195–201.

247. "The Theology and Times of William of Tripoli, O.P.: A Different View of Islam." *Theological Studies* 69 (2008): 80–98.

2009

248. "Karl Rahner's Remarks on the Schema, 'De Ecclesia in Mundo Hujus Temporis,' in the Draft of May 28, 1965." *Philosophy and Theology* 1–2 (2008): 331–39.

249. "Paul Tillich and Karl Rahner: A Bibliography." *Bulletin of the North American Paul Tillich Society* 35 (2009): 5–6.

250. "A Teaching Scarcely Imagined in Europe." *Religious Life Review* 48 (2009): 236–44.

251. "Theologie in den USA: Realitätsnah und kirchlich engangiert." *Wort und Wahrheit* 50, no. 2 (2009): 54–59.

2010

252. "Being a Ministering Church: Insights from History." In *Lay Ecclesial Ministry: Pathways Toward the Future*, edited by Zeni Fox, 53–66. New York: Rowman and Littlefield, 2010.
253. "Johannes B. Lotz, S.J., and Martin Heidegger: A Conversation." Translation of Johannes B. Lotz. *American Catholic Philosophical Quarterly* (2010): 127–31.
254. "Paul Tillich and Karl Rahner: Similarities and Contrasts." *Gregorianum* 91 (2010): 443–59.

2011

255. "Der amerikanische Rahner: Vom Einfluss eines deutschen Theologen auf den Katholizismus in den USA." Karl Rahner-Archiv (Munich), Oktober 2011; *Texte* [online]. Freiburg Universität, Oktober, 2011.

2012

256. "Extraterrestrials and Religious Questions." *Journal of Cosmology* 20 (September 1, 2012). http://journalofcosmology.com/. Accessed November 15, 2014.
257. "The Salvation of Extraterrestrials." *Huffington Post. Religion.* July 16, 2012. http://www.huffingtonpost.com/thomas-f-omeara-op/salvation-of-extraterrestrials_b_1671783.html. Accessed November 15, 2014.
258. "Thomism (Theology)." In *Britannica Online Encyclopedia.* http://www.britannica.com/EBchecked/topic/592919/Thomism. Accessed November 15, 2014.
259. *Vast Universe: Christian Revelation and Extraterrestrials.* Collegeville, MN: Liturgical Press, 2012.

2013

260. *Albert the Great: Theologian and Scientist: Bibliographic Resources and Translated Essays.* Edited by Thomas F. O'Meara. Chicago: New Priory, 2013.
261. "Max Müller, His Philosophy and His Journey." *Heythrop Journal* 54 (May 2013): 385–96.
262. "Resources and Recent Publications on Albert the Great and His Theology." In *Albert the Great: Theologian and Scientist: Bibliographic Resources and Translated Essays,* edited by Thomas F. O'Meara, 1–19. Chicago: New Priory, 2013.
263. *Scanning the Sign of the Times: French Dominicans in the Twentieth Century.* Edited with Paul Philibert. Hindmarsh, Australia: ATF Theology, 2013.
264. "What's the Message on the Runway for Baroque Fashions?" *National Catholic Reporter* 49, no. 7 (January 18–31, 2013): 21–22.

2014

265. "Martin Heidegger's Remarks Following the First Mass of a Newly Ordained Priest." *Philosophy and Theology* 26 (2014): 267–78.
266. "A Theology of Church and Ministry." In *The Theology of Cardinal Walter Kasper: Speaking Truth in Love*, edited by Kristin M. Colberg and Robert A. Krieg, 129–38. Collegeville, MN: Liturgical Press, 2014.
267. "Vast Universe and Extraterrestrials: Threat or Mystery for the Christian Faith?" *New Theology Review: A Catholic Journal of Theology and Ministry* 26, no. 3 (September 2014): 71–75.

N.B.: This listing does not contain the author's book reviews.

Contributors

Stephen Bevans is a priest in the Society of the Divine Word (SVD) and is Louis J. Luzbetak, SVD, Professor of Mission and Culture (Emeritus) at Catholic Theological Union, Chicago. Among his books are *Models of Contextual Theology* (Orbis Books, 2002), *Constants in Context: A Theology of Mission for Today* (with Roger Schroeder, Orbis Books, 2004), and *A Century of Catholic Mission* (edited, Regnum Books, 2013). In 2014 he was appointed a member of the Commission on World Mission and Evangelism at the World Council of Churches.

Michael A. Fahey, SJ, scholar in residence at Fairfield University, Connecticut, obtained his doctorate from the University of Tübingen. He taught ecclesiology in Montreal and Toronto for twenty years before holding the Emmett Doerr Chair in Catholic Theology at Marquette University. Former president of the Catholic Theological Society of America and former editor of *Theological Studies*, he also served as executive secretary of the Orthodox/Catholic Consultation for the United States Conference of Catholic Bishops.

Richard R. Gaillardetz is the Joseph Professor of Catholic Systematic Theology at Boston College. He is the coauthor, with Catherine Clifford, of *Keys to the Council: Unlocking the Teaching of Vatican II* (Liturgical Press, 2012) and the author of a volume forthcoming in the fall of 2015, *An Unfinished Council: Vatican II, Pope Francis, and the Renewal of Catholicism* (Liturgical Press, 2015). Gaillardetz was president of the Catholic Theological Society of America from 2013 to 2014.

Edward P. Hahnenberg holds the Jack and Mary Jane Breen Chair in Catholic Theology at John Carroll University. His books include *A Concise Guide to the Documents of Vatican II* (St. Anthony Messenger Press, 2007), *Awakening Vocation: A Theology of Christian Call* (Liturgical Press, 2010), and *Theology for Ministry* (Liturgical Press, 2014). He is currently a delegate to the US Lutheran-Catholic Dialogue.

Mary Ann Hinsdale, IHM, is Associate Professor of Systematic Theology at Boston College. She is the author of *Women Shaping Theology* (Paulist Press, 2006). She is currently completing a book on ecclesiology employing ethnography and feminist perspectives.

Natalia Imperatori-Lee is Associate Professor of Religious Studies at Manhattan College in Riverdale, New York. She teaches in the areas of contemporary Catholicism, US Latino/a theology, and gender studies. She holds a PhD in systematic theology from the University of Notre Dame. Dr. Imperatori-Lee is currently working on a monograph for Orbis Books on the importance of narrative in Catholic ecclesiology.

Paul Lakeland is the Aloysius P. Kelley, SJ, Professor and Director of the Center for Catholic Studies at Fairfield University. A native of the United Kingdom, he has taught Catholic ecclesiology, liberation theology, and religion and literature at Fairfield for the past thirty-four years. His most recent book is *A Council That Will Never End: Lumen Gentium and the Church Today* (Liturgical Press, 2013).

Vincent Miller is the Gudorf Chair in Catholic Theology and Culture at the University of Dayton where he teaches courses in systematic theology, theology and culture, and globalization and technology. He is the author of *Consuming Religion: Christian Faith and Practice in a Consumer Culture* (Continuum, 2003) and a blogger for *America Magazine*. He is currently writing a book on the impact of globalization on moral responsibility, solidarity, community, and the church.

Susan K. Wood, SCL, is professor of systematic theology at Marquette University. She serves on the US Lutheran-Roman Catholic Dialogue, the North American Roman Catholic-Orthodox Theological Consultation, and the International Lutheran-Catholic Dialogue. She has published *Spiritual Exegesis and the Church in the Theology of Henri de Lubac* (Eerdmans, 1998), *Sacramental Orders* (Liturgical Press, 2000), and *One Baptism: Ecumenical Dimensions of the Doctrine of Baptism* (Liturgical Press, 2009). She is the editor of *Ordering the Baptismal Priesthood* (Liturgical Press, 2003) and coeditor with Alberto Garcia of *Critical Issues in Ecclesiology* (Eerdmans, 2011).

Index